Tracing Connections
Voices of Systems Thinkers

editors
Joy Richmond
Lees Stuntz
Kathy Richmond
Joanne Egner

foreword by
Jay W. Forrester
founder of System Dynamics

Copyright © 2010 isee systems, inc., and The Creative Learning Exchange
Chapter 10 copyright © 2010 Peter M. Senge
All rights reserved. No part of this publication may be transmitted or reproduced in any form by any means without explicit permission in writing from the publishers.

STELLA® and *iThink*® are registered trademarks of isee systems, inc.

isee systems, inc.
31 Old Etna Rd Suite 7N
Lebanon NH 03766
603-448-4990 | www.iseesystems.com

The Creative Learning Exchange
27 Central Street
Acton, Massachusetts 01720 USA
978-635-9797 | www.clexchange.org

Printed in the United States of America

ISBN 978-0-9704921-2-8

Text printed on 70# Finch Opaque, a Forest Stewardship Council-certified paper, manufactured from elemental chlorine-free (ECF) pulp with 30% post-consumer waste. All of the post-consumer recycled fiber is chlorine-free process.

The wood fiber used to make this paper is independently certified to come from responsibly managed forests. The Forest Stewardship Council is a global organization working to eliminate habitat destruction, water pollution, displacement of indigenous peoples, and violence against wildlife. FSC certification is administered through the Rainforest Alliance's SmartWood program. For more information: www.fscus.org | www.smartwood.org

The post-consumer waste fiber in the text stock is derived from paper that has been used, collected, and de-inked, then resupplied to the paper manufacturer. The use of post-consumer fiber reduces the amount of paper going to landfills where it decays and produces methane gas, a greenhouse gas emission.

Over ⅔ of the energy needs to make the text stock were met by on-site, renewable resources—a mix of emission-free hydropower and biomass. Finch uses this power to make both their pulp and their paper.

Design and production: Jenna Dixon, Bookbuilder
Proofreader: Rebecca Siegel
Text: Arno Pro | Display: Hypatia Sans Pro
Cover type: Titillium, an open-source type designed by students at Urbino Accademia di Belle Arti, Italy

1 2 3 4 5 6   10 11 12 13 14

To Barry

Contents

Foreword by Jay W. Forrester ix
Preface by Joy Richmond xi

   Introduction: The Thinking in Systems Thinking—Eight Critical Skills   2
      Barry Richmond

1 Barry Richmond's Influence on Systems Thinking: 22
   From Academia to Widespread Accessibility
      Ali Mashayekhi

2 Systems Thinking for Anyone: Practices to Consider   30
      Steve Peterson

3 Teaching by Wondering Around: Learning About the World Naturally   52
      Frank Draper

4 Changing School Culture: Creating Student-Centered Classrooms   66
      Tracy Benson

5 Modeling for High School Students: Teaching Critical Thinking   80
   through System Dynamics
      Diana M. Fisher

6 Romeo and Juliet in Brazil: Use of Metaphorical Models   94
   for Feedback Systems Thinking
      John Morecroft

7 The Value of Critical Thinking Skills: Modeling Price   120
   and Inventory Dynamics
      Corey Peck

8 Finding System Dynamics: An Exploration in International Development   142
      John L. Newman

9 The Power of the Situation: Modeling Classic Experiments   166
   in Social Psychology
      James K. Doyle, Khalid Saeed, Jeanine Skorinko

10 Education for an Interdependent World: Developing Systems Citizens   186
      Peter M. Senge

Foreword

Jay W. Forrester

Barry Richmond was a pioneer in system dynamics. By creating the user-friendly STELLA and *iThink* software, he opened computer simulation modeling to a far larger field of participants. But Richmond had much broader visions and insights.

Starting with his 1979 doctoral thesis, "Government Growth in a Fixed Economy," he demonstrated his concern for the big picture and the important issues in society. Through most of his career, he saw K-12 education as the key to creating a better world.

Barry's STELLA became the software of choice in pre-college education for understanding how things change through time. He devoted much time to conducting training seminars for teachers. Through that emphasis on education, he played a major role in launching system dynamics as a foundation under the new kind of education that is now beginning to prepare students for the more complex world that they will inhabit.

For many years, Richmond lectured, wrote papers, and led conferences on the habits of mind for systems citizens. His goal was a public with sharper insights and a better understanding of the troubling issues in society. He has led us all to think more deeply about the goals of education.

We have lost a leader, a pioneer thinker, a friend and colleague, who, in his short time with us, has set higher goals for us and focused our thinking.

JAY W. FORRESTER *is the Germeshausen Professor Emeritus of Management at the Massachusetts Inititute of Technology*

Preface

Joy Richmond

The idea for this book came from two directions. One inspiration was a desire to do something as a tribute to my dad, Barry Richmond. He was an eminent systems thinker, innovator, and a pioneer in the field of systems thinking. Our family and the systems thinking community had an overwhelming feeling of loss and grief after my dad's life was cut short by a sudden fatal heart attack in 2002. He was in the prime of his career, very busy with his company, isee systems, which develops systems thinking software, and with consulting engagements all over the world. My dad was committed to bringing systems thinking to every corner of the globe because he wanted to make the world a better place. He saw how this powerful thinking tool could help people make better decisions and change their lives.

After his sudden passing, my family and I talked with some of his closest colleagues and friends. Together, we decided the best way to pay tribute to him would be to help get the word out about systems thinking—Barry's enduring passion. He felt so strongly that if people could think better, they would understand more. This understanding would translate into better decision making, which will benefit people, the environment, and the world. This book is one way to help spread systems thinking. It will leave you with a better understanding of what systems thinking is, who is using it, and why applying systems thinking is so important in this world of growing interdependence.

The second inspiration for the book was the book Barry himself always wanted to write about systems thinking. Although he wrote the user guides to his software, published a number of major systems thinking articles, and made many notes about what he wanted to write, he never had the time to actually write the book. Barry was an excellent writer and the task of trying to write something in his place would be extremely daunting! His vision was a book about systems thinking and the concept of systems citizens, a term that he coined and talked about extensively just prior to his passing. Some of the authors in this book discuss systems citizens and explain in more detail what Barry was talking about when he used the term.

Because we couldn't write the book for Barry, we decided to have a book written in tribute to him by his friends and colleagues who share his passion for systems thinking. The purpose of this book is the same as Barry's purpose for the book he wanted to write: to spread the concept of systems thinking. The proceeds from this book will support and train educators in systems thinking through the Creative Learning Exchange, helping further Barry's mission of getting systems thinking into the hands of as many people as possible.

The introduction for this book is a combination of some of Barry's published works:

- *An Introduction to Systems Thinking with STELLA* (isee systems, inc., 1992–2004)
- *The Thinking in Systems Thinking* (Pegasus Communications, 2000)
- "Systems Thinking: Critical Thinking Skills for the 1990s and Beyond," *System Dynamics Review,* 9 (2): 113–133.

This excellent introduction provides the foundation for the rest of the book. The book is made up of ten independent chapters, each written by different authors. They do not need to be read in sequence. We hope at least one of these chapters will intrigue you enough to continue on your path to becoming a systems thinker.

Enjoy the book and pass it on to someone when you are done so you can help us spread the word about systems thinking!

Acknowledgments

Thanks to all of the contributing authors who made this book a reality; Jay W. Forrester, for his wonderful foreword; Jenna Dixon, for advising and pulling everything together into a beautiful book; Willow Reed and Karen Kaliski, for their writing assistance and help copy editing; Rebecca Siegel, for proofreading; Karim Chichakly, for providing input to models and figures; and Weiping Liu, for help with transferring photos of Barry.

This book has been a wonderful project for the four of us editors and has provided a chance for so many in the systems thinking community to come together and share their stories.

Introduction

The Thinking in Systems Thinking:
Eight Critical Skills

Barry Richmond

> This chapter serves as the introduction to the book. It is a combination of some of Barry's published works on systems thinking skills. He defines eight critical thinking skills that are necessary to evolve our thinking, learning, and communicating capacities. Each author will address how these skills apply to their own work.

I have been writing and re-writing this guide (*Introduction to Systems Thinking with STELLA*, 1985–2000) for fifteen years. I always begin by reeling off a litany of serious challenges facing humanity. And, you know what? The list has remained pretty much the same! There's homelessness and hunger, drug addiction and income distribution inequities, environmental threats and the scourge of AIDS. We've made precious little progress in addressing any of these issues over the last couple of decades! Indeed, you could make a strong case that, if anything, most (if not all) have gotten worse! And, some new challenges have arisen.

So what's the problem? Why do we continue to make so little progress in addressing our many, very pressing social concerns?

My answer is that the way we think, learn, and communicate is outdated. As a result, the way we act creates problems. And then, we're ill-equipped to address them because of the way we've been taught to think, learn, and communicate. This is a pretty sweeping indictment of some very fundamental human skills, all of which our school systems are charged with developing! However, it is the premise of systems thinking that it is possible to evolve our thinking, learning, and communicating capacities. As we do, we will be able to make progress in addressing the

> It is the premise of systems thinking that it is possible to evolve our thinking, learning, and communicating capacities.

> **Barry Richmond's** educational training culminated with his Ph.D. in System Dynamics from MIT in 1979. He then accepted a teaching position at Dartmouth College as an Assistant Professor in the Thayer School of Engineering. Barry was one of the most popular and well-respected teachers at Dartmouth for eight years. In 1985, he founded High Performance Systems (now isee systems), a software development and consulting business, with systems thinking as its foundation. Barry dedicated the rest of his life to teaching people all over the world how to live by systems thinking principles. His expertise was respected worldwide. He was granted the 1989 Jay Wright Forrester Award, a prestigious honor awarded by the System Dynamics Society. The award was for producing the STELLA software, his pioneering work, which revolutionized the system dynamics modeling process.

compelling slate of issues that challenge our viability. But, in order to achieve this evolution, we must overcome some formidable obstacles. Primary among these are the entrenched paradigms governing what and how students are taught. We do have the power to evolve these paradigms. It is now time to exercise this power!

I will begin by offering operational definitions of thinking, learning, and communicating. Having them will enable me to shine light on precisely what skills must be evolved, how current paradigms are thwarting this evolution, and what systems thinking can do to help. In the course of this chapter, I will identify eight systems thinking skills. They are:

- 10,000-meter thinking
- system-as-cause thinking
- dynamic thinking
- operational thinking
- closed-loop thinking
- scientific thinking
- empathic thinking
- generic thinking

The processes of thinking, learning, and communicating constitute an interdependent system, or at least have the potential for operating as such. They do not operate with much synergy within the current system of formal education. The first step toward realizing the potential synergies is to clearly visualize how each process works in relation to the other.

Thinking

Thinking is something we all do, but what is it? The dictionary says it's "to have a thought; to reason, reflect on, or ponder." Does that clear it up for you? It didn't for me.

I will define thinking as consisting of two activities: constructing mental models and then simulating them in order to draw conclusions and make decisions. We'll get to constructing and simulating in a moment. But first, what the heck is a mental model?

It's a "selective abstraction" of reality that you create and then carry around in your head. As big as some of our heads get, we still can't fit reality in there. Instead, we have models of various aspects of reality. We simulate these models in order to "make meaning" out of what we're experiencing, and also to help us arrive at decisions that inform our actions.

For example, you have to deal with your kid, or a sibling, or your parent. None of them are physically present inside your head. Instead, when dealing with them in a particular context, you select certain aspects of each that are germane to the context. In your mind's eye, you relate those aspects to each other using some form of cause-and-effect logic. Then, you simulate the interplay of these relationships under various "what if" scenarios to draw conclusions about a best course of action, or to understand something about what has occurred.

If you were seeking to understand why your daughter isn't doing well in arithmetic, you could probably safely ignore the color of her eyes when selecting aspects of reality to include in the mental model you are constructing. This aspect of reality is unlikely to help you in developing an understanding of the causes of her difficulties, or in drawing conclusions about what to do. But, in selecting a blouse for her birthday? Eye color probably ought to be in that mental model.

> In order to achieve this evolution, we must overcome some formidable obstacles. Primary among these are the entrenched paradigms governing what and how students are taught.

As the preceding example nicely illustrates, all models (mental and otherwise) are simplifications. They necessarily omit many aspects of the realities they represent. That statement is a paraphrase of something George Box once uttered: "All models are wrong; some models are useful." It's important to dredge this hallowed truth back up into consciousness from time to time to prevent yourself from becoming "too attached" to one of your mental models; nevertheless, despite the fact that all models are wrong, you have no choice but to use them—no choice, that is, if you are going to think. If you wish to employ non-rational means (like gut feel and intuition) in order to arrive at a conclusion or a decision, no mental model is needed. But, if you want to think, you can't do so without a mental model!

> I will define thinking as consisting of two activities: constructing mental models and then simulating them in order to draw conclusions and make decisions. . . . what the heck is a mental model? It's a "selective abstraction" of reality that you create and then carry around in your head.

Constructing mental models

Whether the mental model being constructed is of an ecosystem, a chemical reaction, a family, or a society, three fundamental questions must always be answered in constructing it. They are: (1) What elements should be included in the model—or, the flip side—what elements should be left out? (2) How should the elements you decide to include be represented? (3) How should the relationships between the elements be represented?

Selecting activities. Deciding what to include in a mental model, in turn, breaks into two questions. How broadly do you cast your net? This is a "horizontal" question. And, how deeply do you drill? This is a "vertical" question. Developing good answers to these two questions requires skill. And, like any skill, this one must first be informed by "good practice" principles, and then honed through repeated practice.

Systems thinking offers three thinking skills that can help students to become more effective in answering the "what to include" question. They are: *10,000-meter thinking, systems-as-cause thinking,* and *dynamic thinking*.

> **10,000-meter thinking** was inspired by the view one gets on a clear sunny day when looking down from the seat of a jet airliner. You see horizontal expanse, but little vertical detail. You gain a "big picture" but relinquish the opportunity to make fine discriminations.

The first systems thinking skill, *10,000-meter thinking*, was inspired by the view one gets on a clear sunny day when looking down from the seat of a jet airliner. You see horizontal expanse, but little vertical detail. You gain a "big picture" but relinquish the opportunity to make fine discriminations.

The second systems thinking skill, *system-as-cause thinking*, also works to counter the vertical bias toward including too much detail in the representations contained in mental models. *System-as-cause thinking* is really just a spin on Occam's Razor; that is, the simplest explanation for a phenomenon is the best explanation. It holds that mental models should contain only those elements whose interaction is capable of self-generating the phenomenon of interest. It should not contain any so-called "external forces." A simple illustration should help to clarify the skill that's involved.

> **System-as-cause thinking** holds that mental models should contain only those elements whose interaction is capable of self-generating the phenomenon of interest.

Imagine you are holding a slinky, as shown in Figure I-1a. Then, as shown in Figure I-1b, you remove the hand that was supporting the device from below. The slinky oscillates as illustrated in Figure I-1c. The question is: What is the cause of the oscillation? Another way to ask the question: What content would you need to include in your mental model in order to explain the oscillation?

The two most common causes cited are: gravity and removal of the hand. The *system-as-cause* answer to the question is: the slinky! To better appreciate the

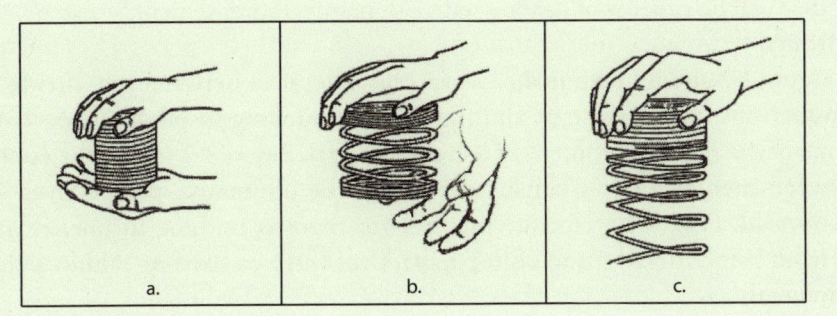

Figure I-1. Slinky does its thing

merits of this answer, imagine that you performed the exact same experiment with, say, a cup. The outcome you'd get makes it easier to appreciate the perspective that the oscillatory behavior is latent within the structure of the slinky itself. In the presence of gravity, when an external stimulus (i.e., removing the supporting hand) is applied, the dynamics latent within the structure are "called forth." It's not that gravity and removal of the hand are irrelevant; however, they wouldn't appear as part of the "causal content" of a mental model that was seeking to explain why a slinky oscillates.

The third of the so-called "filtering skills" (systems thinking skills that help to "filter" out the nonessential elements of reality when constructing a mental model) is called *dynamic thinking*. This skill provides the same "distancing from the detail" that *10,000-meter thinking* provides, except that it applies to the behavioral—rather than the structural—dimension.

> **Dynamic thinking** encourages one to "push back" from the events and points in time to see the pattern of which they are a part. The implication is that mental models will be capable of dealing with a dynamic, rather than only a static, view of reality.

Just as perspectives get caught-up in the minutiae of structure, they also get trapped in "events" or "points," at the expense of seeing patterns. In history, students memorize dates on which critical battles were fought, great people were born, declarations were made, and so forth. Yet in front of and behind each such "date" is a pattern that reflects continuous build-ups or depletions of various kinds. For example, the United States declared its independence from England on July 4, 1776. But prior to that specific date, tensions built continuously between the two parties toward the ensuing conflict. In economics, the focus is on equilibrium points, as opposed to the trajectories that are traced as variables move between the points.

Dynamic thinking encourages one to "push back" from the events and points in time to see the pattern of which they are a part. The implication is that mental models will be capable of dealing with a dynamic, rather than only a static, view of reality.

Figure I-2 should help make clearer the difference between the "divide and conquer"-inspired viewpoint and the systems thinking-inspired perspective in terms of the resulting content of a mental model. Figure I-2 makes the contrast between mental models constructed using the alternative perspectives look pretty stark. That's an accurate picture. Yet there is nothing to prevent models from being forged using both perspectives from co-existing within a single individual.

Until the average citizen can feel comfortable embracing mental models with horizontally-extended/vertically-restricted boundaries, we should not expect any significant progress in addressing the pressing issues we face in the social domain. And until the measurement rubrics on which our education system relies are altered to permit more focus on developing horizontal thinking skills, we will continue to produce citizens with predilections for constructing narrow/deep mental models. The choice is ours. Let's demand the change!

> Until the average citizen can feel comfortable embracing mental models with horizontally-extended/vertically-restricted boundaries, we should not expect any significant progress in addressing the pressing issues we face in the social domain.

Representing activities. Once the issue of what to include in a mental model has been addressed, the next question that arises is how to represent what has been included. A major limit to development of students' skills in the representation arena is created by the fact that each discipline has its own unique set of terms, concepts, and, in some cases, symbols or icons for representing their content. Students work to internalize each content-specific vocabulary, but each such effort contributes to what, in effect, becomes a content-specific skill.

Systems thinking carries with it an icon-based lexicon called the language of "stocks and flows." This language constitutes a kind of Esperanto, a lingua franca that facilitates cross-disciplinary thinking and, hence, implementation of a "horizontal" perspective. Mental models encoded using stocks and flows, whatever the content, recognize a fundamental distinction among the elements that populate them. That distinction is between things that accumulate (called "stocks") and things that flow (called "flows"). Stocks represent conditions within a system—i.e., how things are. Flows represent the activities that cause conditions to change. Some examples of accumulations are: *Water in Clouds*, *Body Weight*, and *Anger*. The associated flows are: *evaporating/precipitating*, *gaining/losing*, and *building/venting*. Figure I-3 should help you to develop a clearer picture of the distinction between a stock and a flow.

To gain a quick idea of why the distinction matters, consider the illustration in Figure I-3b. Suppose a person whose weight has been increasing decides to take

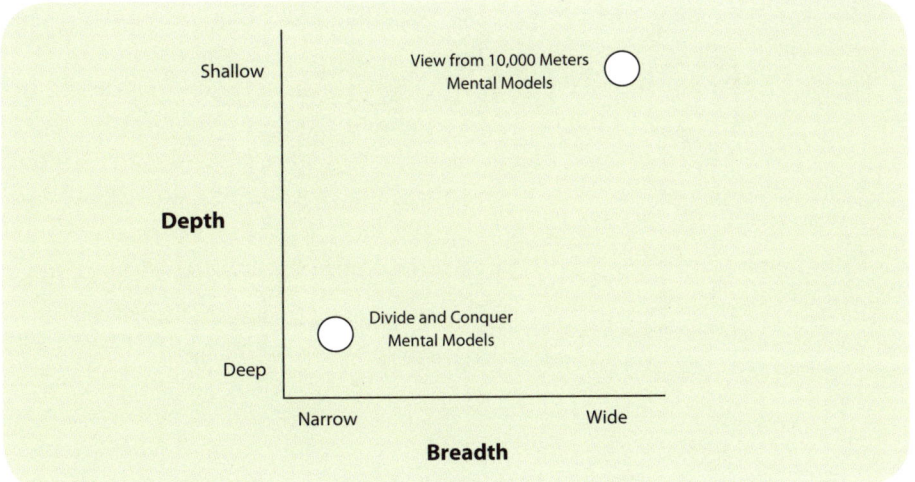

Figure I-2. The content of divide and conquer-inspired versus systems thinking-inspired mental models

some action to address the situation. First, they successfully eliminate all junk food snacks from their diet, and do not eat more at regular meals to compensate for doing so. Second, they implement a rigorous aerobic exercise program—to which they religiously adhere. This means the person will have lowered the volume of the *gaining* flow (i.e., reduced caloric intake) and increased the volume of the *losing* flow (increased caloric expenditure). So what happens to this person's *Body Weight*?

Did your answer include the possibility that it would still be increasing? It should have! Look at Figure I-3b. The reason the person may still be gaining weight is because decreasing the rate of *gaining* (the inflow), and increasing rate of *losing* (the outflow), will only cause *Body Weight* (the stock) to decrease if *gaining* actually drops below *losing*. Until this occurs, the person will continue to gain weight—albeit at a slower rate! Take a moment to make sure you understand this reasoning before you proceed.

When the distinction between stocks and flows goes unrecognized—in this example, and in any other situation in which mental simulations must infer a dynamic pattern of behavior—there is a significant risk that erroneous conclusions will be drawn. In this case, for example, if the inflow and outflow volumes do not cross after some reasonable period of time, the person might well conclude that the two initiatives they implemented were ineffective and should be abandoned. Clearly that is not the case. And, just as often, the other type of erroneous conclusion is drawn: "We're doing the right thing, just not enough of

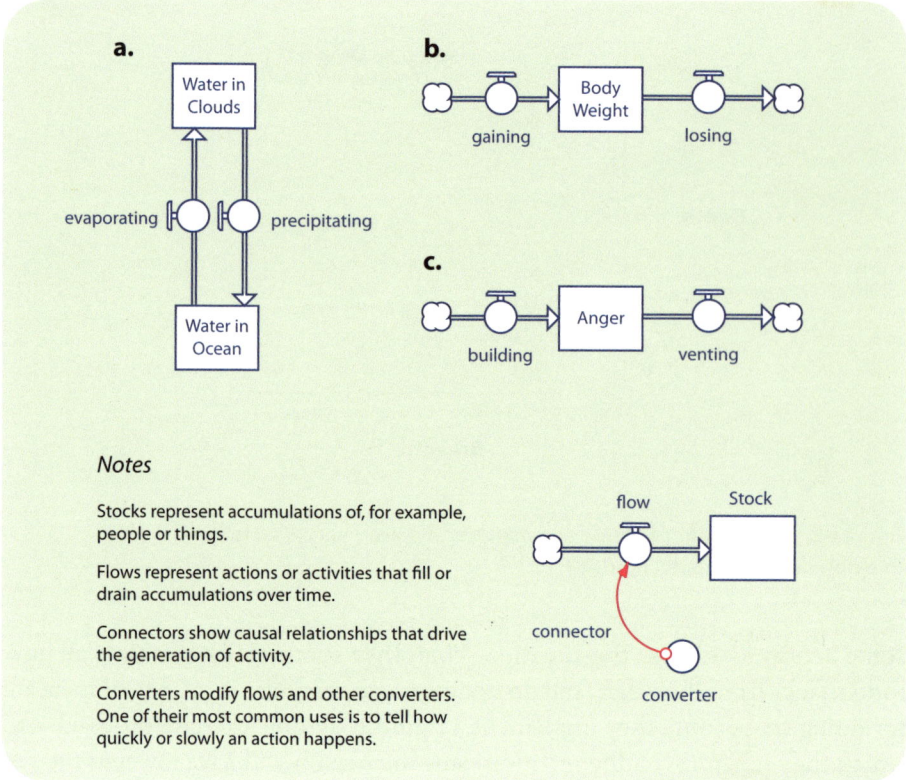

Figure I-3. Distinguishing between stocks and flows, using the STELLA software tool

The concepts of accumulation and flow are content-independent. In whatever specific content arena they are used, their use contributes to building the general content-representation skill!

it!" Redoubling the effort, in such cases, then simply adds fuel to the fire.

In addition to helping increase the reliability of mental simulations, using stocks and flows in representing the content of a mental model has another very important benefit. The benefit derives from the fact that the concepts of accumulation and flow are content-independent. Therefore, in whatever specific content arena they are used, their use contributes to building the general content-representation skill! Figure I-4 seeks to capture this idea via the links that run from each of four specific content-representing activities to the building of a general content-representation skill.

There's a second important idea illustrated in Figure I-4. Note the two Rs. They stand for the word "Reinforcing"—which is the type of feedback loop they designate. The loops work like this . . .

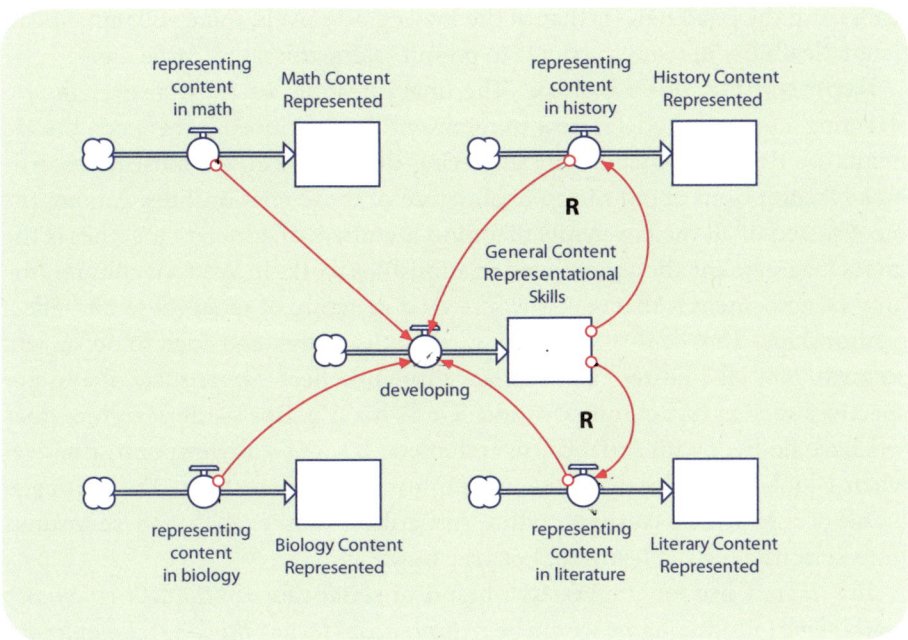

Figure I-4. Developing general content representation skills by representing specific content

As general content representation skills build, they facilitate each specific content-representing activity—though, to keep the picture simple, the link to only two of the specific arenas is illustrated. Then, as students engage in specific content-representation activities, because they are using a content-transcendent language to do so, they develop general content representation skills—a virtuous learning cycle! The cycle creates synergy because all content arenas benefit from activities that go on in any one of them! Now, instead of one content arena interfering with learning in another, each helps to accelerate learning in each of the others. (This is an example of another of the systems thinking skills, *closed-loop thinking*, discussed a little later in this chapter.)

To be able to "speak/write" effectively in the language of stocks and flows requires that students build a fourth systems thinking skill, a very important one: *operational thinking*. Teaching the language of stocks and flows, and the associated *operational thinking* skills, at an early point in the formal education process (e.g., fourth, fifth, and sixth grade) would be a huge step toward enabling students to develop a better set of representing skills. It would, at the same time, leverage development of students' horizontal thinking

> **T**o **think operationally** is to ask, "How does the process work?"

skills. And the good news is that, at the lower grade levels, there still remains sufficient flexibility in many curricula to permit taking this step. Carpe diem!

Representing relationships. The final question we must answer in constructing a mental model is how to represent the relationships between the elements we decide to include. In answering this question, we must necessarily make assumptions about the general nature of these relationships. Among the most sacred of all the covenants that bind members of a society together is the implicit agreement about how such relationships work. In Western cultures, the implicit agreement is that reality works via a structure of serial cause-and-effect relationships. Thus-and-such happens, which leads this-and-such to occur, and so forth. Not all cultures "buy" serial cause-and-effect (some subscribe to perspectives such as "synchronicity" and "God's hand"). But Western culture does.

I have no beef with serial cause-and-effect. It's a useful viewpoint; however, when I look more closely at the assumptions that characterize the particular brand of it to which Western culture subscribes, I discover that these assumptions seriously restrict learning! Let's see how.

The name I use for the Western brand of serial cause-and-effect is *laundry-list thinking* (another name would be *critical success factors thinking*). *Laundry-list thinking* is defined by a set of four meta assumptions that are used to structure cause-and-effect relationships. I use the term *meta* because these assumptions are content-transcendent. That is, we use them to structure cause-and-effect relationships whether the content is literature, chemistry, or psychology, and also when we construct mental models to address personal or business issues. Because we all subscribe to these meta assumptions, and have had them inculcated from the "get go," we are essentially unaware that we even use them! They have become so obviously true, they're not even recognized as assumptions any more. Instead, they seem more like attributes of reality.

But as you're about to see, the meta assumptions associated with *laundry-list thinking* are likely to lead to structuring relationships in our mental models in ways that will cause us to draw erroneous conclusions when we simulate these models. I will identify the four meta assumptions associated with *laundry-list thinking*, and then offer a systems thinking alternative that addresses the shortcomings of each. Here's a question that I'll use to surface all four assumptions:

> **What causes students to succeed academically?**
> Please take a moment and actually answer the question.

If you did produce a laundry list, it probably included some of the variables shown on the left-hand side of Figure I-5. This figure belies four meta assumptions about cause-and-effect relationships implicit in the laundry-list framework. Let's unmask them!

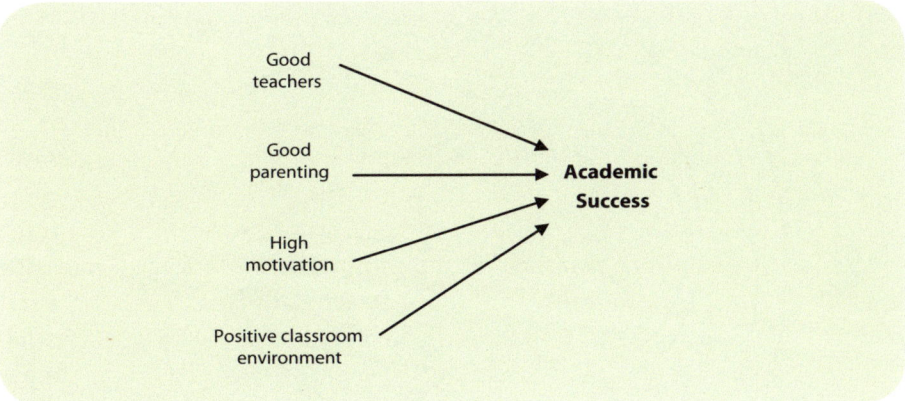

Figure I-5. A laundry-list thinking mental model

The first meta assumption is that the causal "factors" (four are shown in Figure I-5) each operate independently on "the effect" ("Academic Success" in the illustration). If we were to read the story told by the view depicted in the figure, we'd hear, "Good teachers cause Academic Success; Good parenting causes..." Each factor, or independent variable, is assumed to exert its impact independently on Academic Success, the dependent variable.

To determine how much sense this "independent factors" view really makes, please consult your experience.

Isn't it really a "partnership" between teachers and parents (good open lines of reciprocal communication, trust, etc.) that enables both parties to contribute effectively to supporting a student's quest for academic success? And don't good teachers really help to create both high student motivation and a positive classroom environment? Isn't it the case that highly motivated students and a positive classroom environment make teaching more exciting and enjoyable, and as a result cause teachers to do a better job? I could continue. But I suspect I've said enough to make the point. The four factors shown in Figure I-5 aren't even close to operating independently of each other! They operate as a tightly intertwined set of interdependent relationships. They form a web of reciprocal causality! The picture that emerges looks much more like Figure I-6 than Figure I-5!

So, there goes the first meta assumption associated with *laundry-list thinking* (i.e., that the causal "factors" operate independently). Now let's watch the second laundry-list meta assumption bite the dust! The second assumption is that causality runs one way. Look back at Figure I-5. Notice that the arrows all point from cause to effect; all run from left to right. Now steal another glance at Figure I-6. Notice anything different?

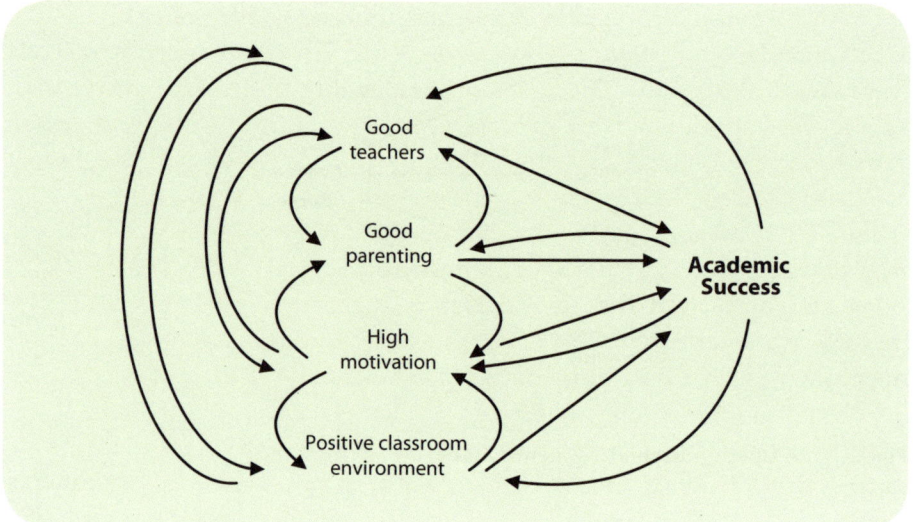

Figure I-6. Effect is also cause

That's right, the arrows linking the "causes" now run both ways! Cause-and-effect comes in loops! As Figure I-6 shows, once circular cause-and-effect enters the picture, the so-called "effect" variable also loses its "dependent" status. It, too, now "causes"—which is to say that academic success stimulates student motivation and a positive classroom environment, just as much as they drive it. Academic success also causes teachers to perform better—it's easier to teach students who are doing well—just as much as good teachers create academic success. And so forth. "Academic Success" is just as much a cause of any of the four "factors" as they are a cause of it! And so, independent and dependent variables become chickens and eggs. Everybody becomes a co-conspirator in a causal web of interrelationships.

> Viewing reality as made up of a web of closed loops (called feedback loops), and being able to structure relationships between elements in mental models to reflect this, is the fifth of the systems thinking skills. It's called **closed-loop thinking**.

The shift from the laundry-list—causality runs one-way—view, to system thinking's two-way, or closed-loop, view is a big deal! The former is static in nature, while the latter offers an "ongoing process," or dynamic, view. Viewing reality as made up of a web of closed loops (called feedback loops), and being able to structure relationships between elements in mental models to reflect this, is the fifth of the systems thinking skills. It's called *closed-loop thinking*. Mastering this skill will enable students to conduct more reliable mental simulations. Initiatives directed at addressing pressing social issues will not be seen as "one-time fixes," but rather as "exciting" a web of loops that will continue to spin long after the initiative is activated. Developing closed-loop thinking skills will enable students to better anticipate unintended consequences and short-run/long-run tradeoffs. These skills also are invaluable in helping to identify high-leverage intervention points. The bottom line is an increase in the likelihood that the next generation's initiatives will be more effective than those launched by our "straight-line causality"-inspired generation.

The third and fourth meta assumptions implicit in *laundry-list thinking* are easy to spot once the notion of feedback loops enters the picture. The causal impacts in laundry lists are implicitly assumed to be "linear," and to unfold "instantaneously" (which is to say, without any significant delay).

> Developing closed-loop thinking skills will enable students to better anticipate unintended consequences and short-run/long-run tradeoffs.

Feedback loops, as they interact with waxing and waning strength, create non-linear behavior patterns—patterns that frequently arise in both natural and social systems. Such patterns cannot arise out of simulations of mental models whose relationships are linear.

The fourth implicit meta assumption associated with *laundry-list thinking* is that impacts are felt "instantaneously." For example, when we look at the factors impacting academic success, the implicit assumption is that each exerts its influence "right now." Take "Positive classroom environment." The idea here is that a good classroom environment—i.e., physical factors like space, light, good equipment, etc.—will encourage students to achieve high levels of academic success. Boost the quality of the physical environment and you boost academic success. Sounds reasonable, but when you draw a more operational picture, the cause-and-effect is not quite so straight-forward. Take a look at Figure I-7.

Instead of words and arrows—Positive Classroom Environment → Academic Success—to show causality, Figure I-7 depicts the associated causal relationships operationally. In particular, the figure includes the potentially significant delay between initiating improvements to a classroom environment and the "arrival" of those improvements. Such delays have been known to stretch out for months. In the meantime, it's possible that student and teacher morale might suffer. This, in turn, could stimulate an outflow from the Level of Academic Success before the arrival of the new lab has a chance to stimulate the associated inflow!

> Delays are an important component of how reality works. Leaving them out when structuring relationships in mental models undermines the reliability of the simulation.

Delays are an important component of how reality works. Leaving them out when structuring relationships in mental models undermines the reliability of simulation outcomes produced by those models. Building the *operational thinking* skills that enable students to know when and how to include delays should be a vital part of any curriculum concerned with development of effective thinking capacities.

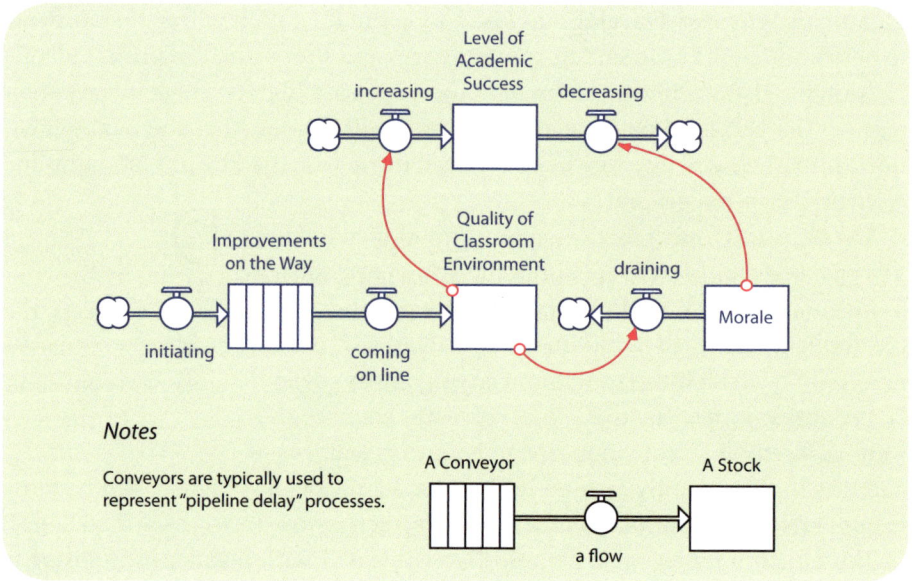

Figure I-7. A non-instantaneous view of academic success

Okay, it's been a long journey to this point. Let's briefly recap before resuming. I asserted at the outset that our education system was limiting the development of our students' thinking, learning, and communicating capacities. I have focused thus far primarily on thinking capacities. I have argued that the education system is restricting both the selecting and representing activities (the two sub-processes that make up constructing a mental model). Where restrictions have been identified, I have offered a systems thinking skill that can be developed to overcome it. Five systems thinking skills have been identified thus far: *10,000-meter*, *system-as-cause*, *dynamic*, *operational*, and *closed-loop*. By developing these skills, students will be better equipped for constructing mental models that are more congruent with reality. This, by itself, will result in more reliable mental simulations and drawing better conclusions. But we can do even more!

Simulating mental models

We're now ready to examine the second component of thinking: simulating. The first component of thinking is constructing mental models. The second component is simulating these models. Throughout the discussion thus far, I've been assuming that all simulating is being performed mentally. This is a good assumption because the vast majority of simulating is performed mentally. Simulating is key to the learning process.

Learning

Learning is depicted in Figure I-8. It's a pretty elaborate picture, and a good example of one that should be unfurled one chunk at a time. The first type of learning was identified in the discussion of the thinking process. Call it self-reflective learning. It comes about when simulation outcomes are used to drive a process in which a mental model's content, and/or representation of content, is changed. I've also just alluded to a second type of learning, one that's driven by the communicating process. Call it other-inspired learning. As Figure I-8 suggests, the raw material for this type of learning is: the mental model itself, the simulation outcomes associated with that model, and/or the conclusions drawn from simulating. How much learning occurs depends upon both the quality of the feedback provided—where "quality" includes both content and "packaging"—as well as the willingness and ability to "hear" the feedback.

Figure I-8 also adds a fourth source of raw material for learning: the impacts of one's actions. As the figure suggests, often it is difficult to perceive the full impact because ramifying takes a long time, and spreads out over a great distance. To reflect this fact, the information for this type of learning is shown as radiating off the "conveyor" named *Ramifying*, rather than the stock called *Realized Impacts*. (*Note:* Conveyors are used to represent delays.)

It's useful to spend a little time digesting Figure I-8—which shows the thinking, learning, and communicating system. An important thing to note about Figure I-8 is that all roads ultimately lead back to learning—which is to say, improving the quality of the mental model. Learning occurs when either the content of the mental model changes (via the selecting flow), or the representation of the content changes (via the representing flow). By the way, to make the figure more readable, not all wires that run to the representing flow have been depicted.

There are two important take-aways from Figure I-8. First, the three processes—thinking, learning, and communicating—form a self-reinforcing system. Building skills in any of the three processes helps build skills in all three processes! Second, unless a mental model changes, learning does not occur!

> Learning occurs when either the content of the mental model changes (via the selecting flow), or the representation of the content changes (via the representing flow).

If you refer to Figure I-8, you will see that simulating is a key part of the self-reflective learning loop. Reflecting on the simulation outcomes we generate is an important stimulator of change in our mental models. But what if those outcomes are bogus? What if we are not correctly tracing through the dynamics that are implied by the assumptions in our mental models? That's right. The self-reflective learning loop will break down. In addition, because simulation outcomes are one of the raw materials being made available for scrutiny

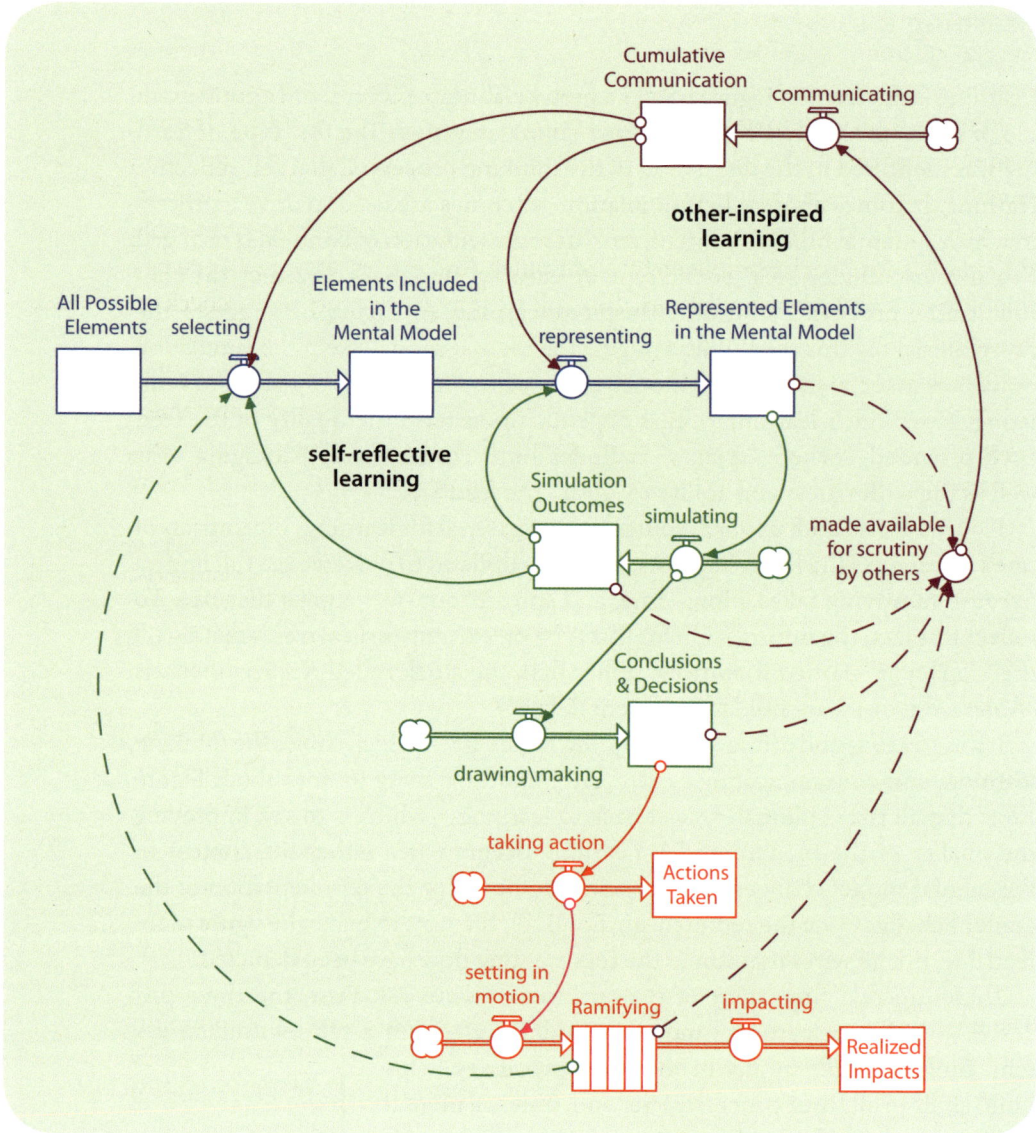

Figure I-8. Map of the learning process

by others in the communicating process, a key component of the other-inspired loop will break down, as well. So, it's very important that our simulation results be reliable in order that the associated learning channel can be effective.

Detailing the reasons for our shortcomings (as a species) in the simulation sphere is beyond the scope of this chapter; however, part of the issue here is certainly biological. Our brains simply have not yet evolved to the point where we can reliably juggle the interplay of lots of variables in our heads. There is, however, growing evidence to suggest that people can hone this capacity.

Systems thinking can offer a couple of things that can help in this arena. The first is the language of stocks and flows. Because the language is both visual and operational, it facilitates mental simulation. STELLA maps really do facilitate mental simulation! But the other nice thing about them is that they are readily convertible into models that can be simulated by a computer. And if you follow good practice in doing your STELLA simulations, they will serve as an excellent sanity check on your mental simulation. Think of the software as a fitness center for strengthening mental simulation muscles. In order to take full advantage of the exercise facility, it's important to acquire the habit of making explicit a guess about what dynamics a particular model will generate before actually using STELLA to generate them. Experience has shown that it is far too easy to back-rationalize that you really knew the model was going to produce that pattern. The collection of rigorous simulation practices is called scientific thinking, the sixth of the systems thinking skills.

> The collection of rigorous simulation practices is called **scientific thinking**, the sixth of the systems thinking skills.

Currently, in the formal education system, very little attention is paid to developing simulation skills. This means that a very important set of feedback loops for improving the quality of mental models is essentially being ignored. The STELLA software is a tool that can play an important role in helping to develop these skills.

Communicating

The next process in the thinking/learning/communicating system is communicating. The communicating I'm talking about must become a vital part of every class! It's the feedback students provide after scrutinizing each other's mental models and associated simulation outcomes (refer to Figure I-8).

The current formal education system provides few opportunities for students to share their mental models and associated simulation outcomes. Well-run discussion classes do this (and that's why students like these classes so much!). Students sometimes are asked to critique each other's writing or oral presentations, but most often this feedback is grammatical or stylistic in nature.

The *empathic thinking* capacity for both giving and receiving feedback on mental models is vital to develop if we want to get better at bootstrapping each other's learning! Many skills are involved in boosting this capacity, including listening, articulating, and, in particular, empathizing capabilities. Wanting to empathize increases efforts to both listen and articulate clearly. Being able to empathize is a skill that can be developed—and is, in some ways, the ultimate systems thinking skill because it leads to extending the boundary of true caring beyond self (a skill almost everyone could use more of). By continually stretching the horizontal perspective, systems thinking works covertly to chip away at the narrow self-boundaries that keep people from more freely empathizing.

> Being able to **empathize** is a skill that can be developed—and is the ultimate systems thinking skill because it leads to extending the boundary of true caring beyond self. By continually stretching the horizontal perspective, systems thinking works covertly to chip away at the narrow self-boundaries that keep people from more freely empathizing.

However, even with heightened empathic skills, we need a language that permits effective across-boundary conversations in order for communication to get very far. And this is where the issue of a content-focused curriculum resurfaces as a limiting factor. Even if time were made available in the curriculum for providing student-to-student feedback on mental models, and empathy were present in sufficient quantity, disciplinary segmentation would undermine the communication process. Each discipline has its own vocabulary, and in some cases, even its own set of symbols. This makes it difficult for many students to master all of the dialects (not to mention the associated content!) well enough to feel confident in, and comfortable with, sharing their reflections. The stock-flow Esperanto associated with systems thinking can play an important role in raising students' level of both comfort and confidence in moving more freely across disciplinary boundaries. Figure I-9 illustrates this notion.

Figure I-9 shows the accumulation of strength in a personal relationship, the accumulation of electrostatic charge on a capacitor, and the accumulation of facts in human memory. Each is represented by the same symbol. As stocks, each performs an analogous function—albeit in quite different contexts—which is to report the status of a condition. In addition, as illustrated in Figure I-9, the logic by which one or more of the associated flows operate is generic. This is, at the very least, a comforting discovery in a world generally perceived to be growing more complex and unfathomable on a daily basis, and in a curriculum rife with detail-dense, dialect-specific content bins. But it also holds the wonderful potential for creating cross-curricular learning synergies. What's being learned in physics could actually accelerate (rather than impede) learning in literature or psychology (and vice versa)! And by building their capacity for seeing "generic structures," students will be simultaneously boosting their capacity for

> And by building their capacity for seeing "generic structures," students will be simultaneously boosting their capacity for making "horizontal" connections in the real world. This last systems thinking skill is **generic thinking**.

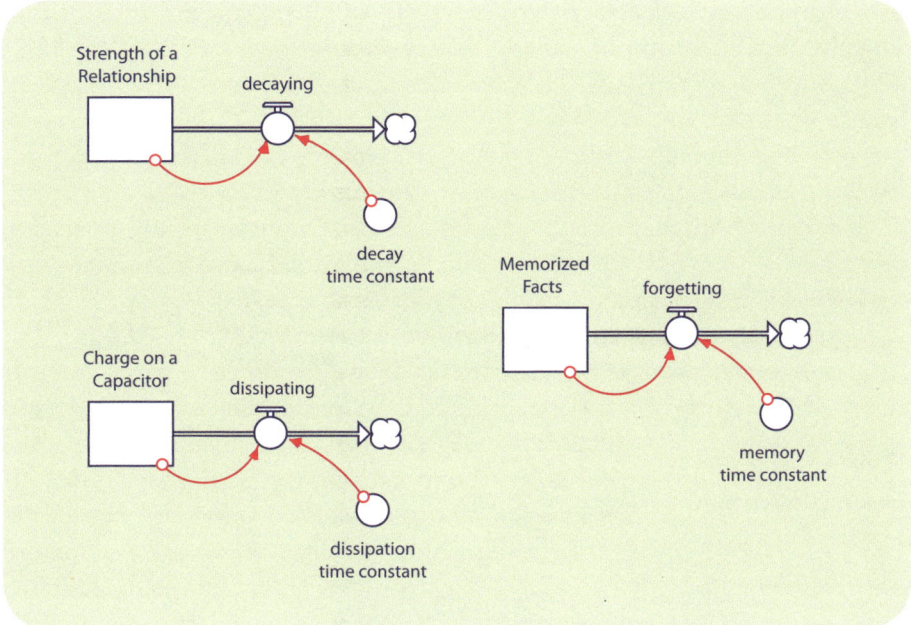

Figure I-9. Generic structure of a dissipation process

making "horizontal" connections in the real world. This last systems thinking skill is *generic thinking*.

Teaching the *generic, operational*, and *empathic thinking* skills needed to "speak/write it" effectively can go a long way toward improving the student communication capacities needed to realize the synergies latent within a multi-discipline curriculum.

This chapter identified eight systems thinking skills that leverage all three processes of thinking, learning, and communicating. Each skill can be readily implemented into today's school systems. The primary barrier to doing so is the view that the mission of an education system is to fill students' heads with knowledge. This view leads to sharp disciplinary segmentation and to student performance rubrics based on discipline-specific knowledge recall. Changing viewpoints—especially when they are supported by a measurement system and an ocean of teaching material—is an extremely challenging endeavor. But the implications of not doing so are untenable. The time is now.

1

Barry Richmond's Influence on Systems Thinking: From Academia to Widespread Accessibility

Ali Mashayekhi

> Professor Mashayekhi explains the role of Barry Richmond in the growth of system dynamics and systems thinking using the software tools that Barry developed.

Barry Richmond came to system dynamics by way of operations research. Operations research is mostly based on linear, restricted assumptions; however, Barry was a broad thinker, and operations research didn't include the foundation and tools he needed to expansively investigate a complex non-linear problem or to explain his thinking.

Barry had studied limits to growth and world and urban dynamics, and he loved the way that Jay Forrester thought about, wrote about, and explained the systems involved. Barry saw that system dynamics offered the power to explore a very complex issue or major problem and to construct an explanation for others. He applied to MIT and joined the MIT system dynamics group to study the field.

As Barry studied and applied system dynamics, he became devoted to making it accessible to everyone regardless of their educational level or particular field of study. His first step was to refer to system dynamics as systems thinking. The new title defined the methodology as a way to think about a problem. Barry was convinced that if both individuals and policy makers had a systemic way to think about and dig into complex problems, to discuss those problems, to share their thoughts in an organized way, and to collaborate on further investigation, many positive advances in social, scientific, and public policy, as well as in other fields, could be made. As a result, he left MIT with a single, ambitious goal: bring systems thinking to a wider audience and apply it without the constraints and

> **Ali Mashayekhi** was born in Khomein, Iran, and received his BSc degree in mechanical engineering from Sharif University of Technology (SUT). In 1974, he entered the System Dynamics Ph.D. program at MIT's Sloan School of Management, where he met Barry when Barry arrived as a new Ph.D. student. Ali's close friendship with Barry was both academic and personal; they lived across the hall from each other in the married students apartments in West Gate at MIT for three years. Ali returned to Iran after he received his Ph.D. in 1978. He is currently a professor of management, teaching system dynamics, organizational learning, and strategic management at SUT. He has also been quite active in teaching, research, and consulting in the United States since 1986.

requirements imposed by academia. That's just what he did.

STELLA was Barry's first major contribution to what would become a set of widely available software applications and educational materials that could be used by anyone. Before Barry invented STELLA, system dynamics models were made with pencil and paper. Each causal loop and stock and flow diagram was drawn, edited, and redrawn as models were refined. The process was tedious and slowed down the systems thinking because as much time was spent on getting the mechanical drawing right as was spent on the critical overall concepts and model outcomes.

Barry's talent for explaining systems thinking concepts and his belief that those concepts should be easy enough for anyone to use developed into the STELLA software. STELLA both engaged beginners and gave advanced systems thinking practitioners a platform for their work. Models could be quickly built, continually improved as thinking changed and expanded, and used to present thinking and outcomes to others.

iThink was developed by Barry after STELLA and it addressed systems thinking for business applications. Other software developers joined the market with applications that incorporated system dynamics and the systems thinking tools that Barry had invented.

Barry was convinced that if both individuals and policy makers had a systemic way to think about and dig into complex problems, to discuss those problems, to share their thoughts in an organized way, and to collaborate on further investigation, many positive advances in social, scientific, and public policy, as well as in other fields, could be made.

Armed with STELLA, his natural teaching skills, and his faith that systems thinking would have a positive impact on any kind of problem solving, Barry began to bring systems thinking to a wider audience. He built relationships with teachers at all grades and university levels across the country. He taught them systems thinking concepts and gave schools software. He also created corporate workshops that taught executives and managers how to improve performance by applying systems thinking to financial, marketing, operations, human resources, and other departmental issues. Of course, he also showed them how systems thinking models illustrated the integration of problems and solutions across departmental lines.

tracing connections

Barry Richmond entered my life in 1974. I had left my home in Tehran, Iran, moving to Boston to pursue a planning and control graduate degree at MIT's Sloan School of Management; however, the Vice President of my university in Iran had encouraged me to study system dynamics. Where better to study system dynamics than MIT in the 1970s where Jay Forrester, founder of system dynamics, was teaching? Although I wasn't sure of my interest, I took a system dynamics course. That one course hooked me; I asked Forrester if I could join his group of students. As a member of that small group of system dynamics pioneers, I found my life's calling and true vocation, and I met many people who would play important roles in my professional and personal life. Barry Richmond was one of them.

Barry and I, with our kids in tow, first met on a playground near the married students' residence. We struck up a conversation that quickly revealed two coincidences: we were both doctoral students in the system dynamics group at Sloan School, and we were across-the-hall neighbors. The proximity of our apartments made it easy for us to become close friends and colleagues. In the evening, after our kids had gone to bed, we would discuss how to conceptualize and analyze a system in relation to a particular problem or talk over many other topics including the national model project in which we were both involved. Barry's questions were always sharp and his explanations were always clear. Like me, Barry had found his calling.

Perhaps most importantly, he invented the concept of learning environments—combining interactive experiences with computer models of real-world issues and problems. These models, based on systems thinking, help us understand how the real world operates and how the problems that we face are generated and can be solved. Some of the best-known learning environments are "Food Chain," "Fly a Cell," and a series developed in collaboration with Harvard Business School Publishing that includes "Balancing the Corporate Scorecard" and "Managing Customers for Profit." Learning environments were created for a variety of disciplines including biology, ecology, and business. They continue to teach, not only about the system they were built to explain, but also more generally about how systems thinking is applied to complex issues.

> Barry developed and documented eight critical thinking skills. Those eight skills continue to serve as a roadmap that begins with attracting a person to systems thinking and continues their involvement by building their skills and competence.

In order to move systems thinkers from simple to more advanced levels of application, Barry developed and documented eight critical thinking skills, which are described in the introduction of this book, "The Thinking in Systems Thinking: Eight Critical Skills." Those eight skills continue to serve as a roadmap that begins with attracting a person to systems thinking and continues their involvement by building their skills and competence.

As you read this book, you'll realize that the leading systems thinkers in the world are connected to Barry. They were his students or his colleagues. And their students and their clients are connected to Barry through the systems thinking concepts that he developed and then taught with his easy-to-use approach.

The best, and most fitting, way to think about how Barry helped build the worldwide community of systems thinkers and how his work continues to influence them is with a model. Such a model not only illustrates Barry's continued importance and presence in this community, but it also shows that any dynamic phenomenon can be explored and illustrated through the use of systems thinking concepts and a model.

A Model of Barry Richmond's Influence on the Systems Thinking Community

Barry's passion for systems thinking and his experience as a professor resulted in the creation of materials (learning environments, books, articles, and training programs) that explained concepts and the creation of applications and software (STELLA and *iThink*) that allowed people to easily make and share models and simulations. He was prolific and his work not only expanded the systems thinking "library," but also kept it current. Figure 1-1 depicts the influence of the software and materials Barry created to support systems thinking education and projects.

> Think of how much easier it is to share ideas that are written down or to explain new concepts in a way that involves your audience and allows them to participate.

Think of how much easier it is to share ideas that are written down or to explain new concepts in a way that involves your audience and allows them to participate. The infusion of software and materials, initiated by Barry, made it possible to reach more students and

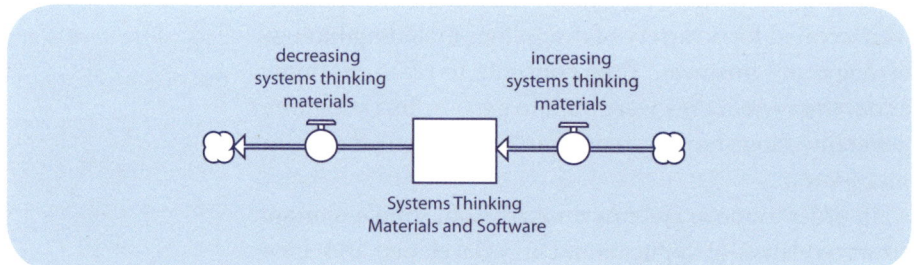

Figure 1-1. Barry created innovative materials and software for systems thinking

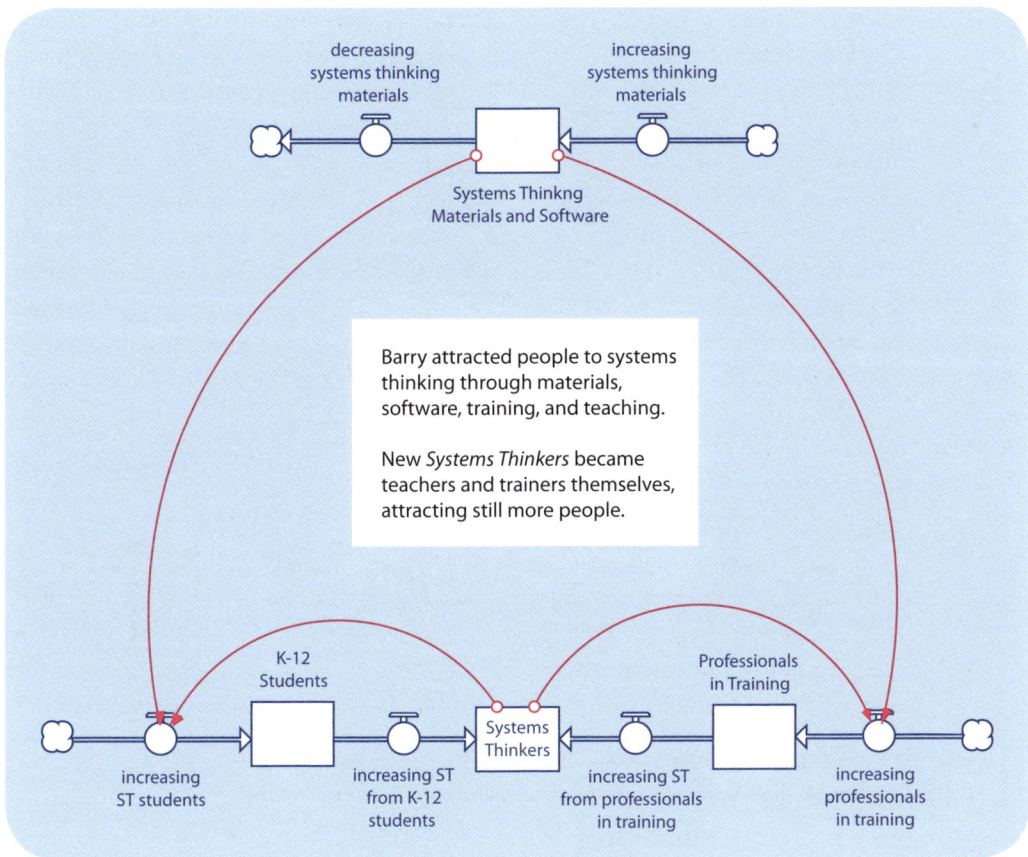

Figure 1-2. The systems thinking materials and training programs offered by Barry increased the number of systems thinkers

professionals who could apply systems thinking to their studies, research, and work.

As shown in Figure 1-2, we can enhance the model to show that expanding the stock of *Systems Thinking materials and Software* builds the stocks of *K-12 Students* and *Professionals in Training*. The outflows of those two stocks add to the stock of *Systems Thinkers*.

Of course, as the number of *Systems Thinkers* increases, the number of available teachers and trainers increases. New *Systems Thinkers* create new training programs that are tailored to particular audiences and disciplines. Models are shared among colleagues, teachers, and students and then refined or applied to new projects.

> The infusion of software and materials, initiated by Barry, made it possible to reach more students and professionals who could apply systems thinking to their studies, research, and work.

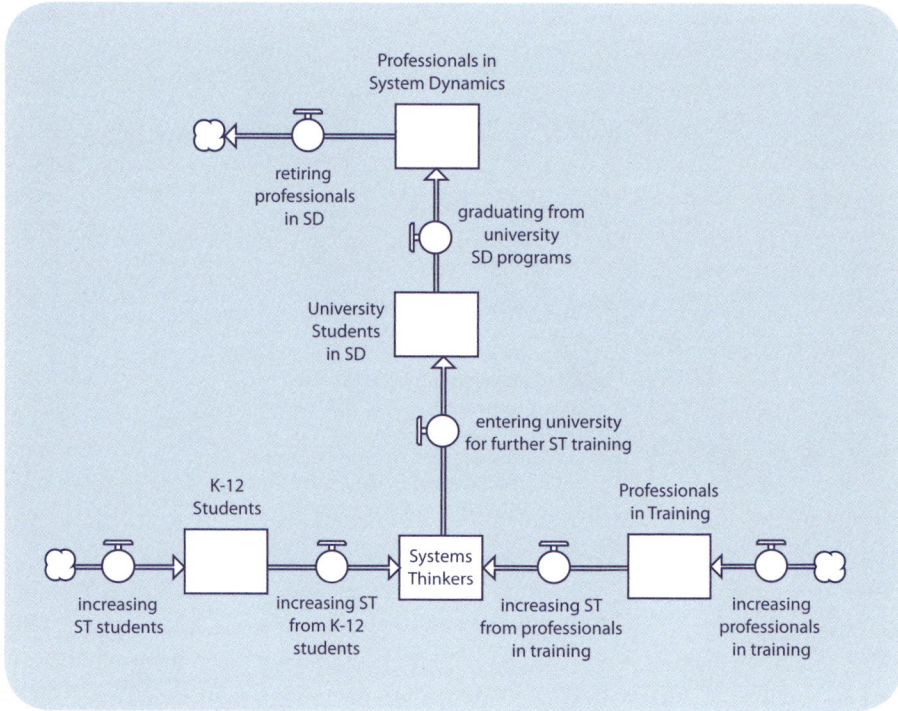

Figure 1-3. Some of the Systems Thinkers, inspired by Barry's work, continued their training in graduate and undergraduate programs

Barry's influence doesn't stop there. Many students and young professionals from the *Systems Thinkers* stock went on to universities, studied system dynamics, and became *Professionals in System Dynamics*, as shown in Figure 1-3.

Their university training made them professional systems thinkers. Their graduation increased the stock of *Professionals in System Dynamics* who went on to create new technologies, author new books and training materials, and devise new educational and training programs. They also increased the teaching capacity in schools and universities, and inside work places, as shown in Figure 1-4.

When we put all the model pieces together, we see the extent of Barry's contribution to systems thinking and the field of system dynamics. The software he invented and the materials he developed made it possible to bring systems thinking into more classrooms, universities, research centers, and businesses. More and more people have become systems thinkers and have advanced to the professional level. Today, the reinforcing loops of the model shown in Figure 1-4 continue to fuel systems thinking. Barry's intelligence, teaching expertise, and passion are still being felt.

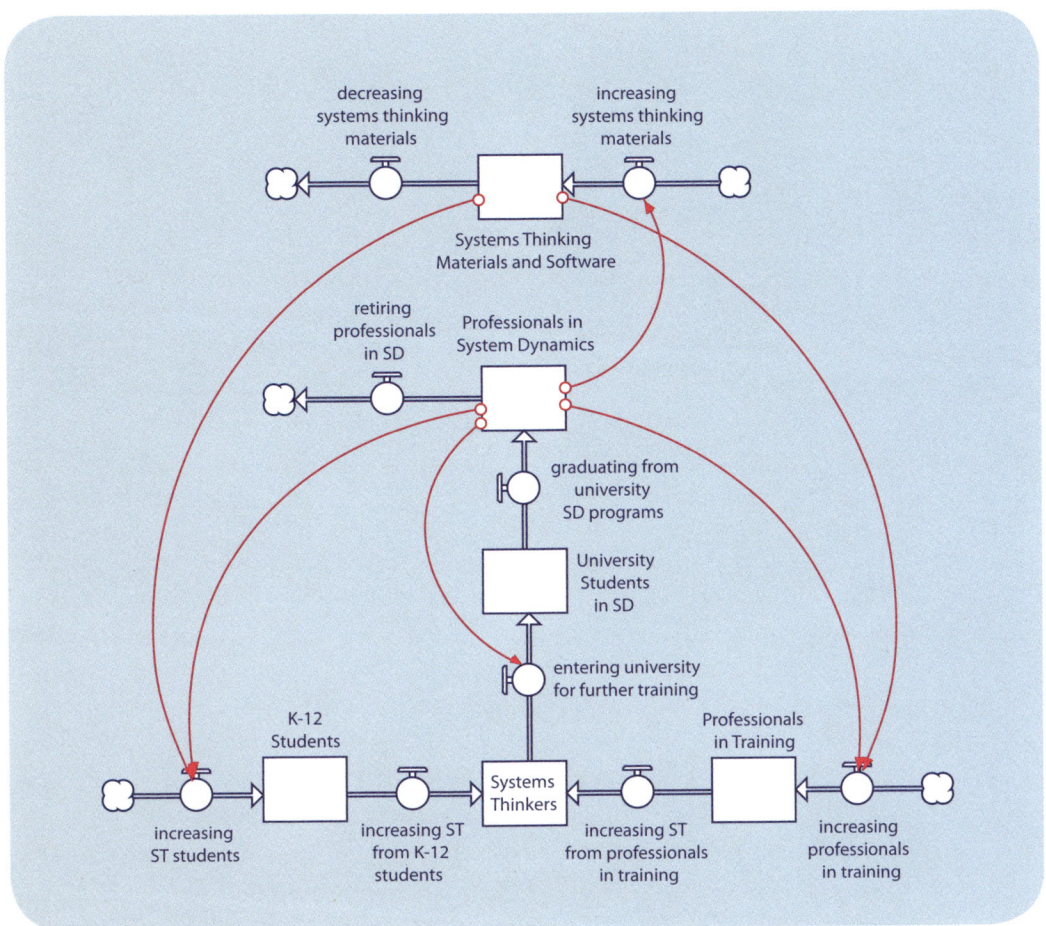

Figure 1-4. Professionals in System Dynamics create more teaching materials and training capacity to fuel further growth in the field

This book serves Barry's mission well in three important ways. First, it points to the wide variety of people, along with many different disciplines, who have benefited from systems thinking. Second, it offers examples that will inspire new systems thinkers. And third, it points to systems thinking resources that are in place and can be used by others.

2

Systems Thinking for Anyone: Practices to Consider

Steve Peterson

> Steve Peterson focuses on how anyone can understand and use systems thinking. He identifies many existing systems problems and discusses how systems thinking is needed to tackle such problems. In addition, he offers some basic steps one can follow to start to become a systems thinker.

I have thought often about Barry's passion for bringing systems thinking to a broad spectrum of professionals and students. At a practical level, a significant, sustained effort is needed to develop high proficiency in building full-blown system dynamics models. But what is the art of the possible for "the rest of us?" If anyone can do this at some level and if everyone should try, then what are the "best practices" associated with doing systems thinking at a less formal and more conversational level?

The depth and rigor of thinking around systems problems can be improved, and basic conversational uses of the systems thinking toolset can yield substantial returns in terms of increased understanding and improved performance. The following discussion identifies and illustrates a small set of systems thinking practices that have significant potential for underwriting effective systems thinking. Although not an exhaustive list, these highly accessible practices typify the approach of many seasoned systems practitioners. As such, they can help form the basis of a development agenda for the systems thinking newbie who is interested in using the systems approach to understand and improve how the world works. Let's begin by painting a broad-brush portrait of some key characteristics of a systems problem and then walk through the five basic practices in some detail.

> **Steve Peterson** met Barry in 1981 at Dartmouth's Thayer School of Engineering, where Barry served as Steve's mentor and thesis advisor. From 1985 to 2003, Steve worked at High Performance Systems, Inc. (now isee systems, inc.). While at High Performance Systems, Steve worked with Barry on many projects:
> - development of the STELLA and *iThink* software packages
> - development of the suite of models accompanying the software
> - design and delivery of consulting engagements using systems thinking
> - design and delivery of systems thinking workshops
>
> Steve currently resides in West Lebanon, New Hampshire, with his family. He is a principal consultant at Lexidyne, LLC, where his current activities include workshop design and delivery, as well as work with non-profits, government (defense and energy), health care, and pharmaceutical companies.

What is a Systems Problem?

Reflect on these questions for a few minutes. What is the most pressing problem currently facing you? Your personal life? Your community or organization? Your country? Your world? Write your thoughts down on a piece of paper.

Figure 2-1, for example, is my personal short list of different levels of systems problems.

For the anxious, apprehensive, or fearful, there certainly is a lot on this list to keep one up at night worrying. How does your list compare? Does your list give you pause?

These problems, which seem more and more prevalent as the world becomes more complex, share some interesting and important characteristics. They are interesting, because the characteristics typify a class of problems that I like to call "systems problems." They are important both because the characteristics point to some weaknesses in the way people often think about issues and because they point to systems thinking as a valuable vehicle for building understanding and improving system performance.

Systems problems share four fundamental characteristics: they are dynamic in nature; they involve multiple players; they are generated by interdependencies; and, finally, they are hard to communicate.

Characteristic 1: Dynamics

The word "dynamics" simply means "change over time." It is a simple concept with powerful implications. In the list in Figure 2-1, "change over time" is

Individual	Striking and maintaining a work-life balance while funding college education for my children
Community	Transitioning from an antiquated junior high school to a modern facility in a time of economic slowdown
Country	Collapse of financial markets
World	Global warming

Figure 2-1. Systems problems at four different levels

> **tracing connections**
>
> I worked with and learned from Barry Richmond for over twenty years. For me, these experiences comprised a remarkable set of opportunities to learn with a very remarkable man. I first met Barry when I was a young, skinny graduate student studying system dynamics at Dartmouth College. Over the ensuing years we worked together at High Performance Systems, collaborating on the development of the STELLA and *iThink* software and on a host of systems thinking-focused projects. The context for these projects ranged from pre-college education to business dynamics to the U.S. agricultural system.
>
> Barry was a man with a great passion for systems thinking. He believed deeply that "systems problems" represent the most pressing issues we face as individuals, as a society, and as a global community. He believed that the framework and thinking skills associated with systems thinking have significant potential to underwrite both the building of understanding and the improvement of performance of these systems. And he believed, very strongly, in "big tent" systems thinking. His view was that anyone can do this stuff at some level, that everyone should try, and that the world would be a better place as a result.

intrinsic to each problem. And yet it is possible and fairly common to view such problems as static in nature, ignoring both how things got to where they are now and how things might change moving forward in time. How often is a dynamic problem mischaracterized as a static one? What are the implications of this mischaracterization?

Characteristic 2: Multiple players with diverse interests

Refer again to the list of systems problems in Figure 2-1, or to your own list. It is apparent that the really difficult issues we face frequently involve multiple stakeholders who have diverse, and often divergent, interests. Like the old consulting fable about the difficulty of herding cats, it can be very difficult for disparate groups to come to a common view. This difficulty is amplified when the players view things from a "me"-centric perspective. In business and government circles, the problems of stovepipes—or silos—within organizations are legendary. Because stovepipes inhibit communication across the organizational chart, issues often are viewed from the perspective of narrowly defined functions or sub-groups. Instead of fostering a big-picture view, stovepipes tend to foster balkanized fiefdoms. In contrast, an approach to problems that moves beyond stovepipes has potential to help players come together around a common set of interests.

Characteristic 3: Interdependencies

A third characteristic of a systems problem is the role that interdependencies between individuals, functions, organizations, regions, or nations play in creating behavior over time. We have often heard that it takes two (working together) to dance; in an increasingly interconnected world, it is even more important to understand how interdependencies drive dynamics. What are the key interdependencies that drive the problem behaviors on your list?

> In an increasingly interconnected world, it is even more important to understand how interdependencies drive dynamics.

Characteristic 4: Hard to communicate

Take an item on your list, and try explaining the essence of the issue to a friend or colleague. Hard, isn't it? By themselves, words are often an inadequate vehicle for explaining dynamic problems driven by the interdependency of multiple players with diverse interests. An important aspect of the systems thinking toolset is its ability to facilitate more effective communication.

> Narrowly focused disciplines in academia, business, and elsewhere can shed light on pieces of a systems problem, but can break down when the problem reflects the interdependency of multiple, disparate actors and processes.

Because of these four basic characteristics, systems problems tend to be very difficult to address using traditional tools, techniques, and frameworks. Static, linear frameworks work well for addressing simple problems, but break down when applied to dynamic, non-linear problems. Narrowly focused disciplines in academia, business, and elsewhere can shed light on pieces of a systems problem, but can break down when the problem reflects the interdependency of multiple, disparate actors and processes. So if you think that the big issues are systems issues, you are likely to be disappointed if you use traditional vehicles for understanding and improving performance. Einstein said it well: "We can't solve problems by using the same kind of thinking we used to create them."

Systems Thinking Practices to Consider

One approach to addressing systems problems is to develop relatively detailed system dynamics models, such as those illustrated elsewhere in this book; however, a major challenge associated with building these models is the substantial learning curve involved. In my experience, it takes intense effort over a sustained period to get really good at building system dynamics models. For most people working to manage school or career, the investment in time and energy required to master the art and science of modeling can simply be too much.

Fortunately, it is possible to make progress as a systems thinker without making such a big investment of time and energy. The key, I think, is to work purposefully to incorporate important systems thinking practices into your daily activities. As these basic practices become internalized, they can support deeper and richer thinking around the structure and behavior of a systems problem, helping to generate better initiatives. Over time, the accumulation of small but continuous investments in a small set of practices can help to make the world a better place.

Here are five practices to consider:

- Think dynamically.
- Expand the boundary of inquiry.
- Get operational.
- Look for feedback.
- Seek to falsify.

These practices arise from and address the four common characteristics of systems issues. In the remainder of this chapter, I describe each of the practices in some detail. For each practice, the discussion will provide the following:

- A definition/description of the practice, identifying its value added
- A set of simple examples of the practice in action
- Suggestions for the next steps that you might take to embed the practice into your own life

Practice 1: Think dynamically

Dynamic thinking involves consideration of how the problem got to the current place, and where one might go from here. Dynamic thinking entails characterizing problems or issues as behavior patterns over time. Rather than simply considering an issue at a point in time ("The economy is in a huge mess!"), dynamic thinking involves consideration of how the problem got to the current place, and where one might go from here. Dynamic thinking often takes the form of a graph of behavior-over-time. You needn't look far to find a phenomenon that can be cast as behavior over time. Consider, as an illustration, the approval rating for U.S. presidents. The public approval of a host of presidents, including Lincoln,

> **Dynamic thinking** involves consideration of how the problem got to the current place, and where one might go from here.

FDR, Reagan, and Clinton, waxed and waned over the course of their tenure in office. Data associated with George W. Bush is particularly interesting. The graph in Figure 2-2 casts this socio-political phenomenon as a set of behavior patterns over time.

Figure 2-2 illustrates three important attributes of dynamic thinking. First, dynamic thinking provides a temporal perspective on a situation. It is certainly true that at the end of his tenure, President George W. Bush's approval rating was extremely low. But it got there through an almost inexorable decline (with a few aberrations that we will note in a minute) from its peak after the events of 9/11 (decline, by the way, is typical in modern presidencies). Meanwhile, the disapproval of the President grew over the period, while the level of indifference (as reflected in "no opinion") remained very low. By providing a dynamic context, this simple graph stimulates thinking and inquiry.

- Why does the popularity of presidents tend to go down during their time in office?
- For President Bush, why did the degree of indifference drop quickly and then remain so low for such a long time? Is this common to modern presidents?
- What might a president do to grow approval ratings in a sustained fashion?

Second, dynamic thinking enables you to put a "stake in the ground" around data. In the initial stages of a client engagement, I will often sketch my "best guess" of some behavior pattern of interest, and then compare that best guess against what the data say. Gaps between my best guess and actual data always provide an opportunity to learn something. In this instance, I was surprised to see the steep drop in the President's approval rating between October of 2001 and January of 2003. Such gaps often cry out for an explanation and further engage the thought processes of understanding what happened, why it happened, and what might be done about it.

> The process of thinking about dynamics, individually and collectively, can go far to help groups come to a shared understanding of the phenomenon of interest.

Another avenue in which dynamic thinking enables you to put a "stake in the ground" around data can be traveled when the data is ambiguous or missing. Consider again your list of pressing problems. Perhaps for one of those problems it is not clear what has happened historically. Or perhaps there are multiple potential trajectories moving forward. Or perhaps different stakeholders have different perspectives. The process of thinking about dynamics, individually and collectively, can go far to help groups come to a shared understanding of the phenomenon of interest.

Systems Thinking for Anyone 37

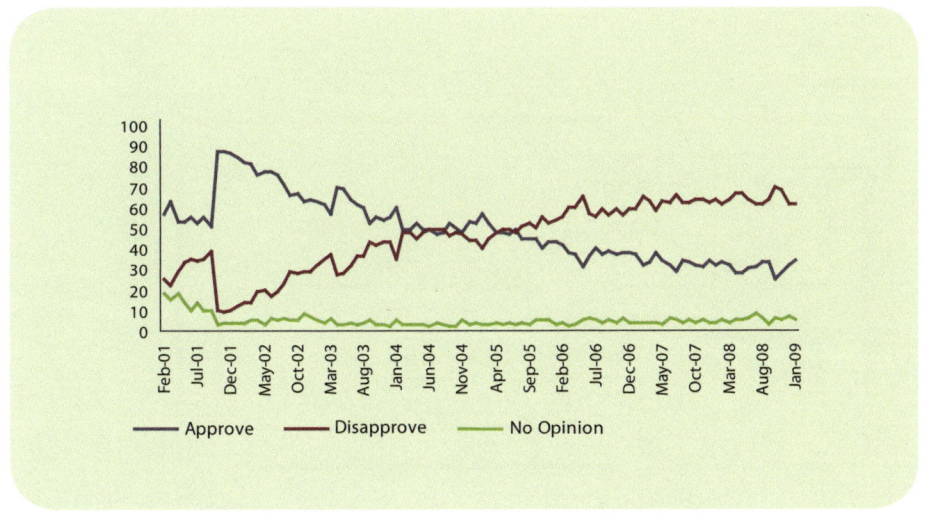

Copyright © Gallup. All rights reserved. Reprinted with permission from http://www.gallup.com.

Figure 2-2. Approval rating of George W. Bush in a behavior-over-time graph

Third, dynamic thinking is generative in the sense that it facilitates inquiry about the underlying processes that have moved the system to its current condition. In the example above, it is clear that external events (particularly 9/11; the beginning of the Afghanistan war; the beginning of the Iraq war; the capture of Saddam Hussein) have had some effect on President Bush's approval rating. But it is also very clear that these "blips" in approval have occurred against a long-term downward trend. One view into the underlying processes that might drive this trend is shown in the simple stock-flow map in Figure 2-3.

The map in Figure 2-3 emerges readily from the approval rating graph (Figure 2-2). The stocks of *Approvers*, *Indifferent*, and *Disapprovers* directly correspond to the concepts displayed as behavior over time. The flows depict the different pathways that people can take while moving among these three stocks. Very productive discussions could emerge around the relative size of these different pathways, the driving forces for each flow, and the relative difficulty in moving people in a sustained fashion from the box of *Disapprovers* into the box of *Approvers*. Maps such as these, because they depict underlying processes, often form the core structure for formal models such as those described elsewhere in this book. And yet, maps such as these can add value by themselves, by forging an initial connection between system structure and system behavior.

> Stock-flow maps can add value by themselves, by forging an initial connection between system structure and system behavior.

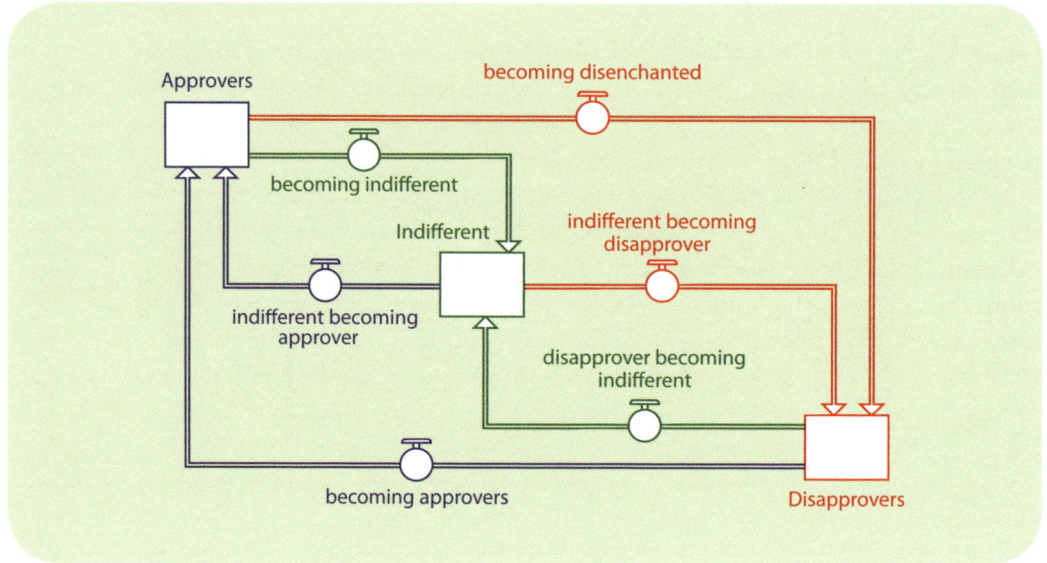

Figure 2-3. Stock-flow map of presidential approval dynamics

Dynamic thinking is one of Barry's critical thinking skills, and is essential to the recognition and diagnosis of systems problems at any level. It turns out that it is relatively easy to begin building your skills in dynamic thinking, as long as you stick with it. Here are a few activities that you might consider:

- Read through the op-ed pages in your favorite newspaper, magazine or online source with a pencil and paper at your side. See if you can capture the verbal description of a phenomenon of interest as a pattern of behavior over time. Try to be as precise as possible about both the units of measure and the range along the horizontal (time) and vertical axes.
- Whenever you encounter a problem or issue expressed as an "event," look beyond the event to see if there is a pattern of events over time. Ask yourself: "How did the system get to its current state? How might it evolve moving forward in time?"
- Focus on learning from the data. It is always the case that you will learn something, particularly if you have first bounded or put a "stake in the ground" around what you think has happened over time.
- Engage others in the process of thinking dynamically. Check your thinking with others. Seek their input. An alternate perspective can often clarify and refine your thinking.

Practice 2: Expand the boundary of inquiry

I really hate to travel by airplane these days. While I am mildly annoyed by the security screenings and some of the other minor hassles of air travel, one thing that really and literally pains me is the tightly defined system boundary often adopted by my fellow passengers. Let me describe it to you.

I'm pretty tall at 6'4", and I'm no longer the skinny guy that I was in my graduate school days. I'm also pretty frugal with client money when I travel. So, typically you'll find me traveling toward the back of the plane in the cheap seats. Leg room there leaves something to be desired. Once I have folded myself into my seat, I am anxious for the duration of the flight, anticipating the moment when the person in the seat ahead of me plugs their noise-canceling headphones into their iPod, yawns, stretches, reaches down, pushes the little button on their armrest . . . and *crushes my legs* as they "sit back and relax."

This dynamic, which I experience pretty much every time I travel by airplane, illustrates the problems of a narrowly-defined boundary of inquiry when dealing with a systems problem. All too often, the person in front of me defines his boundary of inquiry as "me and my seat." Because this area of interest is defined narrowly, actions are taken which can result in unintended consequences and unnecessary pain. In a relatively trivial system consisting of passengers on an airplane, these narrowly-defined boundaries lead to small violations of the social contract, eroding whatever communal spirit exists between passengers. In less trivial systems, the unintended consequences associated with a too-narrow boundary of inquiry can make the difference between success and failure of an initiative. Broadening the boundary of inquiry adds value by increasing the likelihood that you will be thinking about a larger set of relevant relationships that underlie problem behavior. This, in turn, increases the likelihood that you will identify, anticipate, and effectively manage the full suite of consequences of an initiative.

> Broadening the boundary of inquiry adds value by increasing the likelihood that you will be thinking about a larger set of relevant relationships that underlie problem behavior.

A few examples will help to solidify the value added that comes from expanding the boundary of inquiry. First, consider the initial response to the events of 9/11. In the United States, this response was overwhelming and bipartisan; indeed, there was widespread global outcry. *Le Monde* captured the prevailing sentiment well: "We Are All Americans." In many quarters, both in the United States and throughout the world, the response to 9/11 was to seek out and destroy the terrorists responsible.

One very simple representation of this prevailing mental model is shown in Figure 2-4. This little map, with one stock and one outflow, has several compelling features. It is simple. It is direct. It is clear. It is actionable. Unfortunately, because the boundary of inquiry is very narrowly defined, this map can lead to

> Stocks represent accumulations, in this case, the accumulation of *Terrorists*.
>
> Flows represent actions or activities that fill or drain accumulations over time. In this case, the flow called *eradicating* acts to remove *Terrorists* from the system.
>
> The cloud at the end of the flow represents an infinite sink. In this case it indicates that *Terrorists* are removed forever.

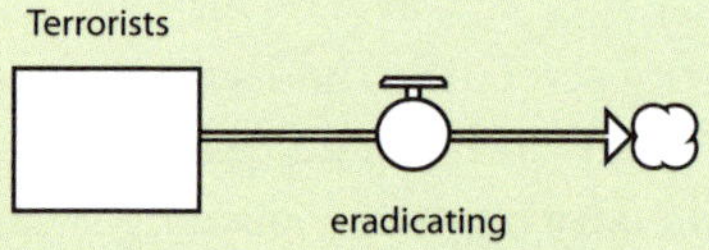

Figure 2-4. A simple representation of the "seek and destroy" mental model

significantly erroneous policy conclusions. In this map, once terrorists are eradicated, that is the end of the story.

But is this the whole story? Contrast the simple map with one that is developed from an expanded boundary of inquiry, shown in Figure 2-5. In this map, it is easy to see how an initial set of efforts to eradicate terrorism can lead to a buildup in enmity toward the United States, which in turn can open up the supply lines associated with recruiting and training new terrorists. Efforts to reduce the number of terrorists can set into motion processes that—over time—could dampen (or even reverse, depending on the strength of feedback) the effect of the initiatives. Also shown on the map (in green) are potential levers for changing system behavior. You might take a few minutes to think through the implications of these different levers as vehicles for reducing terrorist activity.

A second example illustrating the value of expanding the boundary of inquiry comes from the area of public health. According to the Centers for Disease Control and Prevention, prevalence of type 2 diabetes in the United States is projected to double by 2050. This represents an epidemic of epic proportions. The numbers are staggering. According to the CDC (http://www.cdc.gov/diabetes/news/docs/lifetime.htm), one of every three Americans is likely to develop type 2 diabetes over their lifetime. For Hispanic females, the risk is 1 in 2! Type 2 diabetes is extremely challenging. It can be managed at some level, but at this point in time it cannot be cured. It is associated with a host of other medical conditions, including renal failure, blindness, slow healing wounds, and coronary artery disease. To a very large extent, type 2 diabetes appears to be a "lifestyle" chronic illness, associated with obesity, diet, and a sedentary lifestyle.

A narrowly defined boundary of inquiry might lead to a simple representation of incidence and prevalence of type 2 diabetes, highlighting the implications for the nation's health care budget. Figure 2-6 provides a simple map of incidence, prevalence, and the associated incurring of costs.

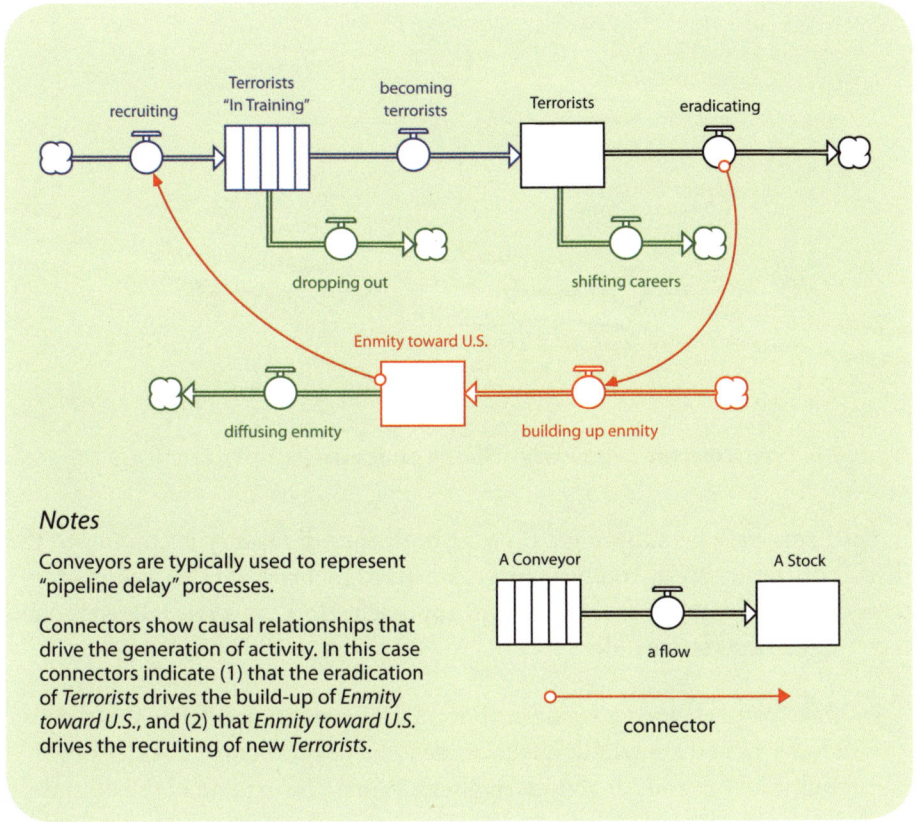

Figure 2-5. A more sophisticated representation of terrorist dynamics

As far as it goes, this simple map (Figure 2-6) can be helpful. It provides a very clear picture of the relationship between the population of type 2 diabetics and the associated health care expenditure. But the policy space increases dramatically with a simple expansion of the boundary, as suggested in Figure 2-7.

With a small expansion in the boundary of inquiry, we can begin to visualize and then address the longer term processes that give rise to type 2 diabetes, perhaps with a positive impact on the system's trajectory. For example, it might be possible to develop targeted public health initiatives (for example, around sustaining a culturally relevant healthful lifestyle) that might slow the influx of people into the pre-diabetic state. Or, it might be possible to develop screenings and lifestyle improvements for pre-diabetics, moving them back into the healthy population *before* type 2 diabetes develops. By lowering the stock of pre-diabetics over time, these initiatives could potentially create a future different than that implied by the CDC projection.

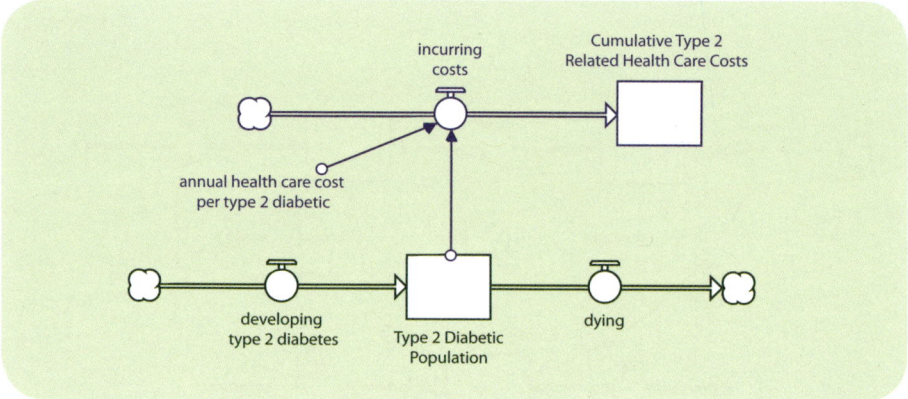

Figure 2-6. Type 2 diabetes—incurring of health care costs

For many people, adopting a broader boundary of inquiry is counter to the default operating style. You have to work hard to incorporate this aspect of "systems citizenry"[1] into your thinking and approach. Here are a few relatively "low-tech" suggestions to consider:

- Make yourself conscious of the boundaries—often implicit—that exist whenever you are working with some issue or problem. Consider how your thinking and/or actions might change if you expanded the boundary of inquiry.
- Get in the habit of thinking through unintended consequences of your actions. This inevitably leads to a healthy expansion in the boundary of inquiry. When you decide to chart a course of action around some systems problem, ask: "What other processes am I setting into motion? How might those processes come back to get me?"
- You may find it helpful to develop some facility in using stocks and flows to represent simple systems and processes. As described in the next section, stocks and flows are extremely powerful tools for representing the essence of how a system is put together.
- Always look behind you before you lean back in the airline seat. Remember, it may be my legs that you're about to crush.

One of the challenges in expanding the boundary of inquiry is in discovering the sweet spot—the optimal degree of expansion that enables you to shed light on thorny aspects of a systems problem. While it is true that everything is connected to everything else, in my experience it is not often useful to make cosmic

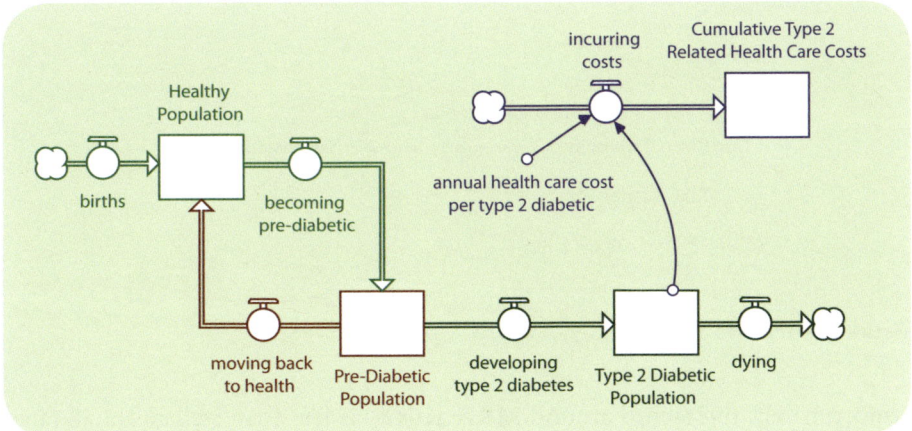

Figure 2-7. Type 2 diabetes—expanding the boundary of inquiry

connections when dealing with real-world systems problems. Instead, you might try a more incremental approach. Start with the prevailing thinking, whatever it is, and then try to expand the boundary by one or two degrees, as illustrated in the diabetes discussion above. See how far that gets you. Iterate as needed.

Practice 3: Get operational

Getting operational about system structure requires you to focus on understanding how underlying processes are put together. Rather than asking, "What are the factors that influence this process?" you are asking, "How does this process work?" You are seeking to understand the essence of how interdependencies operate in the system. The distinction between "factors" and "operational" approaches has important implications for how you think about systems problems. When you get operational, you increase the likelihood that you will identify the actionable levers for improving system performance. When you get operational, you are engaging in Barry's skill of operational thinking. As an illustration of the distinction between "factors" and "operational" approaches, consider the world of mergers and acquisitions (M&A). Often, M&A activity is undertaken because there is hope that the resultant organization will perform better along some dimensions. In the business press over the past 10 years, you will find words like "synergy" or "increased reach" or "shareholder value" associated with discussions of contemplated M&A activity.

> Getting **operational** about system structure requires you to focus on understanding how underlying processes are put together.

> When you get operational, you increase the likelihood that you will identify the actionable levers for improving system performance.

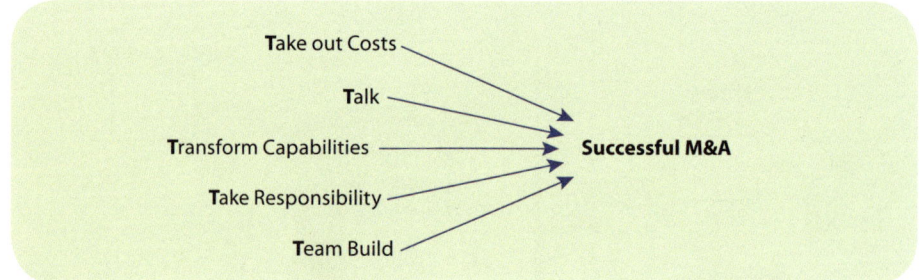

Figure 2-8. The Five T-Factors framework

Unfortunately, the record around M&A activity is less than stellar. The ill-fated Daimler-Chrysler and AOL-Time-Warner mergers come readily to mind.

I recently had the opportunity to work with a client to build understanding of why M&A so often misses the mark, and what an organization might do about it. At the outset, I discovered that the client used what they called "The Five T-Factors" framework (Figure 2-8).

A simple laundry list like that in Figure 2-8 is often used. Perhaps you have developed a list like this, either individually or in a group setting. If you are like me, you have certainly encountered such lists in your educational experience ("Here are the six factors that caused the Civil War . . ."). It is important to note that such lists are *not wrong*. In this instance, each of the five T-Factors is connected in some fashion with a successful M&A; however, the problem is that the factors do not help you to identify *where*, *when*, and *how much* to intervene in the system in order to improve performance. "Getting operational" with the client around each of the five T-Factors turned out to be very productive.

For example, "Team Building" is a great idea in pretty much any context. In many organizations, team building entails the development of highly-connected-to-the-organization individuals who are willing to go the extra mile to achieve the organization's goals. Highly committed people tend to require less management "care and feeding," and their activities tend to build the organization's reputation as a "good" employer. By contrast, highly malcontented people tend to require significant care, feeding, and management, and they can undermine the organization's reputation.

A simple map that provided an organizing framework for our operational view of team building is shown in Figure 2-9. In the map, there are three categories of employees—*Malcontented*, *Contented*, and *Committed*. Flows move employees between the three categories. Flows also represent hiring activities, exits, and the influx of employees to the combined organization as a result of the M&A.

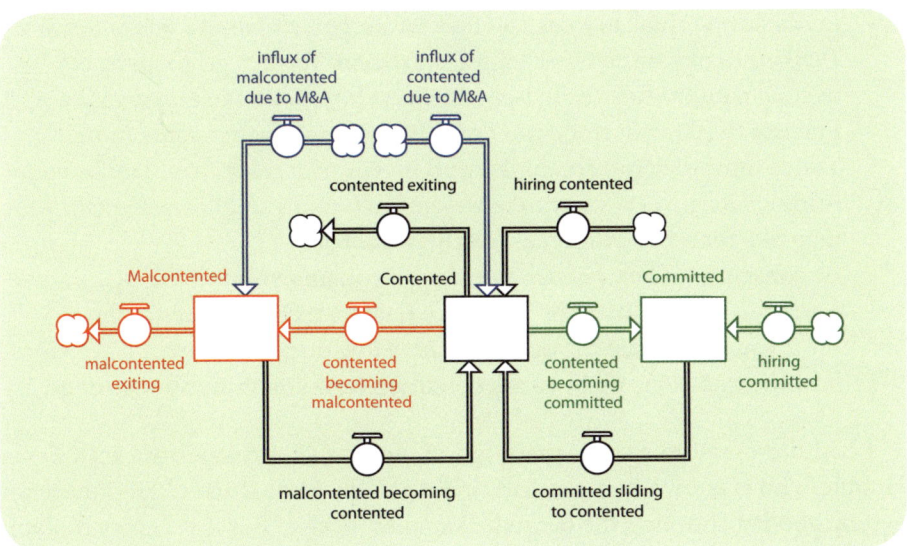

Figure 2-9. M&A team flow dynamics

This map (Figure 2-9) proved exceedingly helpful in pushing forward the thinking about how leadership might facilitate the development of highly committed, highly productive teams during the transitional stress associated with M&A. Based on discussion around this map (as well as subsequent analysis with the resultant model), it became clear that an initial focal point for intervention was around the stock of *Malcontented*. Because of the substantial difficulty in "making" disconnected team members become more connected, and because of the almost viral quality of the spread of discontent and cynicism within an organization (particularly under stressful conditions such as a merger or acquisition), the client team realized that it was essential to monitor the size of the pool of malcontents and facilitate their graceful exit early on in the project. Focusing exclusively on some of the more concrete tasks associated with a merger (for example, taking out costs associated with redundancies in processes, or integrating information technology systems) can allow malcontent dynamics to gain a foothold, causing committed individuals to "slide" and undermining leadership efforts to team-build.

According to Neal Sedaka, "Breakin' up is hard to do." It may well be that developing the habit of getting operational is even harder. And yet, it may well be the foundational practice for those of us who do this stuff for a living. I believe that it is an essential practice if you want to deal productively with systems problems. In order to develop this practice, you might begin by doing some of the following:

- Learn how to think in stock and flow terms. Barry's *Introduction to Systems Thinking* books are an excellent place to begin. You can get them by connecting with the folks from isee systems at http://www.iseesystems.com.
- Practice thinking in stock and flow terms. Then practice some more. Take a topic that you are thinking about (in your work, your family, your reading, etc.). See if you can represent it as stocks and flows. Explain your map to a friend or colleague. Get their feedback.
- Be conscious of *how* you are thinking. If you find yourself asking questions that begin with, "What are the factors that influence this . . ." see if you can re-cast the questions as, "How does this work . . ." Watch how the questions that you ask condition how you think about things!

I had the pleasure several years ago of sharing an airplane row with Ernie Hobbie, who is known in basketball circles as "The Shot Doctor." His advice for getting good at shooting the basketball applies nicely: "But if . . . every day you practice, practice, practice, then you have a chance to break bad habits" (http://vault.sportsillustrated.cnn.com/vault/article/magazine/MAG1069290/2/index.htm).

Practice 4: Look for feedback

Feedback is a *huge* concept in the systems thinking and system dynamics communities. Feedback is operative whenever the current status of the system (along one or more attributes or dimensions) drives activities which, in turn, change the status of the system moving forward in time. As a result, feedback is very closely tied to the performance of a system. Feedback relationships provide the "fine structure" that ties together stocks and flows in real-world systems. Feedback is what makes systems problems so interesting and challenging to address.

When I say, "look for feedback," I do not mean that you should be asking your colleagues to offer candid evaluations of your performance (although you might find that to be a good idea). The practice of looking for feedback will enrich your view of causality. A simple view of causality says, "A causes B, and that's the end of the story." A feedback-enhanced view of causality says, "A causes B, and over time B impacts A." This enriched view of causality can help you to better understand the interdependencies that drive dynamics of growth, decline, instability, or equilibrium-seeking in systems. In addition, by encouraging you to think about underlying interdependencies whose strength changes over time, looking for feedback subtly changes how you look at the "solution" to systems problems. Rather than "fixing" a problem once and for all, the mind set becomes one of how to orchestrate a set of ongoing processes to shape the dynamics over time.

To illustrate this change in mind set, think for a moment about gang behavior and violence among youth. A simple view of causality in this instance might look something like Figure 2-10. This is a straightforward picture that makes a lot of empirical sense. In many areas, gangs are responsible for violent activity. This view suggests a "fix" of removing gangs. No gangs, no violence!

A feedback-enhanced viewpoint enriches the picture considerably (Figure 2-11). In so doing, the diagram facilitates thinking about interdependencies and how one might shape the system rather than fix the problem once and for all. In Figure 2-11, there is a link back from violence to gangs. This link reflects the notion that gang-related violence creates a context that influences the further development of gangs. For example, youth who experience (either directly or indirectly) gang-related violence may become affiliated with gangs in order to regain a sense of control, safety, or protection. To the extent that this vicious cycle exists in a neighborhood, it can drive the system into a "trapped state" from which it may be very difficult to emerge.

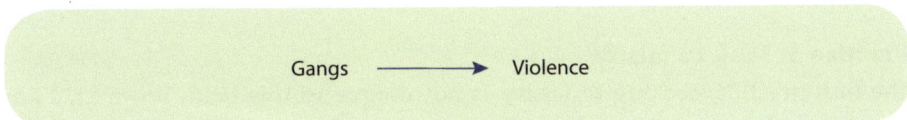

Figure 2-10. A straight-line view of causality

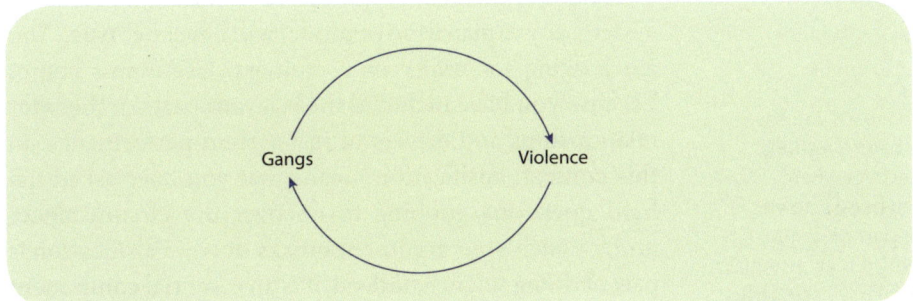

Figure 2-11. A closed-loop view of causality

This practice of surfacing feedback emerges from an internalized perspective that causality is circular in nature. It is what Barry called closed-loop thinking. This is not something that you can prove; it is a perspective that you develop over time. For many, internalizing a feedback perspective first requires shedding habits of straight-line thinking. As you encounter assertions about causality (in your work, your reading, and your interaction with others), try to diagram the causality of the situation. A simple word-and-arrow diagram should do the trick. Then, see if you can close the loop. Write down the avenues of inquiry that emerge when you close the loop. Before long, you will find that you will be looking for feedback as a matter of habit.

As you develop the practice of looking for feedback, it can be easy to go overboard. In my experience, there is a significant return associated with developing a mindset that views causality as circular rather than straight-line in nature. An additional increment of value can come as you use causal loop diagrams (not presented here, but readily accessible from sources such as Pegasus Communications, http://www.pegasuscom.com) to represent feedback relationships; however, diminishing (and often negative) returns tend to emerge if your diagrams begin to take the form of a plate of spaghetti and meatballs. If you finding yourself losing an operational, "how does it work" focus, you may be going a bit over the top.

Practice 5: Seek to falsify

The fifth practice, seeking to falsify, is not unique to this field; however, I am convinced that it is essential to effective use, both conversationally and more formally, of the systems thinking tools and framework.

Barry used to say that the all-around value of this stuff was its ability to help you build a better argument. Because it is always a selection and abstraction of the real system, any explanation or model will never be "true." You are looking for utility or usefulness. Usefulness comes because you have included the relevant parts of the interrelationships and drivers of real system performance. In this context, falsification means that you have asked the hard questions, probing to uncover the circumstances under which your argument breaks down. Falsification is part of doing science; indeed, it is an essential component of Barry's scientific thinking skill. Seeking to falsify adds value in two ways. First, it helps you to build confidence in the utility of your effort. Second, it provides a vehicle for engaging others in the process of pushing forward the thinking on an issue of interest, building team ownership of the work product.

For formal simulation models, a host of testing approaches can be applied in an effort to falsify. For more conversational approaches, simple "thought experiments" can go far to help identify weaknesses in the thinking, areas where the boundary might be expanded, and the like. The idea of a thought experiment involves asking a "what if" question around some piece of how the system is put together, and then relating that to system performance. "What if I pushed the system in such-and-such a way, how might it respond in the real system, and does my current theory account for this?" "What would happen to this dynamic if I expand some aspect of my boundary of inquiry?" It is sometimes useful to use analogies and simple physical processes to help in the think-through process.

Physicists seem to be particularly adept at "falsification," often using simple thought experiments and demonstrations to understand where theories or real systems break down. A particularly compelling example of this practice in action occurred after the demise of the space shuttle *Challenger* in 1986. During the subsequent presidential commission investigation of the disaster, Richard Feynman provided a simple demonstration of the extreme conditions that apparently were not considered in the launch of the shuttle, identifying the circumstances under which the O-ring seals were susceptible to failure. A web search using the words "Feynman O ring" will lead you to a video of this demonstration.

In my own work, I have found it exceedingly helpful to share a simple stock and flow map such as those illustrated above with colleagues and clients, explaining the map to them and then asking them to help us all get smarter, by challenging and improving the thinking that is embedded within the map. When done non-defensively, the explanation of current thinking, the solicitation of input, and the incorporation of insight from the team can go far to help people to come to an improved common understanding. This, in turn, has potential to improve the outcome for a systems problem. You might try adapting this general approach to your own purposes.

Wrap-Up

Systems problems are ubiquitous, and they constitute some of the biggest challenges that we face individually, as a community, corporately, nationally, and globally. The difficulty in tackling systems issues stems from the unique characteristics of each (dynamics, multiple players with diverse interests, driven by interdependencies, difficult to communicate) when lined up against the tools, frameworks, and techniques that typically are used to address these issues. It is a huge challenge!

The tools and frameworks of systems thinking have potential for addressing systems problems; however, one major challenge is that it is too difficult for many people to invest the time and energy required to be facile at building full-blown system dynamics models. Fortunately, lower time and energy investment pathways can improve an individual's approach to systems issues. The pathway outlined here involves sustained, low-level investment in simple practices. By consistently engaging in the practices of thinking dynamically, expanding the boundary of inquiry, thinking operationally, being sensitive to feedback, and seeking to falsify, it is possible to improve thinking about systems problems, yielding better solutions and potentially resulting in an improved world. I believe, as did Barry, that small changes in one's approach to systems problems have potential to underwrite substantial changes in system performance. Wouldn't that be cool?

The challenge, as with so many other aspects of life, is to condition oneself to work at it so that these practices become second nature. You can't just read about it; you have to *do* it. In the words of Tom Magliozzi of *Car Talk* fame:

> ... listening does not lead to understanding; doing does lead to understanding. Does the cobbler teach his son how to cobble by telling him about it? Does the doctor learn to perform appendectomies by reading about them? No. They *do it* ... (http://www.cartalk.com/content/features/ATC/Education/r-rlast15.html)

Go get 'em!

Note

1. *Systems citizen* is a term coined by Barry and used in a number of chapters throughout this book. Systems citizens view themselves as members of a global community. They strive to understand the complexities of today's wordly systems and have the ability to tackle problems with an informed capacity to make a positive difference.

3

Teaching by Wondering Around: Learning About the World Naturally

Frank Draper

> Frank Draper discusses how he has integrated systems thinking into his teaching of science to high school students. The chapter is rich with illustrations of how he has transformed the way he teaches since he learned systems thinking. His students are learning more and his classes are so much fun he has had to open another section to accommodate all the students who want to take his course.

Systems thinking, like any thinking paradigm, should be invisible—a natural way that people think about the world. In Barry Richmond's words, it should be "the water we swim in." Just as most of us don't really deliberately choose to use inductive reasoning for a specific problem and deductive reasoning for a different problem (we just figure stuff out), people do not have to consciously know they are using systems thinking for any particular problem. Instead, we should always be thinking in terms of feedback and circular causality. This principle also has to be applied to the teaching and to the learning of systems thinking and system dynamics. People do not have to know they are learning about the science of systems thinking or system dynamics. They just need to be taught, from the beginning, that the world is made of dynamic, interconnected systems and that there are tools we can use to understand these dynamic relationships.

> Systems thinking, like any thinking paradigm, should be invisible—a natural way that people think about the world.

Since my early introduction to systems thinking, I have been transforming the science curriculum I teach to have "invisible" system dynamics and systems thinking infused throughout all of my courses. It has

Frank Draper grew up in southern California and received a B.A. in biological sciences from California State University, Fullerton. After working as an industrial chemist, a newspaper columnist, and a park ranger, he earned a B.S. in biological sciences and a teaching certificate from St. Cloud State University in Minnesota. He began teaching middle and high school in Minnesota in 1979. After moving to Arizona in 1986, he earned a M.Ed. in secondary education and a Ph.D. in teaching and teacher education from the University of Arizona. He has been teaching in Catalina Foothills school district since 1986 and teaching the field courses since 1994.

People do not have to know they are learning about the science of systems thinking or system dynamics. They just need to be taught, from the beginning, that the world is made of dynamic, interconnected systems.

been a lengthy but rewarding task. Science, as it is generally taught in our country, is mostly a series of facts unrelated to each other in terms of dynamic relationships. Most states, these days, have a set of curriculum standards with lists of factual pieces of science content that need to be covered, but rarely are any of these connected in any meaningful, real-world system of nature. If relationships are taught, they are usually either through correlations or through the "laundry list of facts." Barry talked about this in his article, "Systems thinking: Critical thinking skills for the 1990s and beyond," as well as in his *Introduction to Systems Thinking Guide*, which form the basis for the introductory chapter of this book.

However, I have been able to cover the state-required benchmarks while embedding them in an integrated, systems-based course. I teach the field courses at Catalina Foothills High School in Tucson, Arizona. The standard field sciences course is open to juniors and seniors, and it fulfills the graduation requirement of a third-year laboratory-based course. The honors, advanced field science course is for seniors who have demonstrated high achievement in the standard field science course and wish to delve deeper into the variety of sciences that involve outdoor research.

These courses integrate many sciences, combining anatomy, physiology, evolution, biogeography, ecology, geology, hydrology, chemistry, physics, meteorology, anthropology, and astronomy as well as natural resource management into a unified understanding of how nature works. As an example, whenever my students learn one aspect of the natural world, such as the physics of thermodynamics, they also learn how that component affects many parts of the world they live in: plate tectonics, cumulonimbus storm build-up, and the anatomical and physiological adaptations of animals for controlling heat gain and loss.

tracing connections

I met Barry in 1988, when I was teaching eighth-grade science at Orange Grove Middle School in Tucson, Arizona. Gordon Brown, the retired Dean of Engineering from MIT, lived in our school district, and this was my connection. Gordon had a long history with system dynamics from its beginnings at MIT, and he devoted his retirement to getting it established in public schools. Gordon met me in my classroom one spring afternoon, described system dynamics to me, and asked if I would be interested in pursuing it as a way of teaching the interconnections in the world. I was hooked.

That summer Gordon facilitated getting me, along with other Tucson teachers, invited to a two-week system dynamics training course at Stanford University. It was an incredible opportunity. Besides Barry, my teachers included several other contributors to this book: Steve Peterson, Khalid Saeed, and Ali Mashayekhi. During that initial training, I was finally able to put a name, a science, and a set of tools to the indefinable spark I just knew was lacking from my teaching.

After that course, Barry and I met numerous times. As I gained experience teaching system dynamics and systems thinking to both students and teachers, Barry and I had many conversations about learning, especially about learning systems thinking and system dynamics. We would talk, mostly agree and sometimes, rarely, disagree about how people learn systems thinking and how to best teach it. I think we were trying to figure out what it was we wanted to accomplish by teaching people to be systems thinkers.

Systems Thinking Embedded in Physics

My students learn about the physics of thermodynamics by learning about specific dynamic systems in which the laws of thermodynamics play an important role. For example, Figure 3-1 shows a behavior-over-time graph of animal temperature. A model of animal temperature is shown in Figure 3-2. This model was actually modified from a cooling-coffee-cup STELLA model (such as the one on the Creative Learning Exchange website, http://clexchange.org).

By completing multiple runs of the model as shown in Figure 3-3, comparing the size of animals, their insulation, the ambient air temperature, and whether they are warm- or cold-blooded, my students are able to come up with a general statement not only about thermodynamics (the role of ambient temperature and mass in determining heat loss rates), but also general statements about animal adaptations (what problems small animals face compared to large animals in hot

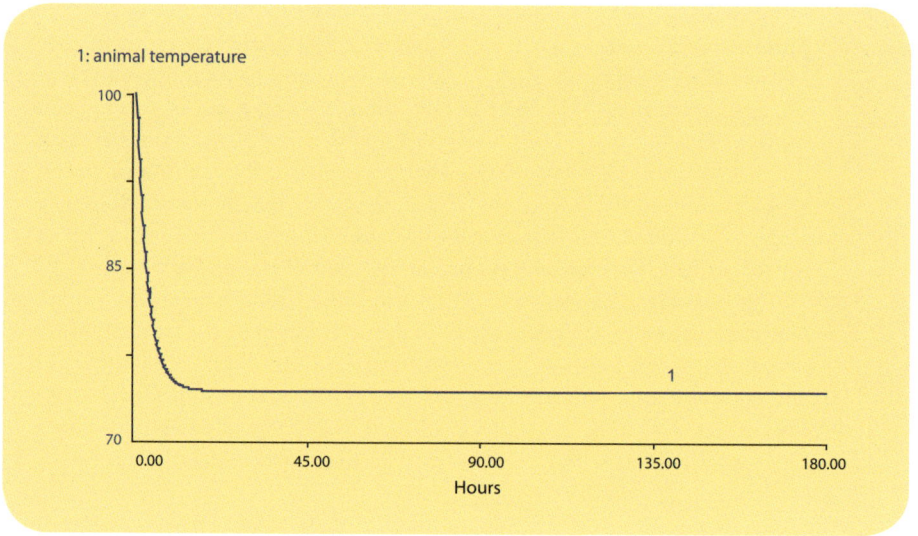

Figure 3-1. Animal temperature over time

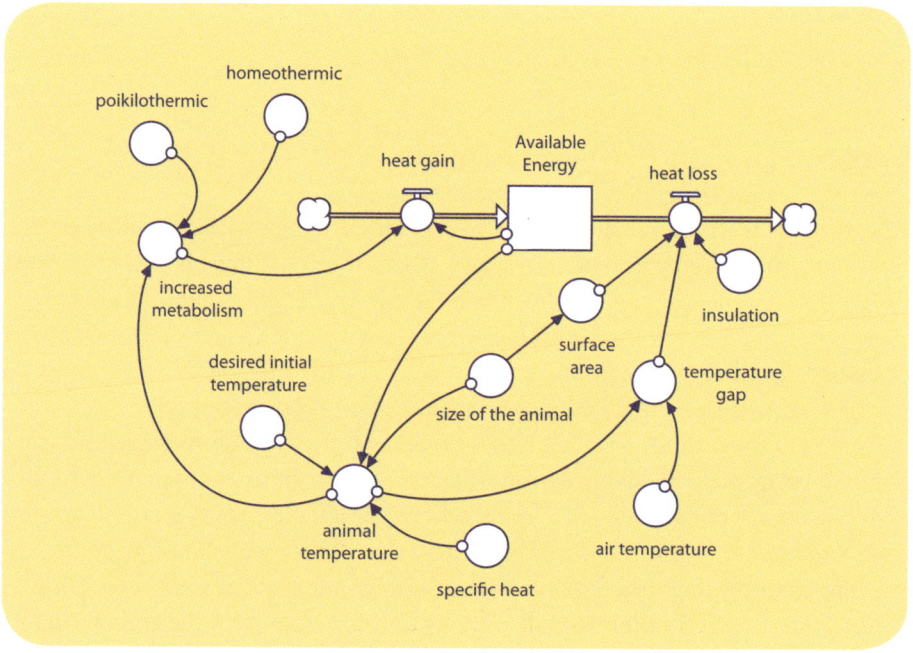

Figure 3-2. Model of animal temperature

and cold environments; what problems cold-blooded animals face compared to warm-blooded animals; what it is that insulation really does for animals).

This is the first STELLA model my students use in my class. I do not discuss STELLA, systems models, systems thinking, or system dynamics. I merely show them how to use the software and off they go exploring the system.

The next day, they explore a U.S. Geological Survey (USGS) website about plate tectonics, thermodynamics, and the rock cycle (http://pubs.usgs.gov/publications/text/dynamic.html). Although not a system dynamics website, the information emphasizes the dynamic nature of plate tectonics and how internal Earth forces interact in complex ways to create the various rock types and geologic features we find in the world.

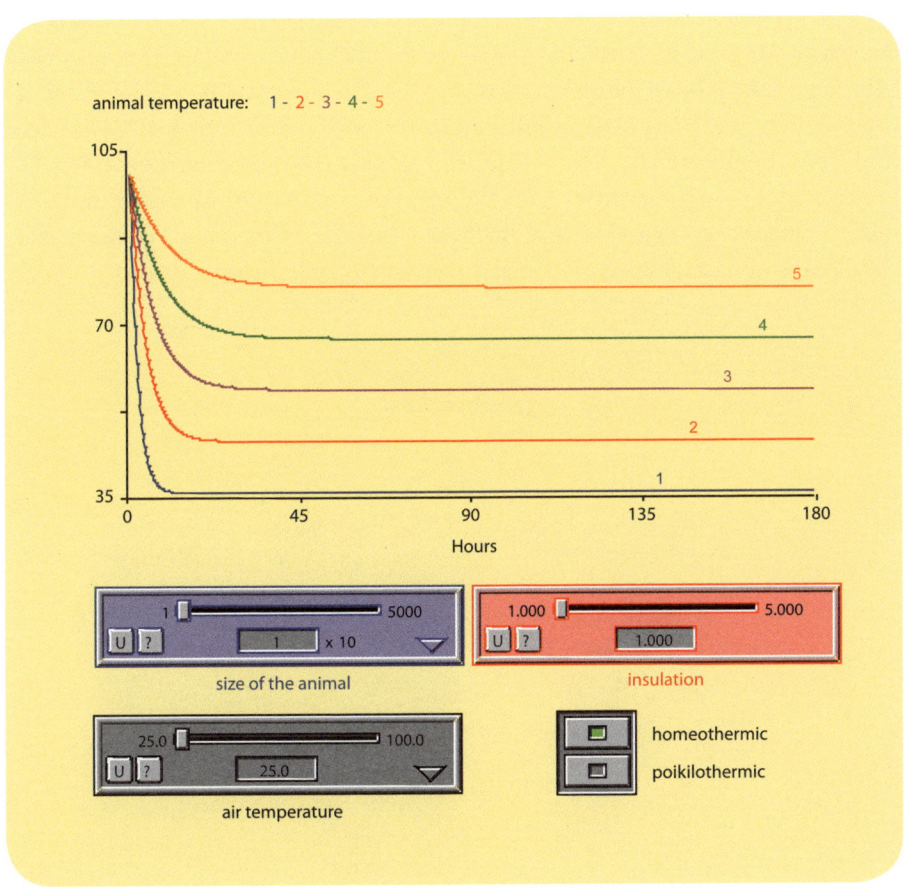

Figure 3-3. Exploring the system with multiple runs

Scientific and Dynamic Thinking

After the initial thermodynamics lesson, the students learn about cumulonimbus cloud build up (towering thunderstorms build up over campus every afternoon at the end of our Tucson summer monsoon season). The feedback relationships between rising warm air, ambient cooler air, vapor-to-liquid phase changes, latent heat release, and the continuing rising of air are presented as a causal loop, without naming the tool itself. My students just automatically draw the loops in their notes and ask questions about the feedback relationships, without ever knowing that this is a basic tool or knowing the name of the tool. Figure 3-4 shows a quick and dirty causal loop I draw for the students during this lab.

I have my students actually "read" through the causal loop. When a wet air mass in the Tucson summer heats up from the sun, its temperature rises; this lowers the density of the air mass (depicted as a negative link). As a result, the air mass rises in elevation. As it rises, the air mass loses heat to the surrounding air and the water vapor undergoes a phase change into liquid. This water phase change releases latent heat from the water that, in turn, heats the air so it continues to rise (depicted as positive links). As the air mass rises, the water droplets continue to cool and eventually form ice crystals and snow. Gravity causes these droplets and crystals to start to fall, causing a downward movement to compete with the upward lift.

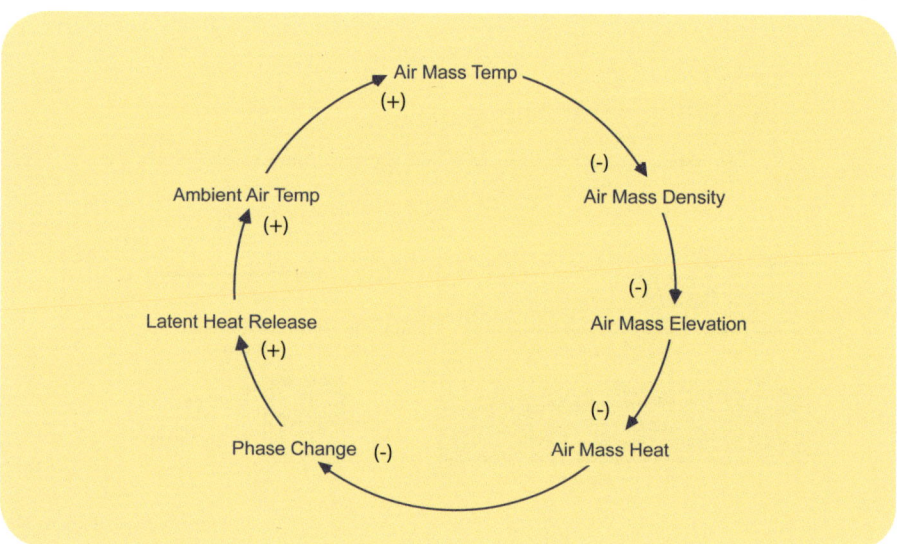

Figure 3-4. Causal loop of temperature

After they show that they understand the circular causality of thunderstorms from this classroom diagram, my students measure the atmospheric pressure, derive the current dew point and use the data in calculations to determine the elevation of condensation or the first phase change in the causal loop. We then go outside and check their math by looking at how high the clouds are building up that day (we can check them against the Santa Catalina Mountains, visible from our school, which rise above 9200 feet). As the towering cumulonimbus clouds quickly build in the afternoon, my students can see the feedback relationship among condensation, cooling, and lift occurring right before their eyes. My students, at this point, are experiencing the results of their own scientific and dynamic thinking.

> As the towering cumulonimbus clouds build in the afternoon, my students can see the feedback relationship among condensation, cooling, and lift occurring before their eyes. They are experiencing the results of their own **scientific and dynamic thinking**.

Closed-loop Thinking and Generic Thinking

In another laboratory exercise, students look at the behavioral and physiological responses of warm- and cold-blooded animals to various external temperature conditions. In this lab, I have the students "talk through" a causal relationship of cold-blooded animals and heat-regulation behavior with me. I have them complete the following prompts:

- "When a poikilotherm's [cold-blooded animal] body temperature is low, it . . . " (My students should answer "lies in the sun.")
- "When its temperature gets to about 36°C or 100°F, it . . . " (My students should answer "becomes active and eats or goes and lies in the shade to cool down a little.")
- "If that cools it down too much, it . . ." (My students should answer, again, "lies in the sun.")

By now they have figured out the circular thermoregulatory behavior of cold-blooded animals. We follow the same set of prompts, but use the hypothalamus gland's behavior for warm-blooded animals and develop the idea of homeostasis. Although they are not aware of it, my students have just practiced both closed-loop thinking and generic thinking in this simple exercise.

> By now they have figured out the circular thermoregulatory behavior of cold-blooded animals. My students have just practiced both **closed-loop thinking** and **generic thinking**.

Operational Thinking

I am not adverse to naming and explaining the tools that I am using. It is just that I have found that if I treat the tools as something special, then my students start to think that systems are special cases of reality, not the way the world works all the time. By the middle of the year, after using STELLA several times, I build, through a classroom discussion, models of population growth, overshoot and collapse, and s-curve limited growth. At this time, I do explicitly discuss the software, the concepts, and the math. By then, my students have a working relationship with STELLA and systems thinking although they don't know it. By the end of the model building exercise, they have had to be explicit in their operational thinking.

So far I have described both the content and the tools the students are using to learn the content. What I am *doing* during these labs is just as important. I am, in Barry's words, "wondering around." Instead of standing in front of the class and directing exercises for the whole class as a unit, I have all four of these labs going on simultaneously, each involving one quarter of the class. Over the course of four days, my students cycle through all of the labs. During that week, I am wandering between the groups—lecturing here, questioning there, just watching someplace else. My job is sometimes knowledge dispenser, sometimes questioner and tester, but mostly coach and mentor.

One of the most important parts of this process is the creation of the tasks my students do. It is critical that throughout the entire four days, my students are confronting what they already think they know with new information that forces them to reconsider how the world works in a whole new paradigm.

The Real-World Context

All of the knowledge and skills my students learn, all of the work they do, is ultimately leading to a better understanding of the real world outside the classroom. My real classroom is outdoors. We have about 10 acres of rather wild desert on campus. It is an active Sonoran Desert wash area that flows with flash floods many times during the school year, but is mostly dry. With over thirty species of birds nesting on campus and many more visiting birds, dozens of plant species, a couple dozen reptile species, and several species of mammals, including a resident bobcat we periodically see catching cottontails, it is a resource not to be taken lightly.

My students come to expect me to ask them to apply all of the classroom "stuff" to the real world. Throughout the year, I constantly draw upon previously learned content to provide a richer context for new material, and using this, I have them explain what we see outside in ever increasing complexity.

The excitement for me comes with the unexpected. I truly cannot predict what we might come across when we are outside. Although my learning goals for each outside trek are very clear, I am ready to suspend them when something important happens right in front of us. Those are the opportunities for my students to apply their systems thinking skills in a new context.

One example of this unexpected opportunity to apply systems thinking skills came today. It is March as I am writing this paragraph. This morning, as we were working on measuring different physical aspects of microclimates, a pair of girls came across what they thought was a dead Desert Spiny Lizard lying in the sand. They called me over to look at it. Several students joined us to look at the reptile. As I approached, I saw its head move just slightly.

"I think the judgment of death is a bit premature," I said.

"Really?"

"His head just moved a little."

A boy who had walked with me asked, "Is he just warming up?"

"What do you think?" I asked. "What's the air temperature you've been measuring?"

"About 68°," he answered.

"So . . . " one of the first girls said, "he's trying to get up to about 100° and is just catching the heat."

"I think so," I said. "But what about the zebra tailed lizards? They aren't waiting like this guy."

"They're a little smaller," a couple of them said at the same time. "They don't take as long to warm up. And the baby lizards, the really small ones, are really racing around."

There it was: scientific thinking without ever planning for it. I just needed to be open for the moment to occur.

These were my second-year, advanced students who had not worked with the animal cooling model for about 18 months. I am convinced, because I have seen

> I am convinced, because I have seen it so often, that the systems thinking worldview helps concepts make so much sense that they are retained better.

it so often, that the systems thinking worldview helps concepts make so much sense that they are retained better.

Such episodes bring up an important point—a point I learned from both Barry and Dana Meadows. Systems thinking and system dynamics, to be truly taught, have to be the way the teacher sees the world and the way he or she lives. Students have to see their teacher personally modeling and using systems thinking to solve problems, to clarify a new phenomenon, and to make sense out of the world. If a teacher does not use systems thinking in his or her own life, then it is merely one more topic or unit that they teach. It becomes school stuff. School stuff is all of that which we "learned" for the test and promptly forgot.

The last conversation I had with Barry, lasting into the early morning hours in Bergen, Norway (and continued on the flight to Oslo the next morning), went deep into a topic I had been working on in my classroom and in the readings. For any deep, lasting learning, teachers and students must enter into a mentor/apprentice relationship in which the teacher is inviting the student into a way of looking at the world and the student is using the thinking tools the teacher is teaching. All of the thinking skills Barry talked about cannot be just "covered" by the teacher, but must be demonstrated through real problem solving by the teacher interacting with the students.

When I do it right, my students see me grappling to understand a complex new phenomenon, either in the field or in the classroom. I look for and encourage those situations when I don't really know what is happening within our world, from something we are observing to some current event in the news. I try to be as transparent in my thinking as I can so that my students observe me spinning my cognitive wheels to put the problem into some kind of context that makes sense.

> It is important that they see that I do not have a "right" or "wrong" answer to the problem, but that I have a mental model—a model that only exists in my head—that I can make explicit.

It is important that they see that I do not have a "right" or "wrong" answer to the problem, but that I have a mental model—a model that only exists in my head—that I can make explicit. And with that mental model, I can come up with an explanation that agrees with the observations and leads me, if the situation warrants, to describe and explain a leverage point that can affect the system in a desired way.

When my students see that both the content and the thinking skills I teach have meaning in the way I approach my own life, they understand that I mean what I say about the world. When you view the world routinely through a systems thinking lens, it is impossible not to use systems thinking.

A System Dynamics Classroom in a Year-Long Context

My classroom, on any given day, would be recognizable to anyone who has been in school. I have specific daily goals, I am covering state-mandated content, and my students are pretty busy. But the long-term structure would not be so recognizable. I do not teach discrete "units" or unified topics of content for two to three weeks or even for an entire term. I pretty much teach everything all the time. I do this because that is how the world is put together.

What I do is to teach a little bit about a lot of stuff at a time, revisit every concept and thinking skill often during the year, and continue to add complexity and functionality as I go. On any given day, my students might be working on two to four different topics, but continuously putting them together into a unified mental model of how the world is structured.

The human mind is so flexible in its ability to move from one thing to the next that students never seem to have a problem juggling many things at once—and never get a chance to be bored. By the end of the year, I am finally able to put some formal, traditional scientific names to concepts and system structures that my students have been building throughout the nine months of a school year.

The denouement for the year occurs in the last week of school. My students—in pairs—take me for a fifteen-minute walk through the desert. During that time they have a set of prescribed information they have to point out to me, but they also have to be able to answer any question I have about anything we might encounter on the walk. My questions vary depending on the skills of the particular students I am testing at the moment, but most are asked to explain, at least once, an on-going phenomenon of which we are just seeing a snapshot.

By using this process, I am able to see whether the students can put an observation into a continuum of time: what happened before to create what we see and what is likely to come later. By the end of school, they get it. The world, as they explain it to me, is not a series of discrete events but a rich, interconnected structure. They cannot explain the distribution of plants on the walk without including hydrology, physics, soil chemistry, weather, and animal pollination and dispersal relationships.

> By the end of school, they get it. The world, as they explain it to me, is not a series of discrete events but a rich, interconnected structure.

My students, in open-ended evaluations at the end of the year, often tell me that they learned more in my course than any other in school, while not having to work as hard. So much of systems thinking *just makes sense.*

Overwhelmingly, students and parents have responded favorably to this kind of teaching and learning. I have room in my courses for 28 students in my one advanced course and 112 in my four first-year courses. I typically get over 40 applying for the advanced course and 225-250 students registering for the first-year course. I have a bit of a soft heart (or head) and have taught an extra section of the first-year course for several years now, teaching 180 students a year about systems thinking by wondering around.

References

Richmond, Barry. "Systems thinking: Critical thinking skills for the 1990s and beyond." In *System Dynamics Review* 9 (2): 113–133.

4

Changing School Culture: Creating Student-Centered Classrooms

Tracy Benson

> Tracy Benson uses classroom stories to describe applications of operational thinking, one of Barry Richmond's systems thinking skills. These stories help illustrate how children and adults use operational thinking to organize concepts and communicate and improve mental models. The stories highlight the influence of systems thinking tools, especially stock-flow mapping and modeling, and reinforce the benefits the tools bring to students and teachers.

1990 was a pivotal year in my systems thinking approach to education. I was hired to join the Orange Grove Middle School in Tucson, Arizona, as their new assistant principal. For the previous three years, I had worked with Principal Mary Scheetz in a neighboring school district. During that time, we often talked about our vision for what middle level education could and should be: the creation of an environment where people with similar visions and passions could work together and do amazing work with young adolescents. Orange Grove Middle School became a place that attracted individuals who challenged themselves as learners, striving to create a school that functioned as a system and that honored the importance and quality of the relationships between all parts of the school. Although at the time we did not have access to current systems thinking terminology, we possessed an innate sense that school systems could be structured, and mental models influenced, so that joy in the workplace and exciting learning environments would be accessible to all members. We believed we could help create a school that could enthusiastically prepare children for the complexity of their adult futures as well as to achieve success by current conventional measures.

We had several mentors along the way who played significant roles in guiding our work together. Dr. Gordon Brown, an Orange Grove neighbor and professor

Tracy Benson earned a B.S. degree in multi-field studies, and then moved to Tucson, Arizona, in 1978 to begin graduate work in exercise physiology and sports science at the University of Arizona.

She taught for nine years, at both the elementary and middle-school levels, as well as being an instructional coach. In order to broaden her ability to make a difference for children, she earned an M.A. in educational leadership from Northern Arizona University and spent seven years at Orange Grove Middle School as an assistant principal and principal.

It was during this time that her journey into systems thinking began as she met and worked with several influential systems thinking teachers and mentors.

None of this time for learning or envisioning systems thinking in schools would have been possible without the long-term support and encouragement of Jim and Faith Waters, who have helped bring the work of systems thinking to schools across the U.S. and throughout the world.

Tracy went on to earn her Ed.D. in educational leadership from the University of Arizona and has been a coordinator of The Waters Foundation, Systems Thinking in Schools project.

Dr. Gordon Brown, an Orange Grove neighbor and professor emeritus from MIT, was our "citizen champion," reminding us that once we had learned about systems thinking and system dynamics, our lives would never be the same. In addition to bringing system dynamics to our school, Gordon connected us with Mr. and Mrs. James Waters, whose guidance and support became an enduring part of the work at Orange Grove, and who, through the Waters Foundation, have helped spread systems thinking and system dynamics in schools well beyond our small middle school. Through the organic energy and synchronicity that flowed through Orange Grove at the time, Gordon Brown also arranged for us to meet Barry Richmond, one of our first systems thinking teachers.

After being introduced to systems thinking, I, along with fellow educators, came to understand that young people could build systems thinking models to help operationalize their understanding of the dynamics of the systems they were studying in a wide variety of subjects including science, social studies, and reading. If models influence the thinking and attitudes of those who see them, as in the case of either computer models or role models, then the level of accuracy models project can weigh heavily on the modeler's mind. As educators learning systems thinking, we recognize the level of skill and practice needed to create realistic models. Luckily for us, George Box's statement, "All models are wrong, but some may be useful," (often reiterated by Dr. Jay Forrester and other system dynamics mentors) reminds us that the models we create will never be perfect or completely accurate (Box 1979); nonetheless, we have learned from experience that the operational thinking used when building models at all levels can be significantly beneficial to teachers and students. Operational thinking requires you to focus on understanding how underlying processes are put together.

tracing connections

As a mentor to educators, Barry Richmond helped us see a whole new perspective of what creating a model of a system could be. He guided and expanded our understanding of the concept of model. He asked and encouraged questions: "How does a system of interest really work?" "What underlying structures create the behaviors we see?" "How can we help others 'see systems'?"

The result of such questions was that, instead of creating a simple model showing individual parts of an ecosystem, we might ask ourselves and our students to create a model showing how elements of an ecosystem, such as populations of different species and components of a habitat, interact to create the dynamic behaviors we observe in the real system. Barry invited us to shift our focus from listing factors that are part of a system to deepening understanding of how systems *really* work. Could students, even those in the younger grades, ask such questions? Could they really create such models?

Experimentation, risk-taking, and learning new skills on the job are not easy for most, including educators. Teachers are expected to know their curricula, to manage classrooms effectively and efficiently, and to provide students with experiences that encompass rigor and relevance. Experimentation and applying "new ways of teaching" that hadn't been used widely in K-12 classrooms was uncharted territory and became quite unnerving for many of us. Luckily, we had Barry and other mentors to guide and expand our understanding of the concepts of systems thinking and dynamic modeling.

By understanding that imperfect models can still be useful, teachers and students are free to use a process of rigorous experimentation and dynamic model construction to gain insight about the systems they study.

Teachers tend to struggle with a number of topics as they learn about systems thinking and system dynamics. Is there a proper developmental sequence when using systems thinking strategies with students? Is it okay to try to incorporate some of the tools if I am still learning about them myself? I remember in-depth conversations about the use of causal loops versus stock-flow maps when operationalizing a problem. We would ask, "Which should come first, loops or stock-flows?" "Is there a proper sequence for introducing specific tools?" Discussions about the distinction between systems thinking and system dynamics were guided by Barry's insight that "the differences are more in orientation and emphasis than in essence." He further described systems thinking as "system dynamics with an aura," which is further described in his paper entitled

> We have learned from experience that the **operational thinking** used when building models at all levels can be significantly beneficial to teachers and students.

"System Dynamics—Systems Thinking, Let's Just Get On with It." It was Barry who encouraged us not to fixate on the details of perfect system dynamics practice, but rather on what was really important for students to learn and investigate. He reminded us that "individuals who generate insights for themselves learn much more than those who are fed them." He would encourage us to refine our own skills and look for new ways to apply those skills and technologies of systems thinking to classroom instruction. A recollection of his advice went something like this: "Don't worry about trying to be perfect system dynamics practitioners; focus instead on how you can help students 'see systems' as they investigate complex problems."

Barry's message focused on what is best for children. To illustrate this message, I share the following stories of students and teachers who have used operational thinking to address particular problems. The stories highlight lessons learned and show the benefits of operational systems thinking. As a teacher and mentor, Barry was truly one of the best; he supported us as we learned directly from our experiences working with young people.

Bryan's Story: Crocodiles and New Insights

Fourth grader Bryan was an eager learner, interested in many things but was often reluctant to conform to day-to-day classroom expectations. As a part of a unit on endangered species, students were asked to choose an animal, then conduct research and prepare a written report that included a stock-flow map. With the knowledge he was free to choose his own animal, Bryan enthusiastically chose to study crocodiles and immersed himself in crocodile research. His stock-flow map included several key variables that had influenced the steady population decline of his chosen species, the crocodile; size of habitat, effects of hunting, and consumer demand for crocodile skins were among the variables.

One year after he completed his project, Bryan was asked to share his work with a group of adults interested in using stock-flow mapping with children. As he was sharing his fourth grade project presentation-style in front of a large audience of adults, he stopped in the middle of a sentence because he realized that as an older and wiser fifth grader, he did not quite agree with particular parts of his fourth-grade model. At that unplanned moment of his talk, he openly shared that his thinking had obviously changed since fourth grade because he noticed he hadn't put in a connector between food and the population stock, and that he needed to both "add and delete some arrows and change a few other parts." The adults in attendance learned that Bryan's stock-flow map did more than help him develop an operational model of his system. The map was a representation of his understanding at a particular time of his cognitive development (fourth grade). As he discovered during his "aha" moment, the sophistication and accuracy of the map could truly improve over time as his own level of thinking and understanding matured.

Stock-flow maps help children represent their current thinking as a visual display. Because the maps help children communicate complex thoughts in a very visual manner, children are able to revisit their thinking and recognize their own growth as their theories and thought processes develop over time, whether that span of time is a day, a week, or even years!

> Because the maps help children communicate complex thoughts in a visual manner, children are able to revisit their thinking and recognize their own growth as their theories and thought processes develop over time.

Eight Grade Math Class: Special Needs to Confident Achievers

Ms. Dunham was an eighth-grade math teacher of children identified as having special needs. These young people had poor images of themselves as students and often expressed self-deprecating comments about their own capabilities, especially in math. Like all students in the school, despite their learning difficulties, they were expected to participate in the same standardized testing as other students. The eighth-grade tests included abstract algebraic concepts that appeared to be far beyond the capabilities of these special needs students.

Since Ms. Dunham was open to different instructional strategies and willing to use them if they could benefit her students, she decided to apply some of the new systems thinking strategies she had recently learned. She taught her students to build simple linear stock-flow models of a shoe factory, to use a hands-on approach to simulate factory manufacturing and consumer spending, to keep track of data in charts and graphs, and then to proceed to build simple STELLA computer models of their economic systems. The computer model simulations helped the students learn the concept of slope and the algorithm y=mx+b; the difference between linear and nonlinear functions; and most importantly, enhanced their view of their own capabilities. One student was overheard saying, "Building these computer models—this is the first time I feel really smart in school."

> One student was overheard saying, "Building these computer models—this is the first time I feel really smart in school."

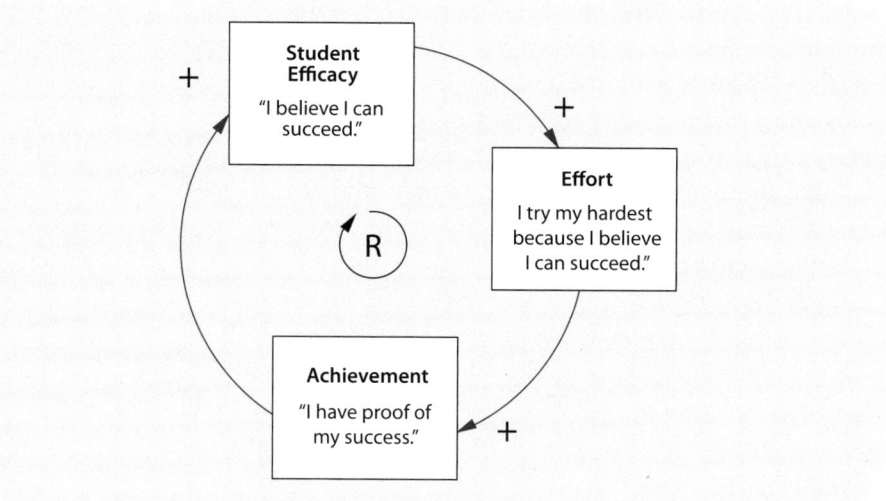

Figure 4-1. Reinforcing loop of student effort and efficacy

Efficacy is a person's ability to produce a desired result. Students who are efficacious believe they have the ability to learn new skills or achieve prescribed standards. By building on a renewed sense of efficacy, this group of once perceived-to-be-struggling math students were asked to teach peers enrolled in the advanced eighth-grade algebra class how to build the same computer models and how the models connected to the algebra concepts they, too, were learning in class. Needless to say, as perception became reality, Ms Dunham's students gained far more from the experience than just enhanced understanding of linear functions and improved performance on written assessments. They discovered a new view of themselves as learners and they projected that positive self-image to their studies and to their interactions with peers.

From this example and other similar documented anecdotes, a theory of efficacy and effort emerges.

This snowballing, reinforcing story, as shown in Figure 4-1, reveals the power of systems tools and strategies. As students learn new ways of representing complex or abstract concepts, they develop a greater sense of self-efficacy, which then motivates them to try harder and persist. Every teacher knows that when students put forth strong effort, they tend to achieve success that, in turn,

> This snowballing, reinforcing story reveals the power of systems tools and strategies. As students learn new ways of representing complex or abstract concepts, they develop a greater sense of self-efficacy, which then motivates them to try harder and persist.

feeds their sense of efficacy. We have learned that students of all backgrounds and capabilities can use systems thinking strategies to help them learn and that capability bolsters their belief in themselves as learners.

Introduction of Systems Strategies in a School Setting: The Bathtub Analogy

As a middle school principal, Mary Quinnan was determined to use systems thinking strategies with her staff as a means for enhancing the overall quality of her school. She had participated in a series of systems training sessions, attended a system dynamics conference, and believed strongly that her staff and students would benefit from a systems thinking approach.

During professional development time with her teachers, Quinnan used causal loop archetypes, behavior-over-time graphs, the ladder of inference, and stock-flow maps (available at http://www.watersfoundation.org) to facilitate in-depth conversations and problem-solving about real school issues. When Quinnan introduced stock-flow maps to her staff, she hung a very large drawing of a bathtub on a white board and then proceeded to explain the dynamics of changing water levels and how the related actions of the faucet and the drain influenced the level changes. Since the familiarity of the bathtub seemed obvious to the teachers, she then posed a series of questions: "If we use the water as a metaphor for student engagement during instruction, what is currently happening to the changing level of the engagement water in your classrooms? What would we need to do to minimize the draining out as when students shut down and disengage in class? What would we need to do to turn up the faucet so that students were motivated and excited to actively participate in class?" These questions led to lively discussions, eliciting numerous ideas to both shut down the drain and turn up the faucet so that there would be increased classroom involvement and participation. Groups of teachers used stock-flow drawings to map out their ideas and to predict the results of new strategies. As with the students, the stock-flow maps helped the teachers visually represent the existing state of their classrooms along with what it would take to increase the engagement accumulation over time.

As Quinnan taught and demonstrated systems strategies when working with her staff, she also encouraged them to use the same strategies in their classrooms as an instructional approach.

A wide variety of efforts contributed to the positive student achievement results at Quinnan's school. Systems strategies played a significant part as a means for making staff collaboration and problem-solving visual and cohesive. As Quinnan

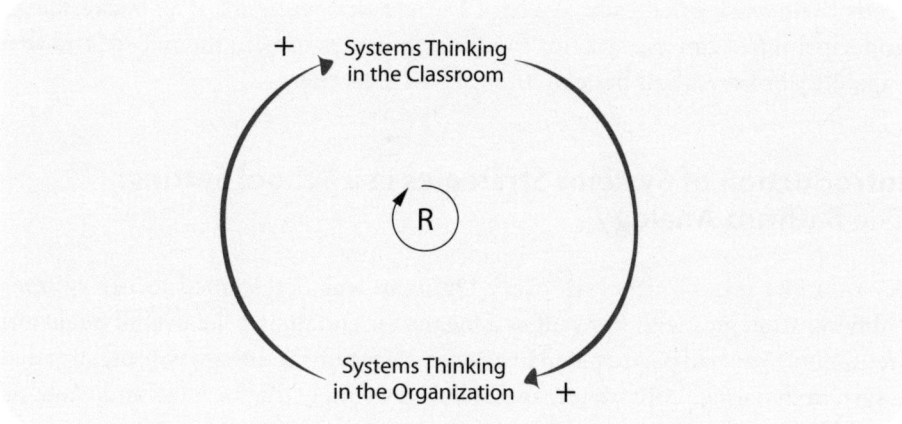

Figure 4-2. Reinforcing nature of the use of systems thinking in the classroom and organization

taught and demonstrated systems strategies when working with her staff, she also encouraged them to use the same strategies in their classrooms as an instructional approach. A feedback loop depicts the reinforcing relationship between the incorporation of systems thinking applied to organizational issues and systems thinking woven into classroom instruction. The reinforcing nature of this dynamic truly contributed to a positive learning environment and enhanced student achievement, as Figure 4-2 indicates.

Systems Thinking in Early School Years

Some adventuresome teachers at Borton Primary Magnet School in Tucson, Arizona thought their very young students (kindergarten, first, and second grades) would benefit from knowing how to build stock-flow models. The teachers saw the value as students identified the stocks, or the main things that change in a system, and the flows that influence the changes. In these primary classrooms, examples of stocks included the amount of soup in a stock pot, amount of water in a bath tub, number of passengers riding in a fictional trolley car, the amount of courage a character develops as described in fiction and nonfiction literature, and the number of people visiting the zoo while on a field trip. Students discussed the nature of the change of the stocks and drew the flows as simple increasing and decreasing

> What was surprising to teachers was the ease with which the students embraced the visual nature of the stock-flow tool.

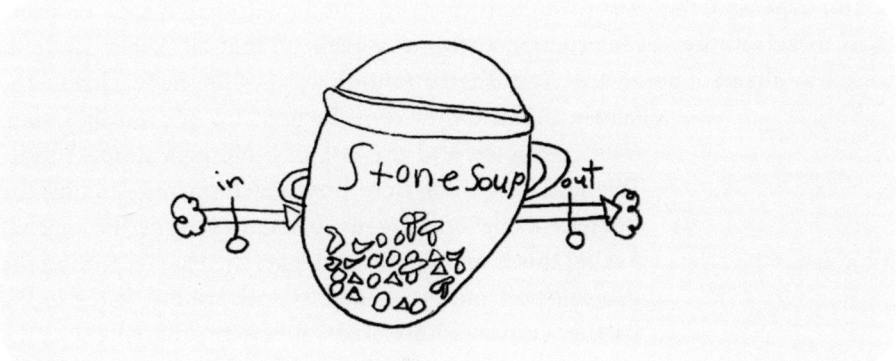

Figure 4-3. Stock-flow map of stone soup drawn by Lizbeth Loreto, kindergartener

rates that either made the level of the stock go up or go down. What was surprising to teachers was the ease with which the students embraced the visual nature of the stock-flow tool.

Stock-flow maps helped children represent their understanding of stories, concepts, and scenarios, not just as static pictures, but as dynamic entities that change over time. Several anecdotes demonstrate how easy it is to underestimate the capabilities of young children. In one classroom a teacher used the book *Stone Soup* to introduce accumulations and rates as stock-flow concepts. Soup in a stockpot was the accumulation (stock) of interest. Parents were invited to come to class and eat the soup from the stockpot. While discussing the outflow of soup in terms of cups of soup served to the parents, one child said, "What about that steam that is coming off the top—isn't that part of the outflow, too? It is not just the soup leaving because we are eating it."

> Stock-flow maps helped children represent their understanding of stories, concepts, and scenarios, not just as static pictures, but as dynamic entities that change over time.

Another example involves a second-grade teacher who was curious as to whether her students were able to build simple computer models using STELLA software. She chose seven of her more verbal, confident students and in less than an hour taught them the basic icons and manipulations of the software. To more effectively introduce computer modeling to the whole class, her plan was to use her seven student-leaders as peer-to-peer guides and pair them with others in the class. After instructing the student guides for 45 minutes, she paired them up with their classmates and asked them to direct their attention to a screen that projected a blank STELLA modeling page. She proceeded to provide basic introductory instruction that included placing a stock on a page and labeling it, and expecting the pairs of students to follow along with her. It took no more than three minutes of instruction before she realized that all of her students were way ahead of her instruction. Their attention was not on the teacher or the screen because they were focused on one another, their own computer, and the task of building a simple model. The student guides were busy teaching and guiding the novices while needing no assistance from the teacher. Seeing this level of independence, the teacher turned the projector off and proceeded to walk around, listen to the partner conversations, and watch with amazement as the students taught and built models with one another. The teacher exclaimed, "It took me practice time and courage to feel comfortable enough to introduce this in my classroom! I invested only 45 minutes of instruction with only seven of my kids, and they don't even need me any more! Why do they catch on so much quicker than adults like me?"

> It took me practice time and courage to feel comfortable enough to introduce this in my classroom! I invested only 45 minutes of instruction with only seven of my kids, and they don't even need me any more!

The teachers of Borton Primary Magnet School continue to be active systems thinking teachers, and their innovative work has been recognized internationally by companies like Microsoft. Students are expected to operationalize their thinking using the visual tools of system dynamics (e.g., behavior-over-time graphs, stock-flow maps, causal loop diagrams, and simple models). Those tools have become part of the learning repertoire for primary school children at Borton Primary Magnet School as they address relevant problems with skill and confidence.

In a student-centered systems thinking classroom, teachers and children, such as those at Borton, are the facilitators of thinking and learning. Children are immersed in practice fields rich in relevant problem-solving, interdisciplinary connections, thought-provoking dialogue, and opportunities for in-depth analysis and synthesis. The Waters Foundation's "Systems Thinking in Schools Project" is focused on supporting teachers in their ability to create such desirable learning environments for children. A systems thinking learning environment is motivating and engaging for even the most reluctant learner, as we saw in the eighth-grade math class. The teachers in Mary Quinnan's school and students like Bryan make it apparent that the visual nature of the systems thinking tools enables individuals to organize, express, and make operational their thinking. Philosopher Rene Descartes once said, "We do not describe the world we see; we see the world we can describe." As systems thinkers learn how to "see systems" by way of operational thinking, the complexity of the world becomes more visible and manageable.

The Goal: Building a Systems Citizenry

The ability to see systems and manage complexity is integral to the development of twenty-first century citizens. In a keynote address delivered to educators in July of 2002, Barry Richmond referred to the importance of developing "systems citizens." Systems citizens view themselves as members of a global community. They strive to understand the complexities of today's worldly systems and have the ability to tackle problems with an informed capacity to make a positive difference. Schools across the United States and throughout the world are actively pursuing the advantages of integrating systems thinking and system dynamics in classrooms and schools. The benefits of such approaches are both immediate to student learning and long lasting, as a systems citizenry is developed and nurtured.

From 1990 through the present, educators from Arizona, California, Colorado, Georgia, Iowa, Massachusetts, Michigan, Missouri, New Mexico, Oregon, Texas, Vermont, China, India, The Netherlands, Singapore, and elsewhere have benefited from Waters Foundation Systems Thinking in Schools training, workshops, and presentations. We are often asked to estimate the number of educators who are integrating systems thinking into their classrooms and schools and the number of children who benefit from this methodology. Responding to this question is challenging because the contagious nature of the work makes it hard to quantify, yet at this point we confidently respond with a number hovering in the thousands. We know that after introductory training, some educators choose to emphasize the language and habits of systems thinking, while others, in addition to the habits, focus on the visual tools and computer modeling that help students operationalize their thinking. One beauty of systems thinking is the ease with which educators can connect and apply any aspect of systems thinking, from the habits to computer modeling, within prescribed curricula and established standards.

Knowing that successful learning environments are characterized by a wide range of teaching strategies that motivate, challenge, and engage students of all strengths and capabilities, educators who are invested in systems thinking approaches have the capacity and tools to create such classrooms, at the elementary, middle, and high school levels. System thinking has been integrated into schools serving urban, rural, and suburban communities and in public, charter, and private school settings.

Barry's message lives on as a new emphasis on citizenry and critical thinking headline educational agendas. In a 2008 report by the Forum for Education and Democracy, "Democracy at Risk: The Need for a New Federal Policy in Education," leading researchers cite the importance of twenty-first century skills that focus on critical thinking. The researchers assert, "We will need to foster major changes in curriculum and assessment to support the critical thinking and problem-solving required for success in the complex society we live in today." Barry Richmond has been an inspiring mentor for K-12 educators, and his legacy continues through the work of systems educators who strive to develop a systems citizenry to lead us through the complexity of the twenty-first century.

References

Box, G. 1979. "Robustness in the Strategy of Scientific Model Building," in *Robustness in Statistics*, edited by R. Launer and G. Wilkinson. Academic Press. 1979. Cited in J. Temple. 1998. "Robustness Tests of the Augmented Solow Model." *Journal of Applied Econometrics* 13: 361–375.

The Forum for Education and Democracy. 2008. "Democracy at Risk: The Need for a New Federal Policy in Education." Washington D.C. http://www.forumforeducation.org.

5
Modeling for High School Students: Teaching Critical Thinking through System Dynamics

Diana M. Fisher

> Diana M. Fisher discusses the process of learning systems thinking. She describes how this process happened for her and how she has continued to develop her ability to teach systems thinking over the years. Diana provides some wonderful examples of how her students have used systems thinking and she offers some helpful tools for new systems thinking practitioners.

I was hooked in ten minutes. The presenter was building a population model using new software called STELLA. As a high school math teacher, I liked the visual representation of the model and the ease of creating graphs and tables, and I saw great possibilities for my math students. When I left the NCCE (National Council of Computer Educators) Conference in Eugene, Oregon in 1990, I started to consider how to use STELLA in my math classes. A new phase in my teaching and learning had begun with the new software and receptive students. I realized, over time, that the software was just the access point to a new way of thinking about certain problems. This was my start on the path to learn to model dynamic systems and bring more holistic thinking to teaching mathematics.

At Stanford University in the summer of 1991, I observed a systems thinking and dynamic modeling training program. Barry Richmond was the main presenter, and that weeklong project was the first time I met him. Then, in June of 1992, I attended the first annual "Systems Thinking in Education" Conference in Tucson, Arizona, featuring Barry as the very passionate and animated keynote speaker.

In 1992, I submitted a proposal for an National Science Foundation (NSF) grant to train high school math, science, and social studies teachers to build

Diana M. Fisher is a teacher at Wilson High School in Portland, Oregon. She has a B.S. and MAT degree in mathematics and is continuing her education in system science and mathematics education. As a high school and university teacher, her primary interest for the last 20 years has been learning and teaching using system dynamics in the classroom.

She has published two books: *Modeling Dynamic Systems: Lessons for a First Course* and *Lessons in Mathematics: A Dynamic Approach*. She has received many honors for her excellent and innovative teaching and was a principle investigator on two National Science Foundation grants focusing on training teachers to use system dynamics in the K-12 curriculum. She has presented at many conferences nationally and internationally to encourage K-12 use of system dynamics.

models of dynamic systems and to write curriculum around those models for use in their classrooms. The proposal was funded in 1993 as the CC-STADUS (Cross-Curricular Systems Thinking and Dynamics Using STELLA) Project. Steve Peterson from High Performance Systems helped get us started. Subsequently, the CC-STADUS grant was awarded exemplary status and a fourth year of funding. A subsequent proposal, CC-SUSTAIN (Cross-Curricular Systems Using STELLA: Training and In-service) was awarded with funding in 1997 for three more years. Barry Richmond and George Richardson, expert system dynamicists, stepped in to help us. They were a powerful influence on our group, not just because they had the depth of understanding of the system dynamics methodology, but because they were consummate teachers. They were caring, compassionate, and really invested in helping us succeed, providing multiple one- and two-day workshops for our lead trainers.

Dr. Edward Gallaher, one of the trainers in our NSF grants, came up with the idea that we should have students participate in a modeling competition, with awards to the first-, second-, and third-place winners. Dr. Gallaher had taught a session on the dynamics of drugs in the body (pharmacokinetics), and had attended training sessions provided by Barry and George. We all liked the idea of a modeling competition, and thus the Sym Bowl Competition began in May of 1994.

Tim Joy, an English teacher from La Salle High School, in Portland, Oregon, who became a trainer in 1994 in the CC-STADUS Project, felt the event should be more of a celebration of student work. He envisioned an expanded event where more student entrants could talk to other students, judges, and adults, explaining their models, and receiving recognition for work well done. So the Sym Bowl Competition morphed into the Sym Fest Exposition.

Being able to choose their own topics for their final modeling projects for the Sym Fest Exposition was very empowering for the students as well as a valuable teaching and learning experience for me. When I started teaching a modeling course using the STELLA software, I developed lessons to help students gain skill with the software and learn how to create basic structures to replicate certain behavior patterns. I also tried to give them some experience with a few of the

tracing connections

In 1991, I met Barry Richmond for the first time. He was the main speaker at a systems thinking/dynamic modeling training program. In 1993, funding came through for our National Science Foundation (NSF) grant to train high school math, science, and social studies teachers to build models of dynamic systems and to write curriculum around those models for classroom use. Subsequently, as funding continued, Barry Richmond and George Richardson stepped in to help us. They were a powerful influence on our group as world-class system dynamicists and consummate teachers—caring, compassionate, and really invested in helping us succeed.

Barry eventually became one of the judges of student projects at Sym Fest as well as a speaker. One comment he made to the entire group of students, teachers, and judges stands out: "The students' collective work floods my heart." One teacher commented that these were not the words of a technician who was just trying to get students to create more correct model structures, but of someone who seeks change.

In the last three years of Sym Fest, Barry not only participated as a judge and speaker, but he also brought T-shirts and copies of the STELLA software for all the students who participated. This was unexpected and overwhelmingly generous—a world-renowned modeler donating his time to work with students and teachers, and a businessman who gave away his software in the hopes that it would encourage students and teachers to continue their study of dynamic behavior and systems thinking. He had a vision to change the world.

---

classic system dynamics scenarios (resource depletion, the spread of epidemics, etc.); however, I also wanted the students to be able to create some models to study problems that were slight extensions of those studied in class.

Initially, I indicated to the students the types of models I felt I knew well enough (to get them off the ground with their projects), and I listed those model types on the board. Never once, in all the years I taught the modeling course, did any student want to design a model from my list. It was a defining moment for me, as a teacher. I'd already told the students they would be able to work on a model that interested them. Since the students knew they were part of an experiment and were excited to be part of a course that was so different from any other they had taken, they were willing to try to create the models they wanted to create, even if I could not always tell them how to solve problems that might arise in their work. What I said was that we, as a group, would try to decide how to overcome each obstacle, try to determine whom we might call for help, and go as far with the model as we could in the time we had to work. This decision made me very nervous. But it was the best decision I made in that and future modeling classes.

For one student, the project meant trying to understand what about cocaine made it addictive, since a person in her family was addicted to cocaine. Many students studied resource depletion issues: forests, salmon, potable water, and food. Others were interested in health issues: smoking and lung cancer, heroin addiction, melanoma, Tay-Sach's disease, asthma, drug receptor binding, cervical cancer, price of treatment during an epidemic, serotonin dynamics, estrogen and osteoporosis, Ebola, hypothermia, alcoholism, AIDS, and cystic fibrosis. Some students wanted to know whether people would have enough energy (power) in the future, or whether the polar bears, or grizzly bears, or eagles would survive, how global warming might be controlled, or how we might lessen crime rates by increasing employment. Students overwhelmingly wanted to understand, more deeply, the important issues of the day.

The Workshops: Training Lead Teachers

After several Sym Fests, the lead teachers involved would take a professional release day and Barry would provide guidance about how we might improve our efforts to infuse systems thinking and modeling into our lessons. Part of the presentation involved creating better model structures, but most of it was about how to get students to increase their understanding of systems. The diagram in Figure 5-1 was given to us as part of a packet of material Barry prepared to help us review what the students had produced at the 2000 Sym Fest.

Barry would build metacognitive models, models to help us think about how we think, about how we might change our behavior as we began to understand the dynamics involved in the systems of learning. His ultimate goal was not to create a better modeler, but to create a better person. He wanted us to become "systems citizens." He tried to capture the process of evolution in a model (Figure 5-2).

As teachers of math and science, we had encouraged our students to build models of physical phenomenon, to try to find valid data and use it as a measure to judge the quality of their models. Barry had a different perspective. He wanted students "to use the incongruities between actual and model-generated outcomes as an inspiration to 'create testable hypotheses' (i.e., to direct their own learning!)." Barry wanted students to use the models to generate understanding and insight. This did not require accurate numbers (per se), but reasonably consistent numbers and diagrams that captured the dynamic process involved in the problem under consideration.

Modeling for High School Students

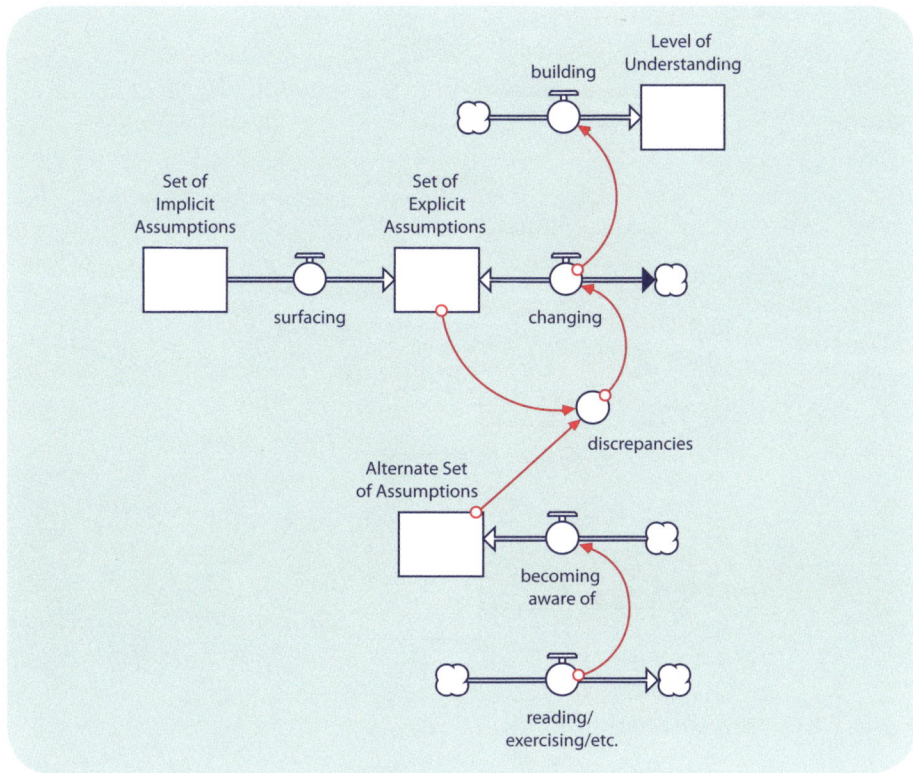

Figure 5-1. Building shared understanding

It is worth noting that Tim Joy was probably the only one who was on Barry's wavelength from the outset and having him as part of our group was invaluable. It took the rest of us some time to change frequencies. I find I have to continue to remind myself of Barry's loftier goal. Tim's insights, due to his nature as well as his knowledge of his field, English, brought a much needed alternate perspective to our work. It reminds me how important it is to have a multi-disciplined approach to learning, for teachers as well as students. Barry connected with Tim from the beginning. But he did not give up on the rest of us. (Thank heavens!)

"All models are wrong! Some models are useful," was one of Barry's favorite statements taken from George Box. He wanted us to de-emphasize our focus on using specific historical numbers and concentrate instead on the feedback structures that were causing the pattern.

Barry wanted students to use the models to generate understanding and insight. This did not require accurate numbers, but reasonably consistent numbers and diagrams that captured the dynamic process involved in the problem under consideration.

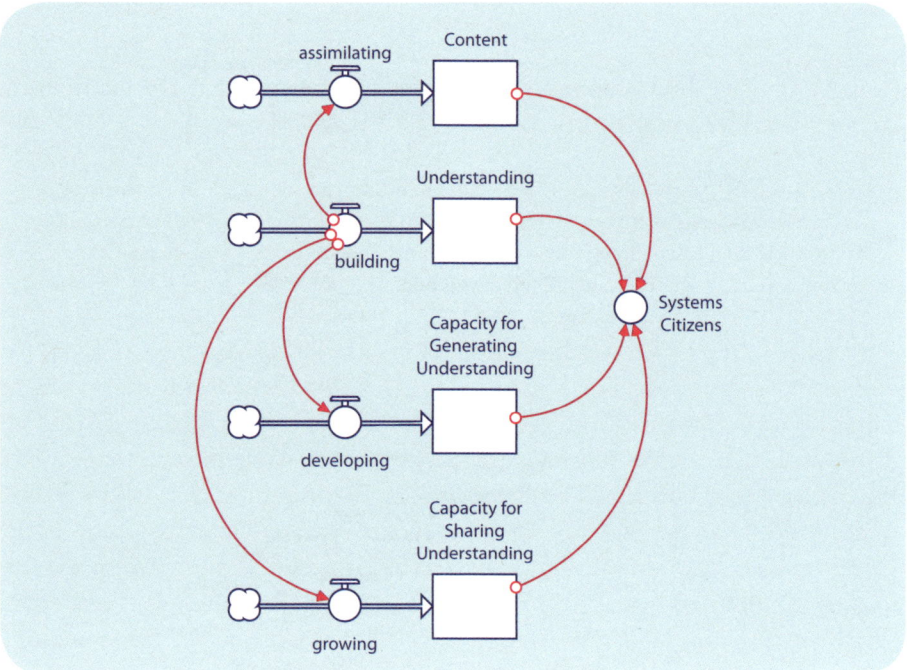

Figure 5-2. Creating systems citizens

He wanted us to use internally consistent numbers. And he wanted students to record the learning that was going on in the building process. "Under what conditions is your model wrong? Why is it wrong?" he'd say. Barry wanted the process to be the focal point. Students learn a lot from their mistakes and can validate a model by identifying the conditions under which the model behaves as expected and when and why it does not behave as expected.

He wanted us to de-emphasize our focus on using specific historical numbers and concentrate instead on the feedback structures that were causing the pattern.

Barry would go through each student model and project, identifying the strengths of each and indicating where the modeling process might lead to more productive learning. He was concerned that students did not address more socially "juicy" topics, like school violence, but instead focused on physical, environmental, or medical science topics, in which students were trying to predict future values. His suggestions could easily have been directed to us, as teachers. I think we (the teachers) had directed our own modeling and instruction to more physical topics because those topics were more comfortable for us and allowed us to use numbers to buoy our confidence that models were being built correctly.

The Teaching Models: Making Understanding Available

Communicating what students learned was another point Barry made in his conversations with us about Sym Fest:

> Focus student attention on gleaning understanding and insight, and on being able to communicate the same, rather than on "proving truth." Designate the project as "gold" if they learn effectively from it, if there is something to learn, and if that something has been effectively made available.

Barry felt we were constraining student creativity by requiring a paper as the only option for communicating the results of their project for the modeling exposition. He wanted us to open the options, especially to consider having students teach others what they had learned, perhaps by using the mapping layer of the software to set up a user interface, perhaps by using the storytelling feature of the software so an audience could understand more easily the design of the student model. He didn't care if we used these features of the software, per se. He wanted the students to go to the next stage—to help their audience understand what they had come to understand in the modeling process. But he anticipated the tools that might help students do that. He had built his software from a deep desire for communication.

Barry felt there were two types of situations that "made understanding available" to others. The first was to develop a guided discovery through a problem. The second was giving a limited model for the learners to critique and modify.

Guided discovery

In guided discovery (with either a teacher or a student as the instructor) the facilitator would unveil a problem in stages. It was necessary for the facilitator to know exactly what s/he wanted to accomplish with the activity in advance. Barry suggested the following steps to help the facilitator tell a story:

1. Begin with explicitly stated learning objectives.
2. Always use a clean, one-screen map/model.
3. Build the bridge starting from *their* side!
4. Simulate early and often; always get a guess!
5. Regularly offer the opportunity to change numbers.
6. Use the storytelling feature of STELLA to unfurl loops/structure.

As a start, after the students presented their models at Sym Bowl or Sym Fest, those of us who had been modeling instructors tried to get our students to create an interface for their models so other students could use them easily. Unfortunately, not every student was interested in doing this, and enough time was not always allocated. But upon reflection, Barry was right. Much learning is realized in the actual building process, but equally as much learning is involved in making the insights gleaned from the model available to others. And the potential impact of the model is multiplied many times if its lessons are made available to others.

> Much learning is realized in the actual building process; equally as much learning is involved in making the insights gleaned from the model available to others.

Extending existing models

The second of Barry's methods for "making understanding available," giving a limited model for learners to critique and modify, surfaced as Barry continued to teach us over the next few years and tried to expand our view of useful modeling experiences for students. We prodded our students to create models from scratch. Barry suggested that much could be learned by allowing students to extend existing models. He suggested that students would be "standing on the shoulders of giants," that it would help in the establishment of model boundaries, and perhaps help eliminate the fear of creation for some students. Barry's hope was that this would open the modeling process to more of a variety of students. The beauty of this suggestion was that it made available serious modeling exercises in courses not specifically dedicated to the teaching of modeling. In a few class periods, students could experience some of the more powerful aspects of the modeling process.

> Barry suggested that much could be learned by allowing students to extend existing models.

Barry suggested this sequence of steps:

1. Begin with a well-constructed, but *obviously* limited model.
2. Ask students to identify the/an obvious limitation.
3. Ask students to "fix" the limitation.
4. Ask students to identify an "issue/limitation" surfaced by the "fix."
5. Continue in this fashion.
6. End the exercise with a final critique identifying the limitations of the model.

Unfurling (unfolding) a model (using storytelling, a very powerful feature of STELLA) and starting a lesson with an obviously limited model are two types of lessons that help the modeler share understanding and are very doable in science, social studies, economics, math, and health classes. These techniques help compress the time students would normally need to understand the basic structure of a model that might serve as the starting point for student exploration. The steps listed above indicate how such a starting point might play out in a classroom, under the direction of a teacher (acting as a facilitator) or as a starting point, after which students are directed to a computer lab to modify a model and explain modifications as part of the lesson. Barry wanted to offer as many opportunities as possible for teachers to adapt his software to different learning/teaching styles. I have not had extensive experience with these techniques, as my focus has always been on having students build models from scratch. But I have had occasion to see very effective use of procedures similar to what Barry suggests above, from the perspective of the student.

On a personal level, starting to teach a modeling course, and using STELLA models in my mathematics courses made me very nervous at times. I had a fear that I would get myself into a situation, in front of a class, where I would not know how to proceed. (Note for readers who are teachers who want to get started and may feel this fear: I recommend experimenting in certain classes, and telling the students that it is an experiment. Students *love* to try something different. If a teacher has good rapport with a class, or just a smaller group of students, s/he will find students very understanding, in fact, more than eager to help work through the kinks in a potential lesson. They take ownership for improving the lesson.) I have found students to be very supportive. It is also good for them to see a teacher in the role of learner, on occasion. As long as they know the teacher is doing her/his homework to try to move the lesson/project forward, the students will be willing to maintain their effort. And every year the process becomes less stressful, and the lessons become more refined. This has been a very important growth process for me.

The End Goal: Becoming Systems Citizens

For Barry, the next step in the modeling process, after communication, was building empathetic skills. He remarked, "having to think about how to make something you know 'available' to someone else, causes you to learn it more deeply, and builds empathetic skills. Empathetic skills are necessary for systems acting/being." He suggested that we help students develop "coaching sequences" for existing models, or models they have created. The coaching sequence, he suggested, might look like this. (The assumption here is that the model has a mapping front end that shows just the basic map without the equations.)

> Having to think about how to make something you know "available" to someone else causes you to learn it more deeply, and builds **empathetic skills**. Empathetic skills are necessary for systems acting/being.

The coach has put the model into steady state. S/he then gives the user a performance challenge. For example, reduce the number of wolves in an ecosystem so the farmers and ranchers are happy they will not have so many predators attacking their livestock. In addition, give the user just enough information to help them get started. For example, give the user a maximum number of wolves that could be hunted and killed each year. Have the user explain what happened to the ecosystem when they killed some wolves and why they think it happened. Then have the user advance to a second model that has at least one additional concept added to the current model.

This second model could be built by the student modeler, based on user feedback about how the output of the previous model might be improved. Or the student might have anticipated what a second-stage model might include and have the new component already designed into the second model. S/he might start the transition to the second model by using a phrase like "I'll bet you were thinking . . ." The second model should allow the user to do better at the given task, "enhance the content or representation of content in the mental model." The user could then perform different tests on the second model, explaining what caused each behavior represented in different simulated runs. In fact, I could not foresee my students doing this until I was able to do this type of coaching myself. I often think Barry taught us how we (teachers) might interact with our students via describing how we might want our students to behave. It was a gentle nudge in the right direction.

> Most of all, he wanted the process to change the way we treated others and how we behaved. He wanted us all to become activists, to behave differently because of our new understanding. He coined this belief as people becoming "Systems Citizens."

In all these experiences Barry wanted both the students and the teachers to internalize what we were learning in the modeling process and to improve our communication with others who were not previously active in the modeling process. But most of all, he wanted the process to change the way we treated others and how we behaved. He wanted us all to become activists, to behave differently because of our new understanding. He coined this belief as people becoming "Systems Citizens."

The concept of systems citizens was, I believe, his ultimate goal. It is likely this concept will evoke the strongest resistance even among those of us who have learned to understand and believe in the systems thinking and system dynamics modeling approach to learning. How many of us who believe that global warming is a serious problem still drive SUVs or plan to purchase an SUV? How many of us do not think about how our words/actions create the problems we deal with each day? How many of us turn on the air conditioner when the air is not that hot, or turn up the heat when we could easily put on a sweater? How many of us live in houses that are much larger than we really need? We need to change our thinking! We need to change our actions! Our best hope is to teach our children the lessons we are learning! But, we need to remember also, they will follow our example.

Although building models and even making the learning that came from building models available is not the level of systems citizenship that Barry wanted us to achieve, it brought the students one step closer to feeling they could understand some issues more completely. Creating systems citizens requires more than any one course can accomplish. Some schools require students to do community service; clubs are usually available that promote environmental responsibility (like recycling, or planting trees); some students spend time with those less fortunate (working in soup kitchens, or helping to tutor other students, or helping build houses for the homeless, or being friendly to new students). These activities provide students an opportunity to internalize what they learn to make a better world. These opportunities require the instruction and example of many teachers, the first and most important being parents. A call to action is the message Barry wanted to accomplish. Exposing students to important issues, empowering them so they can understand the dynamics of many complex problems, is a start. And Barry created the critical stepping stones, along with the systems citizen concept to help go forward in a real world. Building on this base is essential. Unless we all act on our understanding, what good have we done? We don't have to change the world, but we should each be able to change our own lives.

> Unless we all act on our understanding, what good have we done? We don't have to change the world, but we should each be able to change our own lives.

The Final Step: Systems Thinking to Systems Citizen

It is much easier to learn to create a model to study the feedback in systemic problems than to apply those structures and lessons to our own behavior.

Barry wanted us to take the final step.

Ron Zaraza, a science teacher at Wilson High School in Portland, Oregon, was introduced to system dynamics and STELLA in 1991 and, starting in 1993, was co-principal investigator with Diana Fisher on their NSF projects to train teachers to use system dynamics in curriculum for K-12 students. Here, Ron discusses his involvement in the projects.

The K-12 systems community has been extremely fortunate to receive support from both systems academics and practicing professionals. Jim Lyneis, Peter Senge, Steve Peterson, George Richardson, and, of course, Jay Forrester have led the effort to assist us, as teachers, to develop our systems skills as we have experimented with system-based instruction and curriculum. Barry Richmond's role mirrored theirs, but went beyond it in a way that captures Barry's ethics and ideals. Most obviously, Barry was a master teacher himself. As we watched him squatting down to talk to third graders at Sym Fest while they explained their "problem" to him and the logic of their model, it was clear how much Barry enjoyed talking with them, and how energized he was by their ideas. He saw some very sophisticated models done by older kids, but later in the day he kept talking about the younger ones. Those third graders, in turn, had no idea who Barry was, but were really excited by the conversation and some of the ideas they developed from talking with him.

Like the third graders, Barry's work with us "older folks" in Portland reflected the same mix of inspiration and learning, and included a call to us to develop a greater understanding of the power of the tools he was helping us learn.

He was most excited when our models, or our students' models, dealt with politics, personal/community values, fears and expectations, and other quantities that drove social systems. This approach placed us outside our natural comfort zone, but helped us to grow, both in our understanding of system dynamics and in our perception of the world.

Many of us were coming to systems from a mathematics or physical sciences background. Initially, dynamic models were, for us, simply a better way to teach what we were already teaching. System dynamics was a tool rather than a new way of thinking about the world. We saw STELLA models as a more visual as well as a more experimental/interactive approach to problems that were usually solved using algebra or calculus. In particular, STELLA was attractive because of its ability to deal with problems that could be best dealt with using partial differential equations, mathematical techniques far beyond high school students.

Barry supported us tirelessly in that effort, but constantly urged us to step out and consider problems that could not easily be mathematically

Barry firmly believed that people equipped with these skills would bring a level of intelligent decision making not only to the political and business arenas, but also to everyday life decisions.

defined. He saw systems models as most powerful when using "soft variables" (or, as our English and social studies teachers preferred, "rhetorical variables"). He was most excited when our models, or our students' models, dealt with politics, personal/community values, fears and expectations, and other quantities that drove social systems. This approach placed us outside our natural comfort zone, but helped us to grow, both in our understanding of system dynamics and in our perception of the larger world.

Barry's challenge to us was consistent with his most basic hope—that using system dynamic modeling would assist in the emergence of "systems citizens." Barry was passionate about the possibilities for our world as more and more people began to think with a systems perspective. He saw that the systems citizens generated from our collective work would constitute an electorate that understood key systems concepts: delays, different patterns of growth, interconnectedness of actions, natural limits to growth, and, perhaps, most importantly, an awareness of the dangers of unintended consequences. Barry firmly believed that people equipped with these skills would bring a level of intelligent decision making not only to the political and business arenas, but also to everyday life decisions. In his view, a consistent ethic of interdependency and inter-reliance would inevitably emerge.

That perception inspired many of us to revisit our own assumptions, expectations, and ambitions. On the simplest level, for many of us, reading a newspaper will never be the same again. We "quantitative" types began to see a more subjective continuum of values and ideas. Barry inspired me, personally, to move, for the past nine years of my teaching career, into environmental science, one of the rare fields that combines quantitative measurements with qualitative values and assumptions—the perfect playing field for system dynamics students. My change in teaching direction, inspired by Barry, brought me the greatest intellectual excitement and the most profound sense of awe at student thinking in my career.

Barry inspired me, personally, to move, for the past nine years of my teaching career, into environmental science, one of the rare fields that combines quantitative measurements with qualitative values and assumptions—the perfect playing field for system dynamics students.

6

Romeo and Juliet in Brazil: Use of Metaphorical Models for Feedback Systems Thinking

John Morecroft

> John Morecroft shares his story of systems thinking consulting work done with MBA students. He discusses the spectrum of models—from fisheries to "Romeo and Juliet" to global oil production—that he used to illustrate some of the conceptual skills of the modeler and feedback systems thinker.

The attention and imagination of our group of system dynamics doctoral students was captured during our years together by a working paper written by Nathaniel Mass and Peter Senge, "Understanding Oscillations in Simple Systems." I still recommend the paper today.[1] The following excerpt reveals the authors' intention to explain dynamics clearly and rigorously in plain English by interpreting simulations:

> Acquiring a firm intuitive understanding of the possible types of behavior produced by simple first, second and third-order systems marks an important step in learning system dynamics. Such simple systems frequently embody generic structures that recur in a wide variety of complex systems. However, an intuitive grasp of simple oscillating systems often eludes both the beginning student and practitioner alike. Even individuals familiar with the mathematics of dynamic feedback systems often cannot provide a simple non-technical explanation of why a continuous first-order system cannot possibly oscillate, or why a second-order system can. For example, overshoot or oscillation in a system is often explained to result from "system delays" or "inertia." Vague explanations such as these impart little understanding of how decisions being made in a system generate observed problems and behavior.

> This paper presents some arguments we have used in past introductory courses in system dynamics to successfully develop insight into simple oscillating systems.

John Morecroft is Senior Fellow in Management Science and Operations at London Business School where he teaches system dynamics, problem structuring and strategy in MBA, Ph.D., and Executive Education programs.

He has served as Associate Dean of the School's Executive MBA programs and co-designed EMBA-Global, a dual degree program with New York's Columbia Business School. Morecroft is a leading expert in strategic modeling and system dynamics and has written more than fifty papers and journal articles.

He has co-edited three books, written a system dynamics textbook, *Strategic Modeling and Business Dynamics* (Wiley 2007), and he is a recipient of the Jay Wright Forrester Award of the System Dynamics Society and a past president of the society.

His research interests include the dynamics of firm performance and the use of models and simulation in strategy development.

Morecroft has led applied research projects for international organizations including Royal Dutch/Shell, AT&T, BBC World Service, Cummins Engine Company, Harley-Davidson, Ericsson, McKinsey & Co and Mars. Before joining London Business School, he was on the faculty of MIT's Sloan School of Management, where he received his Ph.D. He also holds degrees from Imperial College London and from Bristol University.

The paper analyses a one-level model for the population growth of rabbits in a closed field to illustrate why a first-order negative feedback system exhibits a smooth transition to equilibrium instead of overshoot or oscillating behavior. The paper also analyzes a simple inventory-workforce model to provide an intuitive explanation of the causes of convergent, divergent, and undamped oscillations.[2]

Communicating Feedback Systems Thinking in a Management Environment: The Braskem Course

The dynamic insights we uncovered long ago in MIT's building E40 remain vivid and relevant today—as I discovered in October 2007. I lectured in a management development course that took place in the beautiful Atlantic resort of Guarajuba in the Bahia region of Brazil, 30 miles to the north of Salvador. I contributed two days on "Modeling and Simulation for Strategic Development" during a special international unit in the final week of the MBA program for Braskem, a major Brazilian petrochemical company. There were 35 participants, talented young managers from corporate headquarters and from the main operating divisions including Basic Raw Materials, Vinyl, and Polyolefins.

The international unit was designed for Braskem by Carlos Da Costa, managing partner of Partnership and Learning (P&L), a Brazilian management development firm.[3] I was particularly attracted by the fact that my two days on modeling were positioned between modules on "Managing Across Cultures" and "International Strategy and Management," as shown in Figure 6-1. The culture module was

tracing connections

In autumn 1975, I left England to join the doctoral program at MIT. I remember vividly arriving in Cambridge under New England's crystal blue skies and searching out the headquarters of the System Dynamics Group in Building E40 across from the Sloan School. Here I first met Barry Richmond who, like me, was embarking on a Ph.D. in system dynamics.

Building E40 was not quite what we had expected; it was spartan with brightly painted yellow, red, and blue bare-brick walls. On the second floor, Ph.D. students were dotted around an open-plan area along with researchers and staff. Faculty and senior staff occupied offices around the edge. Grey-metal desks were surrounded by bookshelves and filing cabinets set among rows of sturdy concrete pillars—factory legacies painted bright colors and looking like giant mushrooms sprouting from the floor with inverted mushroom-caps at the ceiling. Now, E40 is much more elegant, but it had its own special charm back then as shared space for newly arrived doctoral students. Our colorful office home was minimalist in décor but memorably spacious. We even found a spare corner to play basketball, with Barry as coach for overseas students.

Our first year was intense. Among the required courses were Principles of Systems 1 and 2, during which we began to acquire modeling skills—not only how to build models but also how to understand their dynamics. Perhaps it was then, in the crucible of problem sets, that Barry's commitment to the clear communication of system dynamics began.

---

delivered by Shalom Schwartz from the Hebrew University in Jerusalem and the international strategy module was delivered by Walter Kuemmerle from the Harvard Business School. This positioning of modules was Carlos' choice and reflected his desire for materials to reveal mindsets and interdependencies in global business and their implications for management. It was an inspired fit with system dynamics and feedback systems thinking.

In fact, Carlos originally asked me to run a business game combining systems thinking, group decision-making, and business acumen. The *Oil Producers' Microworld*, a gaming simulator about the long-term dynamics of the global oil industry, seemed appropriate. But we knew the game should be more than an entertaining black box. Participants should learn enough about feedback systems thinking to appreciate the underlying model and its dynamics.

> The positioning of modules was Carlos' choice and reflected his desire for materials to reveal mindsets and interdependencies in global business and their implications for management. It was an inspired fit with system dynamics and feedback systems thinking.

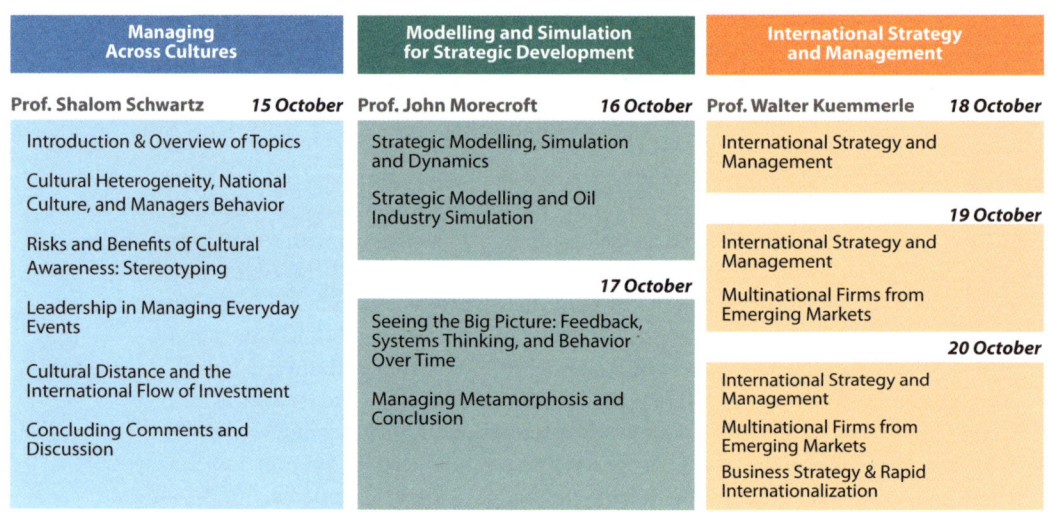

Figure 6-1. Overview of the Braskem course

A Spectrum of Model Fidelity: From Analogue to Metaphorical

Models range in size from large and detailed to elegantly small and metaphorical. The spectrum is illustrated in Figure 6-2. On the left-hand side are analogue, high-fidelity simulators with realistic detail and accurate scaling epitomized by console games such as *Formula 1* on PlayStation. They are so realistic that even Formula 1 drivers use PlayStations before races to practice laps and to learn circuit layouts. People tend to expect business models to be similarly realistic; the more realistic the better. But very often smaller models are extremely useful. As Figure 6-2 suggests, the spectrum of useful models can include illustrative models (of limited detail yet plausible scaling) or even tiny metaphorical models (of minimal detail yet transferable insight).

My favorite example of a metaphorical model is a simulator of "Romeo and Juliet," intended for high school students studying Shakespeare in English literature classes. Clearly, a simulator cannot possibly replicate Shakespeare's play, but it can encourage students to study the play more closely than they otherwise would. By simulating the waxing and waning of love between Romeo and Juliet, students become curious about romantic relationships, both in the model and in the play.[4] A metaphorical model is small and can be explained quickly. As we will see, the "Romeo and Juliet" simulator fits on a single page and involves just a

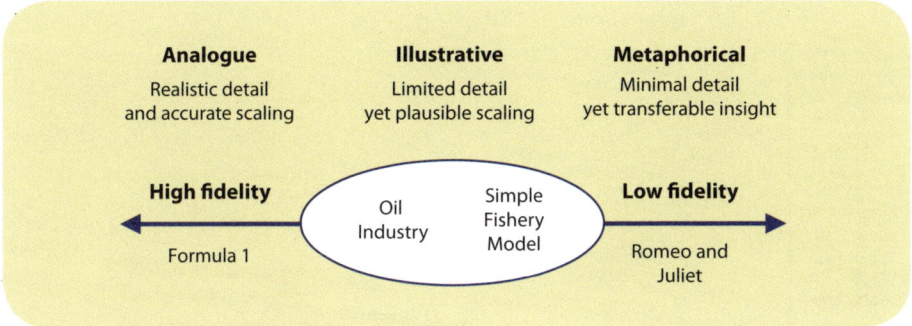

Figure 6-2. Modeling and realism—a spectrum of model fidelity

handful of concepts, a far cry from the large and detailed model that lies behind a Formula 1 simulator.

It is important to realize that business models typically lie somewhere in the middle of this spectrum of model fidelity. In the Braskem program, participants were able to experience this middle range with two more simulators that formed the core of the program. Closest to the metaphorical model is a simple fishery model (just 10 equations) to explain the syndrome of collapsing fish stocks observed in fisheries around the world. Further to the left is the oil industry model (containing 100 equations) used to investigate long-term scenarios for oil price and crude oil production and to shed light on the industry's volatility. Neither of these models are perfect replicas of the industries they represent. Instead they focus on selected dynamics (the behavior over time of catch and ships in fisheries, and the behavior over time of oil price, upstream capacity, and demand in the oil industry) and capture just enough about the feedback structure of the business to explain the dynamics of interest.

Metaphorical Models and Thinking Skills: Pacific Sardine Fisheries

People rarely think of problems in business and society in terms of dynamics and behavior over time. Instead they are preoccupied with events and who to blame when things go wrong. Their ability to express problem situations in dynamic terms needs to be awakened. In the Braskem course, we began with a vivid example from the Pacific Coast sardine fishery. The events in the history of the fishery are described by ecologist Robert Leo Smith.

> The Pacific Coast sardine industry had its beginnings back in 1915 and reached its peak in 1936–1937 when the fishing fleet netted 800,000 tons. It was first in the

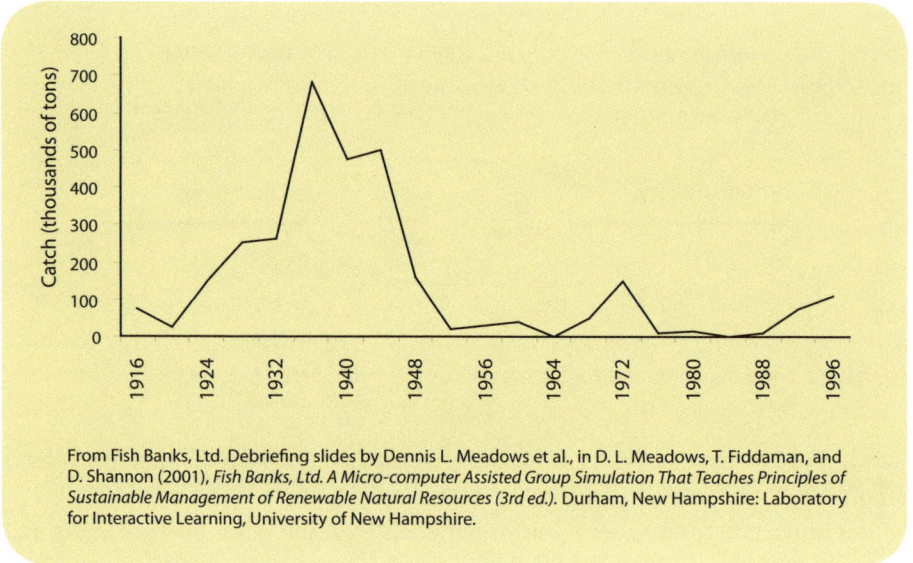

Figure 6-3. Puzzling dynamics in fisheries

nation in numbers of pounds of fish caught, and ranked third in the commercial fishing industry, growing $10 million annually. The fish went into canned sardines, fish bait, dog food, oil, and fertilizer. The prosperity of the industry was supported by overexploitation. The declines in the catch per boat and success per unit of fishing were compensated for by adding more boats to the fleet. The fishing industry rejected all forms of regulation. In 1947–1948 the Washington-Oregon fishery failed. Then, in 1951, the San Francisco fleet returned with only eighty tons. The fishery closed down ... [Oliver Owen, *Natural Resource Conservation: An Ecological Approach*. New York: MacMillan, 1985.]

> Time charts encourage **dynamic thinking**, a vital skill which Barry describes as "the ability to see and deduce behavior patterns rather than focusing on, and seeking to predict, events." Time charts help modelers to identify feedback structures (or interdependencies) that explain the observed behavior patterns.

An important step in modeling is to construct time charts of selected variables in such problem situations. Time charts encourage dynamic thinking, a vital skill which Barry describes as "the ability to see and deduce behavior patterns rather than focusing on, and seeking to predict, events." Time charts help modelers to identify feedback structures (or interdependencies) that explain the observed behavior patterns. For example, Figure 6-3 shows the annual Pacific sardine catch in thousands of tons over the period 1916 to 1996. The highly volatile trajectory encapsulates the unfolding catastrophe facing the fishing community in its bid for growth and prosperity. The annual catch grew remarkably

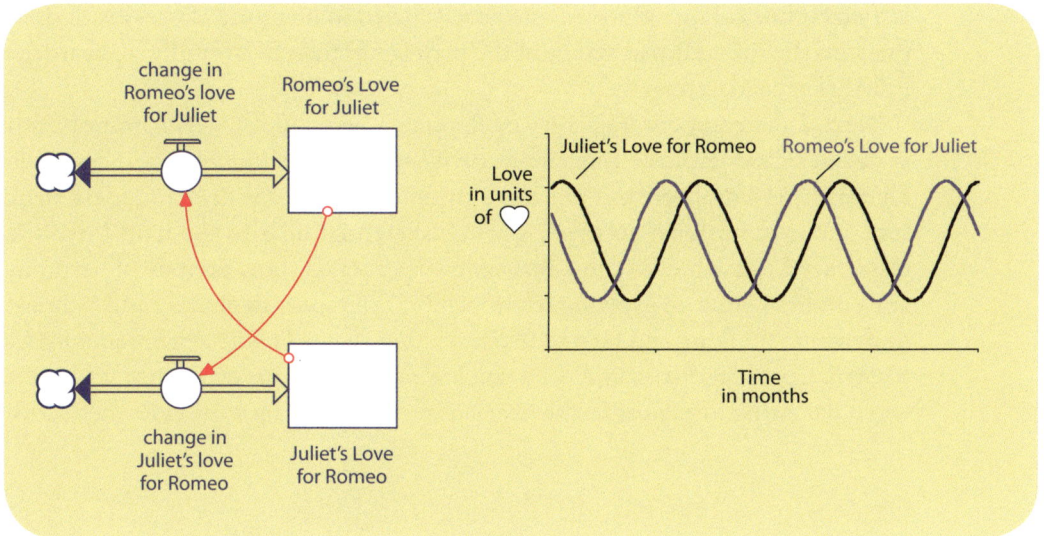

Figure 6-4. Problem situation: Waxing and waning of love between Romeo and Juliet

between 1920 and 1940, starting around 50 thousand tons and peaking at 700 thousand tons—a fourteen fold increase. Over the next four years to 1944, the catch fell to 500 thousand tons, stabilized for a few years and then collapsed dramatically to almost zero in 1952. Since then it has never properly recovered.

Metaphorical Models and Thinking Skills: "Romeo and Juliet"

In the Braskem course, I reinforced dynamic thinking about the rise and fall of fisheries with dynamic thinking about Romeo and Juliet. Admittedly, this is a fanciful example in which a conjecture about varying love in a relationship substitutes for the factual historical time series data found in fisheries; nevertheless, the exercise enables students to consider the time dimension and scaling of love, despite its emotional and intangible nature. I began by sketching on a flip chart the axes of the time chart shown on the right of Figure 6-4. The horizontal axis is time in months and the vertical axis is love in units of love. Not surprisingly, the vertical axis is amusing, but it also provokes serious discussion about how, in reality, one might gauge the strength of an emotional attachment between two people.

I then defined the problem situation as the waxing and waning of love between Romeo and Juliet and sketched the trajectory of *Juliet's Love for Romeo* as a quantity that rises and falls cyclically over time. I admit that the fit between this imagined trajectory and Shakespeare's play is somewhat tenuous, but remember this is a metaphorical model whose purpose (if used in literature classes) is to draw one into the romantic substance of the play rather than to faithfully replicate the full Shakespearian tragedy.[5]

Next, I sketched the trajectory of *Romeo's Love for Juliet,* which, importantly, is out-of-phase with the movement of *Juliet's Love for Romeo*. The phasing in Figure 6-4 is simulated and therefore strictly consistent with the model's structure and assumptions; however, a rough sketch (similar to the kind I drew in class) need not achieve such consistency in order to show periods of harmony and conflict within an evolving relationship. Differences in phasing add richness to dynamic thinking and help to illustrate how events fit within a broader cyclic pattern. Consider, for example, instances of conflict between Romeo and Juliet when her rising love, near to the peaks, is reciprocated by a fall in Romeo's love.

Operational Thinking in "Romeo and Juliet"

Another vital modeling skill is operational thinking, which, as Barry notes, brings discipline to feedback systems thinking. "It's here [in operational thinking] that people must think in terms of units of measure, or dimensions. Physical conservation laws are rigorously adhered to in this domain. The distinction between a stock and flow is emphasized." In the Braskem course, the fisheries example provided an ideal practical situation in which to introduce stocks and flows, and to question why it is so difficult for real fishing communities to achieve a sustainable balance between fish population and fleet size. I omit the detail of this example here, but invite readers to imagine for themselves the aggregate stocks and flows of fish and ships that would form the basis of a simple-yet-plausible model of fisheries.

> In **operational thinking**, people must think in terms of units of measure, or dimensions. Physical conservation laws are rigorously adhered to in this domain. The distinction between a stock and flow is emphasized.

"Romeo and Juliet" served to amplify the operational thinking introduced with fisheries. I began by sketching on a whiteboard just the two stock accumulations shown in Figure 6-4: *Romeo's Love for Juliet* and *Juliet's Love for Romeo*. We discussed the need for units of love in order to quantify the waxing and waning of love. We also discussed how these variations in love would be captured in the gradual filling-up or depletion of the two love stocks. Naturally, that led us to consider the rates of flow that impinge on love: the *change in Romeo's love for Juliet* and the *change in Juliet's love for Romeo*. The important distinction between a stock and a flow is apparent here. Love builds or withers and so a time-dependent story of love can be told. Changes in love (whether Romeo's or Juliet's) are naturally measured in units of love per month which accumulate over time into units of love, thereby ensuring dimensional consistency in the stock and flow networks. Love springs eternal from the heart, depicted as the pool from which new love flows or to which spurned love returns.

By now the whiteboard diagram showed two stocks and two flows, as yet unconnected. To complete the diagram there is a need to recognize the mutual dependence of Romeo and Juliet. They are emotionally entwined. Of course there are many ways to express this entwinement. But two particular and strikingly simple connections are all that are needed to produce the cyclical pattern of love in the time chart. At least that is the dynamic hypothesis. If the *change in Romeo's Love for Juliet* depends on *Juliet's Love for Romeo*, and vice-versa, then an endless cycle of waxing and waning love is possible. This hypothesis came as a big surprise to many people and is a powerful example of a fundamental tenet in system dynamics—that feedback structure gives rise to dynamic behavior. In Figure 6-4 there is a closed feedback loop that weaves its way between and among the stocks and flows of love. There is no need for any external influence to drive the dynamics of love, not even the stars and the moon. The tides of love are self-generating.

From this structural diagram, it is a further step to a full-blown simulator. In my experience, this step is not easy, although it is undoubtedly made more achievable by the self-imposed rigor of operational thinking and the resulting diagram like the one shown on the left of Figure 6-4. In the Braskem program, I asked participants to formulate equations. Initially, they wrote equations for the two stock and flow networks (using as a template the stock and flow equations for fish and ships from the simple fisheries model).

All stock and flow equations have exactly the same syntax because they are accumulations. Like a bathtub, each stock accumulates its inflow (or, in more general terms, the difference between the inflow and the outflow). Modeling software exploits the syntax similarity by automatically writing stock accumulation equations. But it is important for beginning modelers to write such equations for themselves, so they better understand how the intuitive yet vital concept of accumulation is expressed rigorously and mathematically.

After writing equations for the accumulation of love, participants then tackled the tricky task of formulating equations for causal links between the two lovers. I allowed participants the freedom to introduce auxiliary concepts in order to operationally create the links. This exercise, conducted by pairing participants, provoked a lot of thinking and discussion. Participants tried their best to capture the imagined sensitivity of lovers and argued whether Romeo and Juliet respond to being loved in exactly the same way or somehow mirror each other's affections. The model was small enough that everyone managed to formulate a full-set of equations and run simulations. The result was a wide variety of time charts. Some charts showed escalating growth of love while others showed a collapse of love to a permanent state of cold lovelessness (zero units of love).

In the limited time available, nobody was able to reproduce a cyclical pattern of love; nevertheless, the exercise of developing the model and equations provoked much fruitful thought about the relationship between Romeo and Juliet, just as a metaphorical model should. With a bit more time after the course was completed, it was possible to formulate equations that generate cyclicality. They are listed in Appendix 1 and are not especially difficult to understand (see also Appendix 2 for an equation description).[6] But the difficulty of writing equations that mean what you intend (and of being absolutely clear about what you really mean) underscores an enduring challenge of good modeling. It is not easy to build full-blown simulators (even small ones), and there is always room to improve formulation skills; however, the discipline of operational thinking about Romeo and Juliet takes one deeply into the problem situation and, with patience, can yield an insightful simulator. The same applies to business and industry models, and that was the message I wished to convey.

> The discipline of operational thinking about Romeo and Juliet takes one deeply into the problem situation and, with patience, can yield an insightful simulator. The same applies to business and industry models, and that was the message I wished to convey.

Structure and dynamic behavior in "Romeo and Juliet"

A causal loop diagram of the relationship between Romeo and Juliet is shown in Figure 6-5. It was a good opportunity to practice basic diagramming rules in preparation for the multi-loop oil producers' model. Essentially, Romeo and Juliet's love for each other is mutually dependent, and it is this interdependence that forms the closed feedback loop of their relationship. Our picture shows not only love but also changes in love.

As *Romeo's Love for Juliet* grows, it causes the *change in Juliet's love for Romeo* to increase (which is depicted as a positive link). Such increments of love make *Juliet's Love for Romeo* stronger, another positive link. In other words, her love thrives on affection. Romeo is different and he spurns affection. So, as *Juliet's Love for Romeo* grows, it causes the *change in Romeo's love for Juliet* to decrease, (which is depicted as a negative link). Such deductions from (the stock of) love make *Romeo's Love for Juliet* weaker, a kind of positive link.[7] In other words, his love withers with affection and is nurtured by disdain.

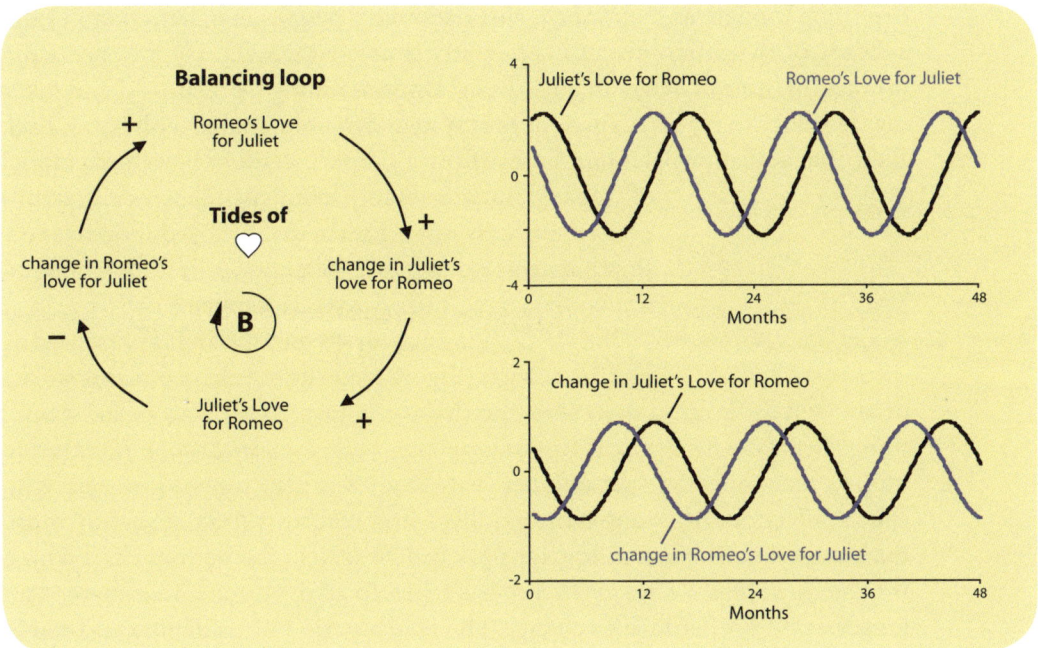

Figure 6-5. Causal loop diagram and simulations of Romeo and Juliet

The four links make a closed loop, which is named "Tides of Love" and is shown as a balancing loop B. This polarity says that the loop counteracts spontaneous change. For example, if *Romeo's Love for Juliet* were to increase (due to an imagined exogenous event like the arrival of spring), then the strictures of their closed loop relationship would bring about a counteracting decrease in his love. In this thought experiment, Romeo's springtime ardor induces an increase in *Juliet's Love for Romeo*, which accumulates. Her greater love in turn induces a decrease in *Romeo's Love for Juliet*, thereby closing the loop and counteracting the original increase. Of course, if Romeo's love were to thrive on affection rather than to wither, his relationship with Juliet would be transformed into a reinforcing loop and their love would grow without bounds.

Behavior Analysis in "Romeo and Juliet" ("Understanding Oscillations")

Simulations of the "Romeo and Juliet" model are shown on the right of Figure 6-5. It turns out that the two are locked in an endless cycle of waxing and waning love, as originally postulated. But the simulations help to explain this puzzling over time (which, as mentioned, surprises many people and alerts them to the subtlety of dynamics, even in apparently simple systems).[8] My interpretation mimics the style of behavior analysis in "Understanding Oscillations" and takes me right back to my first experiences of system dynamics shared with Barry. Back then, the oscillations of interest arose from a simple inventory-workforce model of a factory. But remarkably, interdependencies in a factory bear an uncanny resemblance to the closed-loop relationship between Romeo and Juliet, as further illustrated in Appendix 1 (see http://www.iseesystems.com/tracing).

> Interdependencies in a factory bear van uncanny resemblance to the closed-loop relationship between Romeo and Juliet.

The simulation runs for 48 months and is presented as two time charts (Figure 6-5), the top chart showing stocks of love and the bottom chart showing changes in love. At the start of the simulation, *Juliet's Love for Romeo* is two units of love while *Romeo's Love for Juliet* is one unit. Romeo's affection causes Juliet's love to grow while Romeo's love falls as he spurns affection. After one month, Juliet's love reaches a peak of slightly more than two units. The reason for this peak can be seen in the bottom chart where the *change in Juliet's Love for Romeo* has fallen to zero, meaning that there is no longer cause for her love to change. She is in a period of contented and stable love. But this state does not and cannot last. By month 1, Romeo's love has fallen to zero and the rate of change of his love is at a minimum of minus one units of love per month. He does not share Juliet's stable contentment and his love for Juliet continues to fall, reaching a low of slightly more than minus two units of love by month 5. Of course Juliet notices this marked decline in affection over a period of three months. Her love for Romeo gradually recedes and reaches zero by month 5. By now she is quite upset with Romeo and the rate of change of her love reaches a low of minus one units of love per month. Inevitably, this further deterioration in their relationship causes her love to fall still further, becoming negative in value and reaching a minimum of slightly more than minus two by month 9. Meanwhile, Romeo (the contrarion) feels freed of unwelcome affection and his disdain for Juliet begins to lessen, so that, by month 9, his love returns to zero and is growing at its fastest rate just as Juliet's love reaches its nadir.

> The metaphorical model, "Romeo and Juliet," when developed and completed, presents a good example of **closed-loop thinking**, one of Barry's eight types of systems thinking.

Further shifts in affection are already in train. *Romeo's Love for Juliet* continues to rise for four months, reaching a peak of slightly more than two units by month 13. This surge of affection induces new romantic feeling in Juliet. Her love climbs from its negative depths to a calm neutrality of zero by month 13. But this seeming neutrality does not last as her love continues to grow, spurred on by Romeo's evident and sustained affection. Just before month 16, Romeo and Juliet find themselves back in exactly the same romantic state they were at the start of the simulation. *Juliet's Love for Romeo* is at two units of love and rising, while *Romeo's Love for Juliet* is at one unit and falling. The stage is set for another identical cycle of love.[9] The metaphorical model, "Romeo and Juliet," when developed and completed, presents a good example of closed-loop thinking, one of Barry's eight types of systems thinking.

Dynamic and Operational Thinking about Oil Production

Fisheries and Shakespeare occupied the first morning of the program and paved the way for the *Oil Producers' Microworld* in the afternoon. The *Microworld* is a gaming simulator that captures the dynamic interplay of three groups of oil producers whose combined production determines the world supply of crude oil; however, their reasons for investing and producing are very different. Commercially motivated, independent producers are represented by companies like Shell, Exxon Mobil, and BP Amoco. Politically motivated OPEC producers include the swing producer (Saudi Arabia), and opportunists are represented by developing countries such as Nigeria. The contrast of world views among these diverse stakeholders was well-suited to the international theme of the Braskem program. These world views are bound together in multiple feedback loops, which are coded as the Microworld's diverse alternative futures for the oil industry.

Participants were organized into competing teams who played the role of independents. Teams make yearly upstream capacity investment decisions over twenty-five simulated years, with an objective to make as much money as possible. Success depends on developing investment strategies and policies suited to the selected industry scenario. Scenarios, in turn, reflect the influence on the industry of the other producer groups and their strategic goals, as well as global economic pressures on demand. In the Braskem course, we used a topical scenario entitled "Asian Boom and Bust." The team with the highest cumulative net income in 2020 was to be the winner of the competition.

An important objective of the exercise was for participants to look inside the *Microworld* to understand how the industry is modeled (rather than treating the simulator as a mysterious black box). Therefore the pre-game briefing involved dynamic and operational thinking about the industry.

We began with the turbulent history of oil price, as shown in Figure 6-6, spanning a period of 130 years from 1869 to 2004. There are striking contrasts between periods of price stability, mild price fluctuations, dramatic price surges, and equally dramatic collapses. Between 1869 and 1880, there was extreme price volatility corresponding to the early pioneering days of the oil industry in the Pennsylvania oil regions of the United States. Following the early extreme price fluctuations was an interval of mildly cyclical oil price in the decades between 1889 and 1929. This marked reduction of volatility was brought about by John D. Rockefeller, founder of Standard Oil, who set about controlling supply through ownership of refining and distribution.

In the pre-war and post-war era from 1930 to 1970, the reformed oil industry structure remained in place—almost unchallenged—even as the industry expanded internationally on the back of colossal reserves in the Arabian Peninsula. Throughout this era, spanning four decades, supply and demand were in almost perfect balance—an astonishing achievement when one considers the complexity of the industry.

But new forces were at work, ushering in a new era of oil supply politics. As the locus of production moved to the Middle East, the global political power of the region was awakened, feeding on the appetite of western industrial countries for Arabian oil to sustain their energy-intensive economies and lifestyles. Control over Middle Eastern oil was seized by newly formed OPEC (the Organization of Petroleum Exporting Countries). In 1974, and again in 1978, OPEC exercised its power by decreasing production and forcing up the price of oil. As Figure 6-6 shows, the price doubled and continued to rise to a peak of almost 70 dollars per barrel by 1979—a peak not seen since the early days of the Pennsylvania oil boom in the nineteenth century. So, in the 1970s, after two decades of managed calm and predictability, chaos returned to global oil markets.

After 1978, oil price fell sharply to only 20 dollars per barrel in the mid-1980s. For more than twenty years there were no further upheavals to match the dramatic variations of the 1970s. As the turn of the century approached, oil price was stable and low at 15 dollars per barrel. In fact, many observers at the time believed it would stay low for the foreseeable future. But the industry proved them wrong. Instability reminiscent of the 1920s and early 1930s, triggered by regional wars, power struggles within OPEC, fears of shortage, and extremes of weather started to affect oil production. Price began to rise again in 2001, reaching more than 30 dollars per barrel by 2004. This upward trend continued to 60 dollars per barrel in 2006, and, as we all know, to more than 100 dollars per barrel in 2008 (expressed in constant 2006 dollars).

Clearly, there is a lot to explain in the detail of this fascinating chart covering such a long span of time. It is troublesome that the price of such a vital commodity as oil can vary so much. The implications are enormous for industrialized societies, OPEC states, developing countries, oil companies, chemical companies, and consumers. Western economies are painfully affected when the price of gasoline rises sharply. It is even more painful in OPEC economies when the national budget

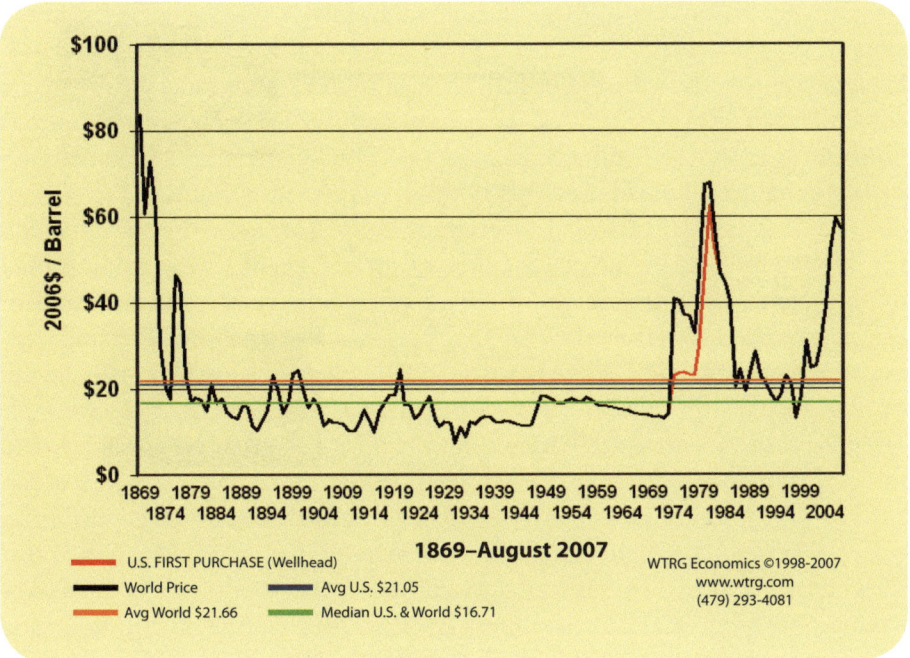

Figure 6-6. Historic crude oil price, 2006 dollars

shrinks in half or less during an oil price collapse. Yet, among the wild extremes of price over 150 years, prolonged periods of stability have been experienced in the 1930s, 1950s, and 1960s. Perhaps such stability is even more remarkable than volatility. Operational thinking about the oil industry can help to explain these episodes. Following is a sample of the operating structure from the *Oil Producers' Microworld* that explains industry stability (see Morecroft 2007, Chapter 8 for more details). The same material was presented to Braskem and gives a feel for the amount of model detail revealed to participants in preparation for the simulation competition.

Oil production capacity expansion by the independent producers

The independents expand production capacity when they judge it is profitable to do so, as shown in Figure 6-7. Note that, in the *Microworld*, this judgment is left entirely up to the discretion of players. The circular symbol is the capacity expansion policy, commonly called capex, that controls the flow of new capacity into the stock of capacity controlled by independents. Figure 6-7 shows the main information sources that are available to calculate the profitability of investment projects.

Independents estimate the development costs of new fields and the expected future oil price over the lifetime of the field. Knowing future cost, projected oil

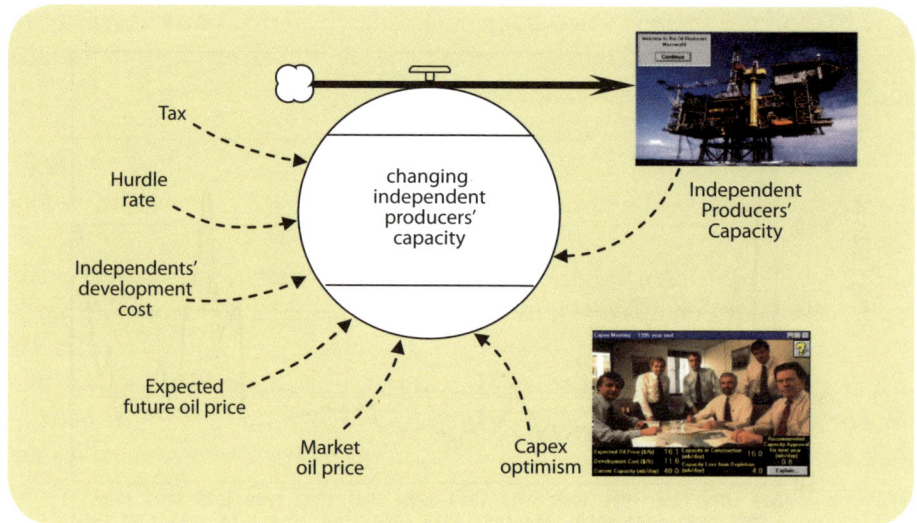

Figure 6-7. Independents' capacity expansion—a commercial worldview

price, likely size of a new field, and the tax regime, financial analysts (or game players) can calculate the future profit stream and apply a hurdle rate to identify acceptable projects. In reality, each project undergoes a thorough and detailed screening, using well-tried upstream investment appraisal methods. The greater the estimated profitability, the more projects exceed the hurdle rate and the greater the recommended expansion of capacity. In addition, a scale effect is represented by information feedback from independents' capacity. The more capacity, the bigger the independents become and the more projects are in their portfolio of investment opportunities.

Executive control of recommended expansion is exercised through capex investment optimism that captures collective investment bias among top management teams responsible for independents' investment. Optimism can be viewed on a scale from low to high. High optimism means that oil company executives (game players) are bullish about the investment climate and approve more capacity expansion than financial criteria alone would suggest. Low optimism means executives are cautious and approve less expansion than recommended. It is important to appreciate the distance from which we are viewing investment appraisal and approval. We are not concerned with the detail of individual oil field projects; rather, we are seeing the commercial pressures for oil production capacity expansion in the aggregate.

Strictly speaking, there is a two-stage stock accumulation process for upstream capacity. Changes in capacity first accumulate as capacity-in-development which, after a time delay, is commissioned and becomes operating capacity.

Output of the "swing producer" of oil

For many years the swing producer in the oil industry has been Saudi Arabia. The role of the swing producer is to vary output, up or down, by just enough oil to defend OPEC's intended price, known in the industry as the "marker price." A producer taking on this role must have *both* the physical and economic capacity to increase or decrease production quickly, by up to 3 million barrels per day in a matter of weeks, in order to absorb unexpected variations in demand (due, for example, to an unusually mild winter or hot summer) and/or to compensate for surprise variations in the output of other producers. The model makes the important assumption that the swing producer always has adequate capacity to meet any call for oil it receives.

Figure 6-8 shows the factors influencing Saudi production policy. Saudi oil ministers are pictured discussing changes in the output of the desert oil fields. Production responds to pressure both from production quotas and from oil price. There are two stock adjustment processes operating simultaneously. Ministers change production in order to meet the swing producer's allocated quota. But they also take corrective action whenever the market oil price deviates from OPEC's intended price. When the price is too low, Saudi production is reduced below quota thereby undersupplying the market and pushing up the market price. Conversely, when the price is too high, Saudi production is

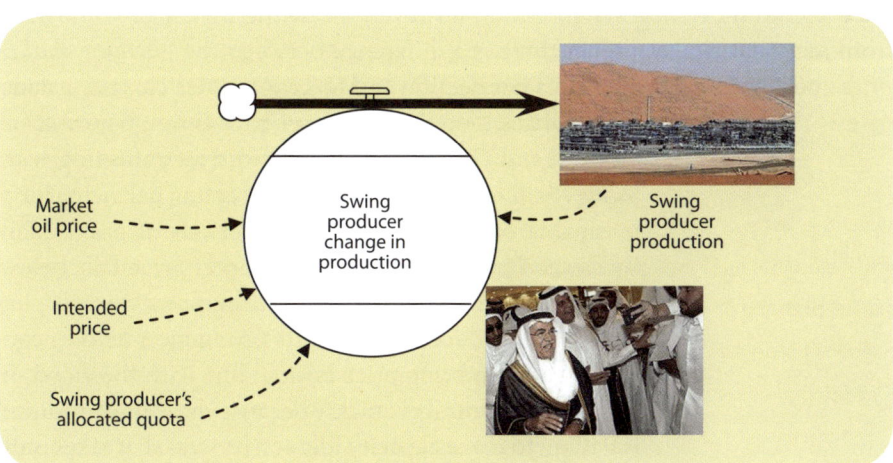

Figure 6-8. Swing producer's policy—a political worldview

increased above quota to oversupply the market and reduce the oil price to the level OPEC is trying to defend. Such ability and willingness to rapidly adjust production is characteristic of any swing producer.

Sometimes the swing producer floods the market with oil in order to drive down the price and gain market share. This punitive mode of production is part of the full model, but is not included in the sample of structure presented here.

Feedback loops in global oil production

Figure 6-9 shows the main feedback loops formed by the independents and by the swing producer. These loops play an important role in balancing supply and demand in the global oil industry. Balancing loop B1 is the industry's main commercial supply loop. A production shortfall stimulates a rise in *Market Oil Price* and an increase in the *price-to-cost ratio*, which makes upstream investment more attractive for commercial oil companies. As a result, there is an increase in *capacity approval* and *capacity in construction*, which eventually leads to expansion of *Independents' Operating Capacity* and actual *independents' production*. Extra production corrects the *production shortfall* and completes loop B1. Because it takes many years to develop new capacity, this feedback loop alone does not ensure that supply always matches demand. Market forces alone cannot stabilize oil price.

> Because it takes many years to develop new capacity, this feedback loop alone does not ensure that supply always matches demand. Market forces alone cannot stabilize oil price.

In fact, price stability comes from the swing producer. *OPEC production* in the lower half of the figure is the sum of *Swing Producer Production* and the *Opportunists' Production*. When the member states are in harmony, they produce according to negotiated quota; however, the swing producer will depart from negotiated quota when there is a difference between the *intended marker price* and *Market Oil Price*. This connection to *Market Oil Price* closes a balancing feedback loop B2 that passes back through *production shortfall* and *OPEC production* before reconnecting with *Swing Producer Production*. This fast-acting balancing loop is capable of creating prolonged periods of price stability as seen in the 1960s. When market price falls below the intended marker price due to a temporary supply glut, the swing producer quickly cuts production below negotiated quota to bring price back in line with the target or marker. The loop acts quickly because the swing producer is willing to make capacity idle—a process that takes only a month or two. Similarly, when market price rises above the intended marker price due to a temporary demand surge, the swing producer quickly re-activates

> Despite OPEC's reputation for aggressive price hikes, the swing producer is in fact a benign and calming influence in the global oil market, boosting or curtailing production in order to maintain stable prices.

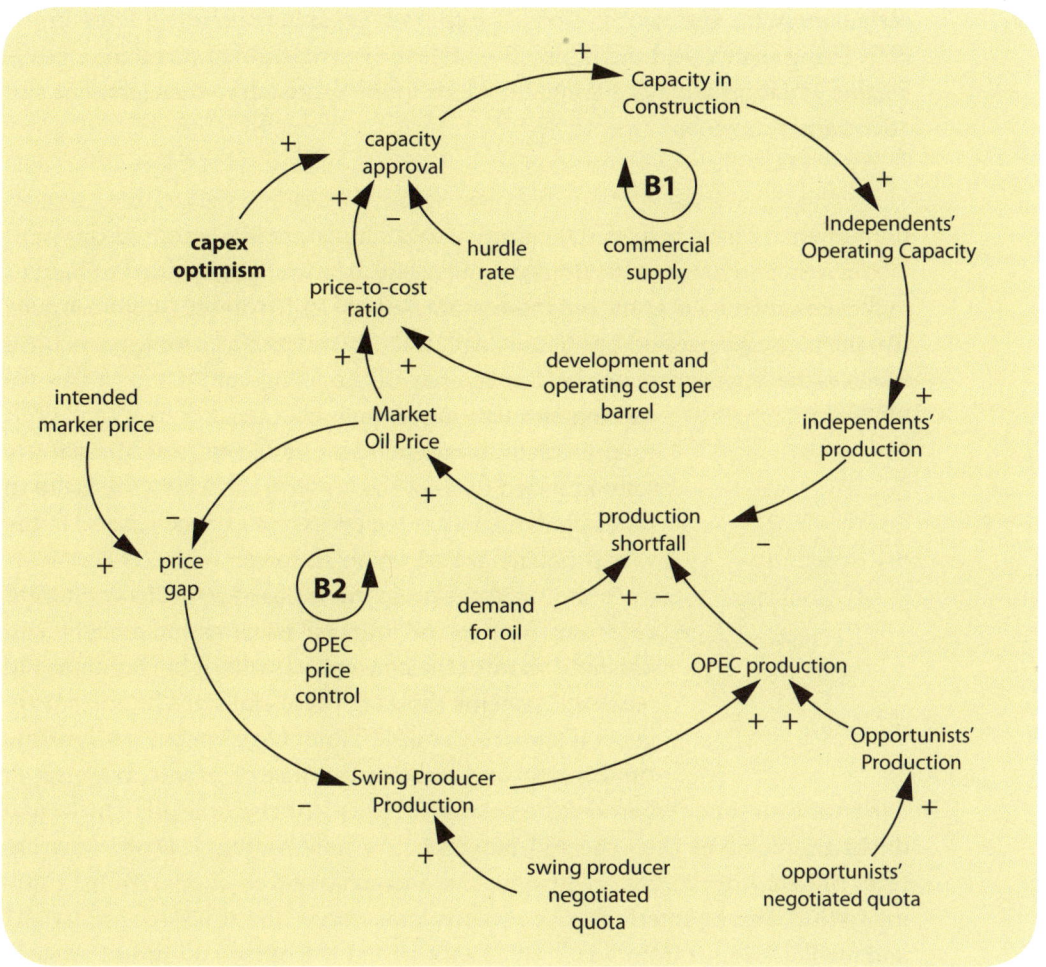

Figure 6-9. Feedback loops involving independents and the swing producer

idle capacity to increase supply and bring price down. Despite OPEC's reputation for aggressive price hikes, the swing producer is, in fact, a benign and calming influence in the global oil market, boosting or curtailing production in order to maintain stable prices.

Similar discussion of the remaining operating policies, stock accumulations, and feedback loops in the oil producers' model completed the pre-game briefing given to the participants. At that point the chosen teams were ready to play the *Microworld*. Like a bevy of earnest Juliets, they pitted their wits against fickle OPEC and global consumers under a scenario of Asian boom and bust. The sought-after prize was evening dinner for the winning team at an elegant restaurant in the Guarajuba resort. The contest was fierce but nevertheless enjoyable. Using an involved and interactive style to systems thinking created not only a game situation but a fundamentally important approach to management situations and problems.

In this paper, I have reviewed the models and simulators used in a two-day module on system dynamics for Braskem managers. Models are intended to help us make sense of our complex and interconnected world, to foresee (amid complexity) the consequences of strategic change, and to avoid pitfalls. Doing so requires much more than technical skills in the use of modeling software or a flair for gaming simulations. People also need conceptual skills to appreciate interdependencies in business and society (often hidden from everyday view) and how they lead to puzzling dynamics in the events we experience and in the very problems we are trying to solve.

> People need conceptual skills to appreciate interdependencies in business and society (often hidden from everyday view) and how they lead to puzzling dynamics in the events we experience and in the very problems we are trying to solve.

In the Braskem program, we used a spectrum of models, from "Romeo and Juliet" to fisheries and global oil, to illustrate some of the conceptual skills of the modeler and feedback systems thinker. These skills are important for general managers as well. Time charts encourage dynamic thinking to find, among the flux of events, patterns of behavior over time (whether it be volatile oil price, the rise and fall of fish catch, fluctuating love, or the expected outcome of a new strategy). From such patterns of behavior there is the imaginative and creative step of operational thinking to find, among interlocking decisions and actions, the stock accumulations and feedback loops from which dynamics arise. In "Romeo and Juliet," there is just one feedback loop which, to the surprise of many, can generate an endless cycle of waxing and waning love. In global oil, the interplay of many feedback loops connecting commercial producers, consumers, and OPEC creates both turmoil and stability in the oil industry and in oil prices. Simulation reliably computes these outcomes, but it is the discipline of feedback systems thinking that makes clear the structure that lies behind simulated behavior. The mysteries of the simulator, and its chosen slice of reality, are revealed so it is no longer a black box.

> Simulation reliably computes these outcomes, but it is the discipline of feedback systems thinking that makes clear the structure that lies behind simulated behavior.

It was the desire to illuminate the thinking behind the *Oil Producers' Microworld* that led to the content of the Braskem course with its blend of large and small models. And so the smallest model, "Romeo and Juliet," became a metaphorical model to awaken feedback systems thinking among one group of managers in a single region of vast and beautiful Brazil. It was part of Barry's quest to bring systems thinking to the world.

References

Mass NJ and Senge PM 1975. Understanding Oscillations in Simple Systems, MIT System Dynamics Group Working Paper, D-2045-2 (available from the System Dynamics Society on a DVD containing the complete D-memo series of the MIT System Dynamics Group).
Morecroft JDW 2007. *Strategic Modeling and Business Dynamics,* Wiley, Chichester.
Owen, Oliver. *Natural Resource Conservation: An Ecological Approach.* New York, N.Y.: MacMillan, 1985.
Radzicki MJ 1993. "Dyadic Processes, Tempestuous Relationships, and System Dynamics," *System Dynamics Review,* 9 (1), 79–94.
Richmond BM 1985. *A User's Guide to STELLA,* High Performance Systems Publications, New Hampshire. (High Performance Systems subsequently became isee systems.)
Richmond BM 1977. Senior Executives System Dynamics Workshop Session II: Inventory-Workforce Model, MIT System Dynamics Group Working Paper, D-2661 (available from the System Dynamics Society on a DVD containing the complete D-memo series of the MIT System Dynamics Group).
Strogatz SH 1988. Love Affairs and Differential Equations, *Mathematics Magazine,* 61 (1), 35. 10.

Notes

1. Oscillations continued to fascinate Barry and became an important part of his repertoire for communicating systems thinking. Already, in 1977, he was conducting workshops in the MIT Senior Executives program using the inventory-workforce model to introduce system dynamics concepts. He begins his workshop notes (Richmond 1977) by stating that the purpose of the session is:

    To illustrate three major system dynamics concepts:
    (1) Internal structure has inherent behavioral tendencies. Structure gives rise to behavior. External factors precipitate response.
    (2) Transferability of structure.
    (3) Difficulty of performing an intuitive policy analysis even with a formal (explicit) model (and a simple one at that!).

    The notes include a structural diagram and equation listing for the inventory-workforce model and simulations (hand-drawn trajectories to join-up character plots) that show how different disturbances in demand (step-increase, ramp, and pulse) all precipitate cyclical variations in inventory, production, and workforce.

Also, the first user guide to STELLA includes a section devoted to the oscillatory dynamics of a predator-prey model, as the following excerpt shows:

> Now here is a tough question for you. Why does this system oscillate? Think about it for a minute. You might want to review the model structure, analyze a few graphs and change some parameters before drawing any conclusions. The model you just constructed is not only a simple model of predator-prey dynamics. It has the generic structure of a pure oscillator. (The structure governing the motion of a pendulum, an oscillator we are all familiar with, is almost identical to your two-stock model.) The key to the oscillatory behavior is in the way the two stocks are linked. When prey reaches a peak, the predator population is at its most rapid rate of expansion. Similarly, when predators are at the low ebb of their cycle, prey population is at its most rapid rate of expansion."

2. The paper begins with a single stock model of the rabbit population in a field to rigorously demonstrate (by simulation) that a model containing a single stock accumulation cannot possibly generate overshoot or cyclical dynamics. A model requires at least two stocks to generate oscillations. The authors develop an inventory-workforce model containing two stocks and only four active equations (eleven equations including constants and initial values) to rigorously demonstrate the origin of undamped oscillations in a second-order system. Realistic extensions to this tiny model are then used to explain both expanding and damped oscillations. These structural variations on the base model are similar to the structural variations that Mike Radzicki adds to his Romeo and Juliet model to investigate dynamics and romantic styles.
3. I would also like to acknowledge Isabella Schiavinato and Soraia Cardoso for their enthusiastic and professional support during the Braskem course. Thanks, too, to Ana Cristina Dias, Coordinator HR at Braskem, who kindly secured permission for details of the course to be included in this paper.
4. The Romeo and Juliet simulator comes from a paper by WPI's Mike Radzicki, published in the *System Dynamics Review* which, in turn, was built on an article by Harvard's Steven Strogatz in *Mathematics Magazine* (see the annotated bibliography at http://iseesystems.com/tracing for more details of both papers). The model's original purpose was to engage the interest of Steven Strogatz's undergraduate students who were studying differential equations. By translating the differential equation model into stocks, flows, and feedback loops Mike Radzicki found it to be a useful model for engaging the interest of students studying system dynamics. English literature students may not understand differential equations, but they can appreciate romantic relationships expressed in the visual language of stocks, flows, and feedback loops.
5. In the model of Romeo and Juliet, it is not their families that keep them apart; instead, it is Romeo's fickleness. Nevertheless, the model does touch on themes such as love, time, fate, and chance that students of Shakespeare are often asked to consider. For example, the Wikipedia entry about Romeo and Juliet mentions that "time plays an important role in the language and plot of the play . . . For instance, when Romeo attempts to swear his Love to Juliet by the moon, Juliet tells him not to, as it is known to be inconstant over time, and she does not desire this of him."
6. The appendices for this chapter as well as for the rest of the book are available at http://iseesystems.com/tracing.
7. The assignment of polarity to this link is tricky because the link corresponds to a bi-flow in a stock accumulation process. Here one could justify a positive link on the grounds of a double negative effect—*deductions* from love make Romeo's love for Juliet *weaker*.

8. Readers can recreate the simulated trajectories and study them more closely by running the Romeo and Juliet simulator that accompanies this chapter and can be found at http://iseesystems.com/tracing.
9. By carefully analyzing the shape of the trajectories for change of love and the areas they enclose, it is possible to prove they are symmetrical around their peaks and, therefore, that a perfect undamped harmonic oscillation is unfolding. Such graphical proof is beyond the scope of this paper, but a similar proof for the inventory-workforce model can be found in the original article on "Understanding Oscillations."

The Loops of Feedback

A verse inspired by 30+ years of system dynamics and a famous song, called "The Streets of London," by British folk singer Ralph McTell. Incidentally, I saw him perform the song live in 2006, at a festival in North Cornwall marking the centenary of the birth of English Poet Laureate John Betjeman.

Have you seen the asset stocks in the multi-looped beer game?
Amplifying orders when consumers drink more beer.
The factory's working overtime and still the stocks are in decline.
Feast then turns to famine, but the reason is unclear.

Refrain (to be sung after each verse):
So how can you tell me that life's optimal.
Don't say we're rational all the time.
Let me take you by the hand.
I'll lead you through the loops of feedback.
I'll show you something that will make you change your mind.

In the Fish Banks model, at the fish rate formulations,
There are non-linear functions confounding fishermen's lives.
Their ships return empty when once there was plenty.
The sudden collapsed fishery is yesterday's surprise.

Have you glimpsed intangibles within the airline simulator
Determining the destiny of People Express?
Declining motivation and service degradation
Feed back to undermine the firm's growth and success.

Have you seen the coiled-up slinky's fascinating oscillations
Showing that in structure dynamic patterns lie?
There's no need for forcing factors only nature's spring-mass strictures
Plus the covert force of gravity's steady tie.

Refrain.

(cont.)

Have you heard of misperceptions, turning into paradoxes
In the way that systems behave over time?
Information overrun and localised rules of thumb
Cause not only cycles but stagnation and decline.

The original "The Streets of London" carried a positive message that life is better than we think, especially when compared with homeless people who roam the streets of London and face real hardship. I wanted to end this song on a positive note too, so I added this extra verse:

In all problem situations, there are hidden feedback loops,
Shaping how events unfold within our times.
Despite complex society there's no need for anxiety.
Just design better policies and we'll all lead better lives.

Optional Ending Refrain (slightly modified):
So even though life is not optimal.
And we're not truly rational in our minds.
Let me take you by the hand.
I'll lead you through the loops of feedback.
Together we'll find something that will lead to better times.

—Based on "The Streets of London"
John Morecroft, March 2007
extra slinky verse for Barry, June 2008

Academic note: The song and its refrain question the views of policy advisers who believe that the rigorous rationality of free markets prevails and will solve the problems faced by society. Instead, we need "loops of feedback" to make sense of our complex and interdependent world.

7

The Value of Critical Thinking Skills: Modeling Price and Inventory Dynamics

Corey Peck

> Corey Peck details an extended client engagement in which Barry's critical thinking skills were incorporated to provide a richer, more actionable understanding of inventory and pricing dynamics in a basic materials market.

I had first been exposed to systems thinking as an undergraduate at Colorado College, and my early experiences at High Performance Systems (now isee systems) began to show me the true power of the approach. Like many young systems thinkers, I was both captivated by this methodology and frustrated that I had never learned about it before! And although I was long on enthusiasm and short on experience, I knew that Barry's key thinking skills provided a solid foundation from which to see the world in a fascinating new light—a perspective I was looking forward to sharing with others.

In addition to developing the STELLA/*iThink* software, High Perfomance Systems had established a consulting operation to provide a systems thinking and/or simulation perspective to clients. With some facilitation and expert supervision, High Performance Systems' clients often found they could use the software and the associated methodology even more effectively. Conversely, such projects allowed High Performance Systems to get valuable feedback and real-world examples to further enhance their software offerings. In one particular case, Phil Odence (then head of High Performance Systems' client services arm) and I had been contacted to help a Canadian client team with what at first seemed like an intractable problem.

The client was a major player in the wood pulp industry—a basic commodity used to create all types of paper products. The industry had traditionally seen big

> **Corey Peck** began his career at isee systems (then High Performance Systems) in 1994 and had the privilege to work closely with Barry throughout most of the next decade. His life, both professional and personal, has been profoundly influenced by the lessons he learned under Barry's mentoring.
>
> In addition to teaching workshops focused on systems thinking and dynamic modeling, Corey specializes in simulations of flow dynamics to inform decisionmakers about the operational realities impacting their strategic choices. Corey, who lives in Colorado Springs, is the managing director of Lexidyne, LLC—a leading systems thinking company and a strategic partner of isee systems.

swings in pricing over a period of years, which was making management hesitant about a major capacity addition they were considering. The proposed plant would take over a year to complete, and the price at which increased wood pulp production could be sold was the main factor in determining the financial viability of the additional capacity. Our team was called in to provide some perspective on the price forecast for wood pulp material. Specifically, the client wanted to have a better idea about the price of wood pulp in the short-term and to have a tool to help analyze likely price scenarios further out. The question with which the management team was wrestling is illustrated in Figure 7-1.

As Phil and I began our work with the team, we first wanted to shift the focus away from a "predict the future" mindset to one that was more cognizant of the true interconnected structure that represented how the marketplace for wood pulp actually worked. After asking some detailed questions, the client told us they had collected a significant amount of historical data on what they had felt were the important dynamic parameters within this market. In some cases, this data existed on the level of the individual producers and specific buyers, but other metrics existed only for the industry as a whole.

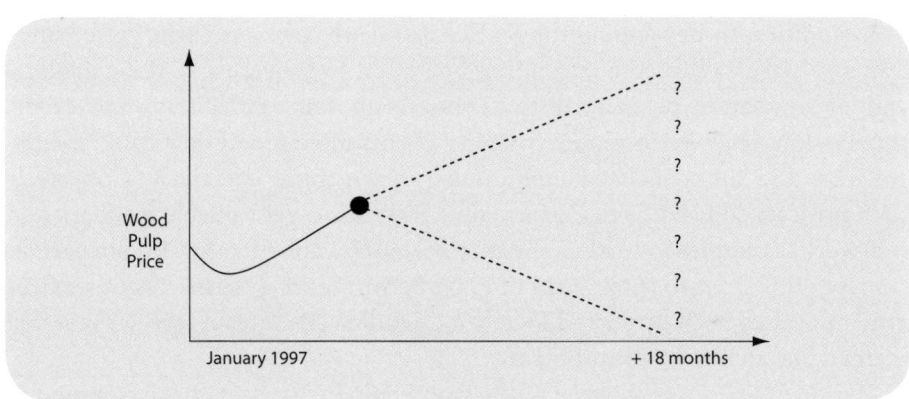

Figure 7-1. The key question: Where is wood pulp price headed?

tracing connections

The year was 1997, and I was a young systems thinker working at High Performance Systems (now isee systems). As part of High Performance Systems' client services team, I would soon be pulled into a client engagement in which Barry Richmond's critical systems thinking skills played a vital role. Barry was a passionate advocate of what he called "The Key Systems Thinking Skills." It is a rare day when I don't use one or more of these thinking skills in both my personal and professional life, and to a large extent my career, has been spent utilizing these thinking skills to help frame and ultimately answer questions in a wide variety of contexts. These key thinking skills will not create "insight on demand," but employing them will often provide a unique perspective and a shift in mindset that can prove to be incredibly valuable.

Statisticians on the client team had been working with the historical dataset and had been able to draw some preliminary correlation-based relationships between some of the variables (such as inventories and price). But, since the variability in all the data was so broad and seemingly unpredictable, such a relationship indicated that predicting inventory (held by both producers and retailers) was the key to forecasting what the commodity price would be. And the team's statistical efforts to develop a predictive model of industry inventory had not been particularly fruitful. In fact, we were told that this failure had ultimately led the client to seek a systems thinking solution!

> We first wanted to shift the focus away from a "predict the future" mindset to one that was more cognizant of the true interconnected structure that represented how the marketplace for wood pulp actually worked.

Operational Thinking

Instead of focusing on the data per se, Phil and I first led the client team through an exercise in which we mapped out the structure of the system, ignoring (at least initially) the specific data associated with it. In a facilitated session, we created a simple structure of the system that incorporated the specific variables of interest and identified how these components fit together. Instead of focusing on all the potential variables of interest, we decided to focus our attention on the "physics" of the system: what was really moving in the industry and where were the accumulations? By focusing on a "main chain" of activity, the team was able to shift

> We decided to focus our attention on the "physics" of the system: what was really moving in the industry and where were the accumulations? ... a great example of **operational thinking**.

from a mathematical construct to a more conceptual framework—a great example of what is known as operational thinking. The simple but informative structure we first developed is shown in Figure 7-2.

Although the map illustrated in Figure 7-2 did not incorporate all of the variables in which the team would ultimately be interested, it did lay out the "physics" of how wood pulp moved through the system. Many on the team immediately wanted to layer in the connections in the system. For example: how commodity price and inventories affected each other and how the activities of *consuming*, *producing* and *shipping* interacted. Phil and I first asked the client team to exercise another thinking skill and mentally simulate this basic stock-flow structure. They soon realized that the model represented quantifiable flow of materials from producers to retailers and ultimately to consumers. In other words, the only things moving into the system were *producing* and *importing*; the only things moving out of the system were *exporting* and *consuming*. As such, the changes in the amount of wood pulp in the stocks of *Producer Inventory* and *Retailer Inventory* should simply be the net result of the flows associated with those stocks over time. Since the team had already collected copious amounts of data on all of these variables, we suggested the first step was to simply populate the basic stock-flow model with historical data to see if, in fact, the numbers added up correctly. When a complete set of data is readily available, plugging in the historical numbers into a defined stock-flow structure is a very simple sanity check for both structural and numerical validity.

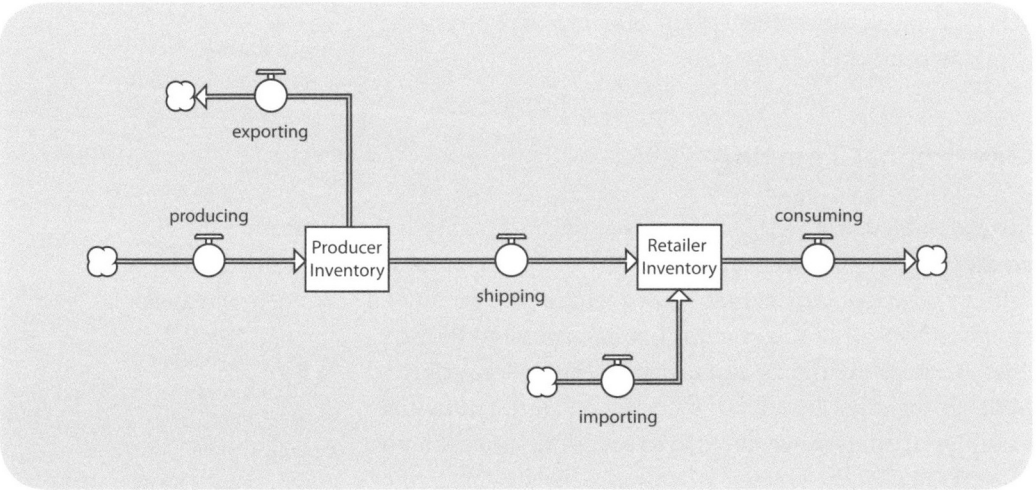

Figure 7-2. Mapping how wood pulp moves through the system

Operational Thinking with Conserved Flow

To the surprise of everyone on the team (Phil and me included), the simulated values for the stocks that resulted from plugging in the historical data for the flows disagreed significantly with the collected data for those accumulations! In looking at the outputs closely, we found that the simulation results (in dashed lines) showed an increased deviation from historical data through time, as shown in Figure 7-3.

Clearly, there was a discrepancy between our proposed structure and the underlying data, sometimes called the "link between structure and behavior" in the parlance of systems thinking. We double-checked both the model and our thinking. Was something included in the basic stock-flow map that shouldn't be there? Or was something missing? With the help of the client team, we determined that the structure of the model was correct, at least in theory. At this point, it was time to re-examine the data piece by piece. A careful study of the sources from which the data was collected identified two key omissions. First, a key industry source had only reported exports of the top five producers, which, in effect, left approximately 25% of exports unreported. Second, the same source had estimated the amount of imports by asking retailers what percentage of their shipments had come from overseas. Although at times such self-reported data is indeed reliable, in this case the estimate was off by a wide margin. It turned

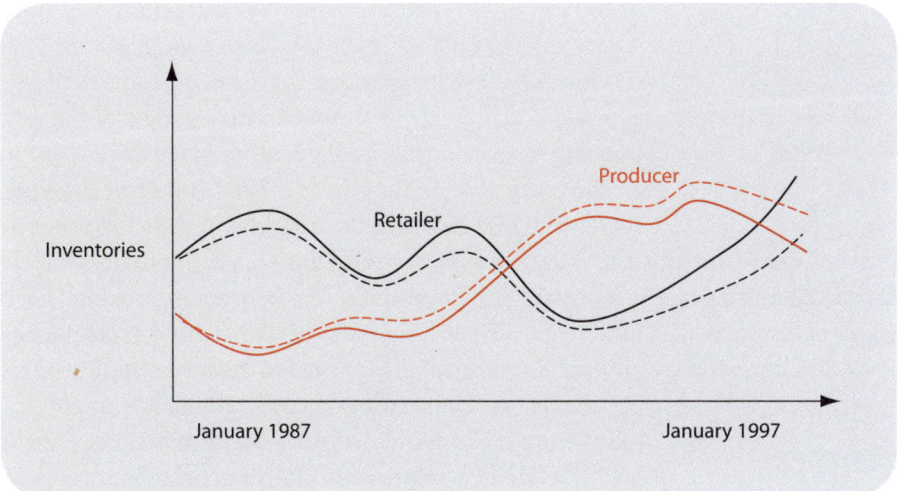

Figure 7-3. Simulation result vs. historical data

> Discovering these data limitations was made possible by using the basic stock-flow model and understanding the relationship (both structural and mathematical) between the elements, a process employing the concept of **operational thinking** with conserved flow.

out that these two key dynamics in the model did indeed exist, but the reported historical "data" associated with them was significantly flawed. Discovering these data limitations was made possible by using the basic stock-flow model and understanding the relationship (both structural and mathematical) between the elements, a process employing the concept of operational thinking with conserved flow.[1]

Dynamic Thinking

With our structure confirmed and our input data verified, the temptation was to expand our basic stock-flow backbone to include the other variables of interest as well as to identify various inter-connections within the system. This tendency is inherent in any client engagement in which data investigations loom large. Having had a bit of technical training in my undergraduate studies, I was itching to extend the model to include the pricing mechanism and perhaps some sort of prediction module (such as a regression equation). But as project manager, Phil instead advocated taking a step back from the details and looking at the aggregate patterns of behavior in the marketplace over time. Doing so was relatively easy, as we now had a solid and verifiable dataset of various industry metrics to drive time-based graphs showing the overall behavior of key variables (such as inventories and price) over time. A very simple time-series graph (as shown in Figure 7-4) was developed that expanded the limited perspective of a simple price forecast to a more complete view of the relationship between price and inventory over time.

> The process of shifting from a single-point-in-time perspective to one in which the variables in question are seen over a longer time horizon is called **dynamic thinking**.

The process of shifting from a single-point-in-time perspective to one in which the variables in question are seen over a longer time horizon is called dynamic thinking—a vital thinking skill on any project using the systems thinking approach. The process of looking "backward" at historical data may seem counter-intuitive for a client whose explicit focus is to develop a forecast for the short- and medium-term; however, the historical perspective resulting from dynamic thinking is often vital to solving problems involving industry projections. First, it begins to identify important patterns of behavior over time that, by themselves, suggest key structural components and relationships. For example, from Figure 7-4, it is clear that there is some sort of inverse relationship here between

> The historical perspective resulting from dynamic thinking is often vital to solving problems involving industry projections.

inventory and price (when one is high, the other tends to be low). Second, plotting different key variables on the same time scale can help identify the dynamics that play out over longer and shorter time frames. For example, the client team originally hypothesized that seasonal demand was what was creating the wild swings in price and inventory. As shown in Figure 7-5, however, the process of dynamic thinking forced everyone to look very closely at parameters on the same time scale,

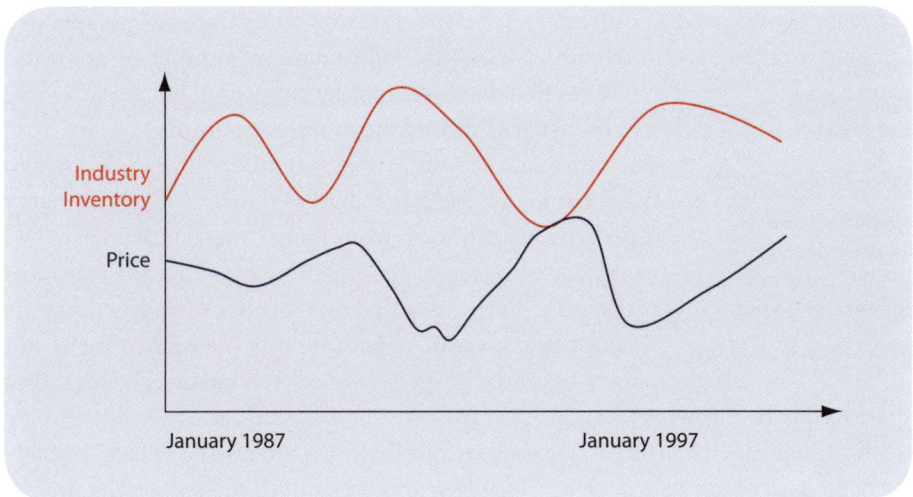

Figure 7-4. Behavior patterns of inventory and price

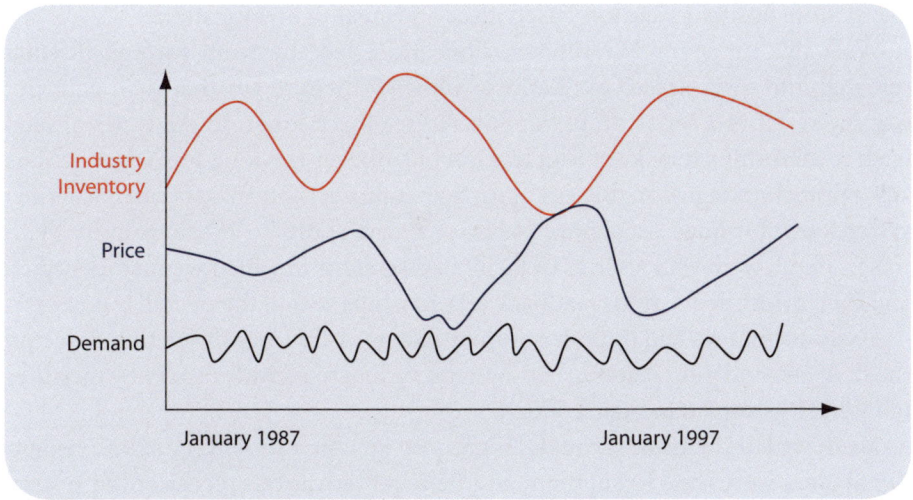

Figure 7-5. Behavior patterns of demand relative to price and inventory

and doing so showed that demand seasonality was smaller in both frequency and magnitude than the corresponding variability in industry price and inventory.

Generic Thinking

Finally, the nature of the historical data patterns began to suggest possible common system structures. The oscillatory nature of the industry led us to help the client team investigate the causes of such behavior from an operational perspective. Digging into the system dynamics literature[2] illuminated a number of examples from a wide variety of industries that displayed similar patterns of behavior. Seeing these cases (from different industries) shifted the mindset of the client team from one of isolation ("our problem is different than that of any other company/industry/market") to one of commonality ("perhaps we can learn from these other, similar cases")—a terrific exhibition of generic thinking. Once the team was on board with the idea that this sort of oscillation dynamic was not uncommon, it became much easier to focus our efforts on understanding and improving the system rather than simply to throw our hands up in frustration or blame various industry players for the problems. The discussions within the team did an about face. Initially we had heard comments such as, "If only we could smooth out seasonal demand," or "Company XYZ added capacity in 1995 and it threw everything out of whack," or "Industry leaders need to stop exporting excess inventory." But through the process of using these key systems thinking skills, the conversations were changing to more positive, solution-based ideas and areas of investigation.

> Seeing these cases shifted the mindset of the client team from one of isolation to one of commonality—a terrific exhibition of **generic thinking**.

With this new-found optimism, Phil and I led the team through further research into marketplace oscillations, allowing them to see that such behavior was the result of a series of interconnected feedback loops. These types of feedback relationships may keep markets in control over the long-term, but various sub-optimal strategies on the part of participating decision-makers can make such systems exhibit huge oscillatory behavior in the short- to medium-term. With this in mind, we began a series of facilitated sessions in which we first identified and then quantified various feedback relationships within the overall industry.

To do so, first we had to flesh out the basic stock-flow backbone that depicted the flow of wood pulp material through the system to include other key variables of interest, as shown in Figure 7-6.

Next, we led the team through an exercise in which some very simple, operational ideas were used to augment and tie together various pieces of the system, as shown in Figure 7-7.

For example, instead of using the historical data for the flow of *producing*, we asked a very general operational question: "How is *producing* determined?" In this case, the math was very simple: *producing* is simply overall industry *Capacity* multiplied by an *operating rate* (which is itself determined by other factors). Similarly, *Price* is set at a point in time and then experiences *changing price* based on a desired *fraction change in price* (determined by the collective action of decisionmakers in the system). Retailer *base orders* (primarily to replace what has been consumed) initially sit in an *Order Book* (sometimes called "order backlog") until they can be filled by producers (*filling orders* with an associated *average time to fill orders*), which in turn triggers *shipping* from *Producer Inventory* to *Retailer Inventory*. As the map began to expand and take shape, the client team immediately started to see the relationships that could be included and which might be the cause of such instability in the system. One by one, they would grab the pen in the conference room, draw a connection between two variables, and describe their mental models of key feedback relationships. "Producers will modify their *operating rate* based on levels of *Producer Inventory* but also on *Price*." "Retailers will only begin *importing* if they are holding too little in *Retailer Inventory*." "*Price* will be impacted by price leverage, which is a ratio of industry-wide inventory to *consuming*." With this flurry of enthusiasm and creativity, Phil and I knew we

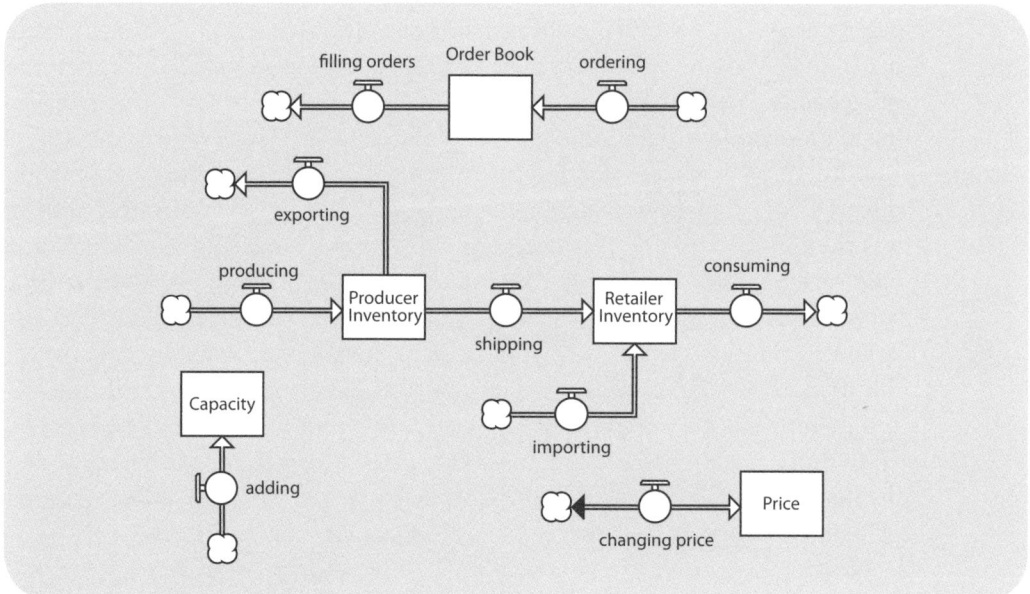

Figure 7-6. Flow of wood pulp material through the system

had started to tap into the collective wisdom of the client team, who were now chomping at the bit to incorporate all of the interactions they hypothesized to exist in the system.

In order to manage this process and keep the modeling process in control, Phil facilitated another session in which key feedback relationships were identified. To keep the model and the associated analysis manageable, the client team was asked to limit themselves to four key drivers for any single variable in the model. These hypothetical relationships were then incorporated into the existing stock-flow model, as shown in Figure 7-8. (For the sake of diagram simplicity, the decision points and influencers related to *exporting*, *importing*, and *adding capacity* are not shown, but were included in the actual case.)

With this rather detailed structure in place, we could now go about quantifying the strengths of various feedback relationships using the collected historical dataset for calibration purposes. To take perhaps the simplest example in the

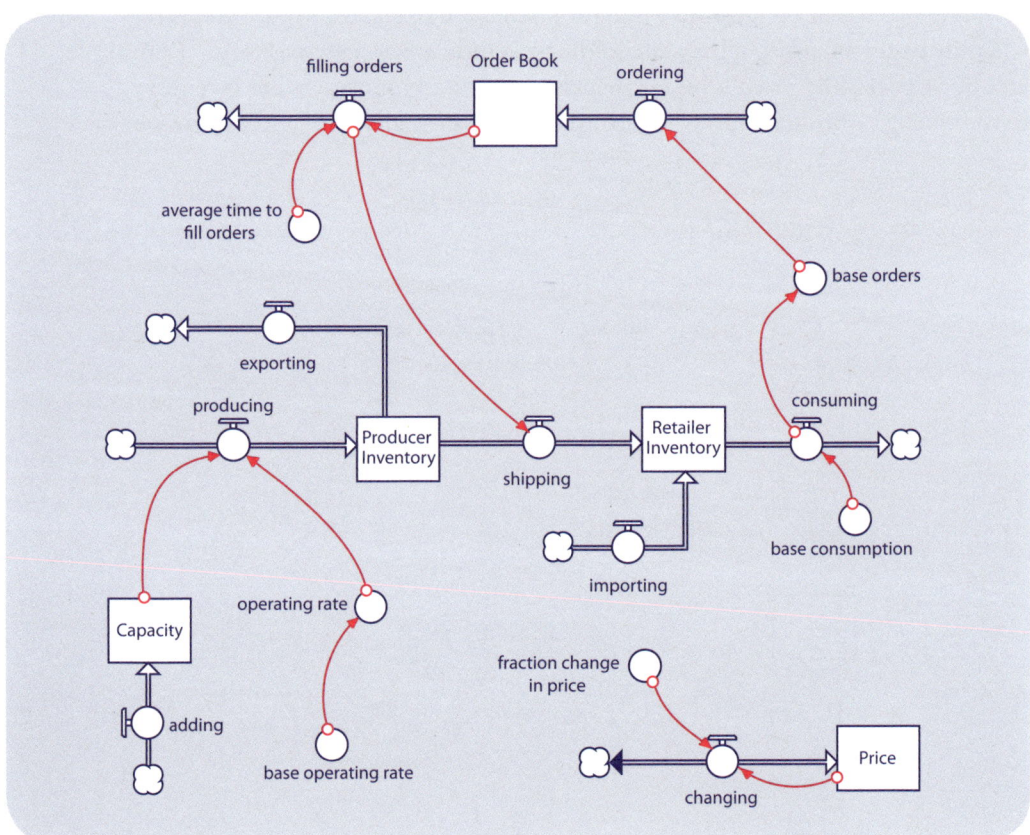

Figure 7-7. Model of the system with key relationships

model, we looked back in the data to relate the *average time to fill orders* (and by extension, *shipping*) with the corresponding values of *Producer Inventory* through time. Our hypothesis was that if producers felt inventory reserves were too low, they would delay shipments as a default inventory management mechanism. The feedback loop here was quite evident: low inventory would cause producers to increase the *average time to fill orders*, hence delaying *shipping* out of *Producer Inventory*, which, all else being equal, would improve the inventory short-fall. This type of feedback mechanism is called a negative (or balancing) loop and is common in many types of inventory systems.

Sure enough, when we plotted the *average time to fill orders* vs. *Producer Inventory*, a clear non-linear relationship emerged (as shown in Figure 7-9).

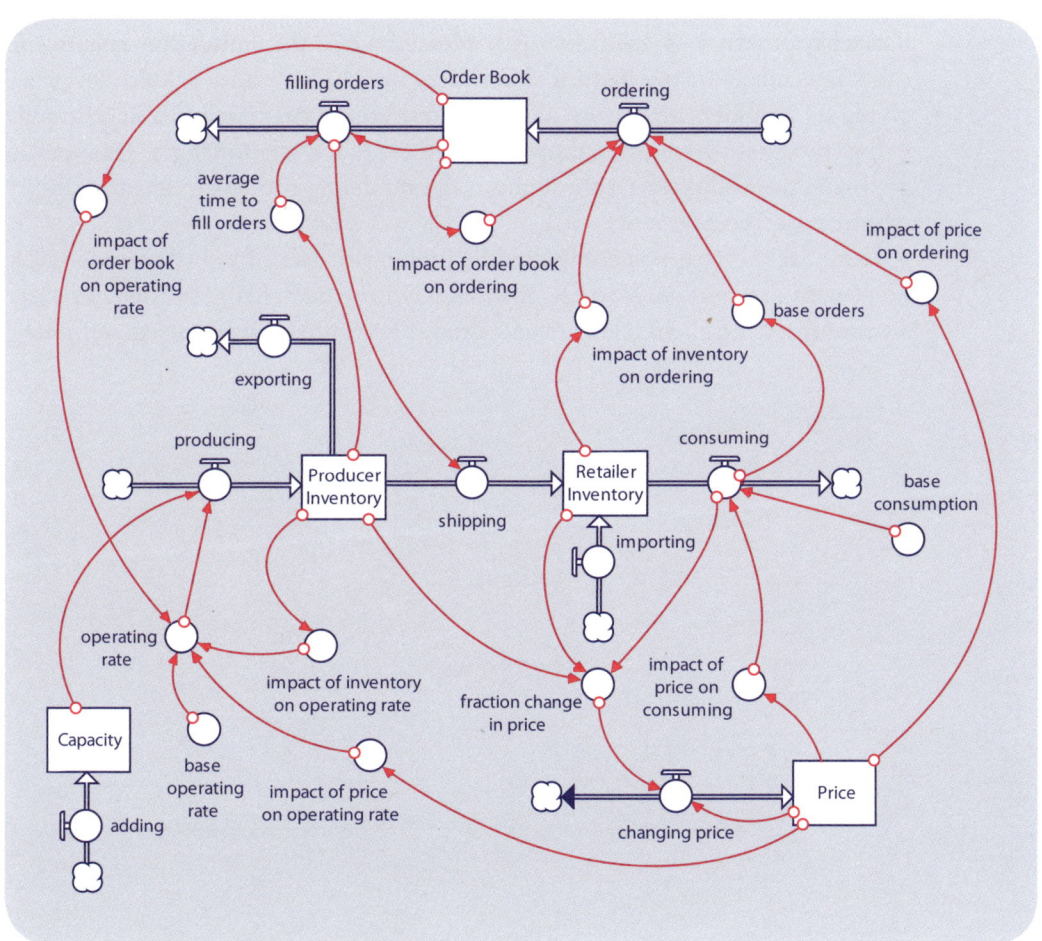

Figure 7-8. Model with added relationships

The implication of these data was clear: producers always used a minimum amount of time (roughly two months) before an order was filled for a retailer, even if the level of *Producer Inventory* was large. When inventories were tight, however, producers would delay even longer before processing orders and shipping wood pulp to the retailers as a way to preserve what little inventory reserves they were holding. With this relationship clearly established in the data analysis, we could simply translate this feedback mechanism directly into our model structure. And in keeping with good modeling practice, this relationship was implemented by itself just to see the impact it had on the system. In other words, Phil and I established this connection in the model to override the historical data for *filling orders* and *shipping* that had existed up to this point and kept all of the other historical data intact. This allowed us to run the simulation with just this particular decision rule embedded in the model logic, as a test to see if our hypothesis was valid. We were pleased when the simulation results still calibrated nicely to the historical numbers for *Producer* and *Retailer Inventory*, giving us confidence that we had rendered this particular dynamic correctly before progressing to other, more involved feedback relationships. This was an approach we would repeat throughout the modeling process to ensure validity of introduced components.

A similar exercise was completed by looking at data of industry-wide inventory relative to *consuming* to see how quickly *Price* had changed. The data analysis confirmed the client team's expectation: a low ratio of inventory to *consuming*

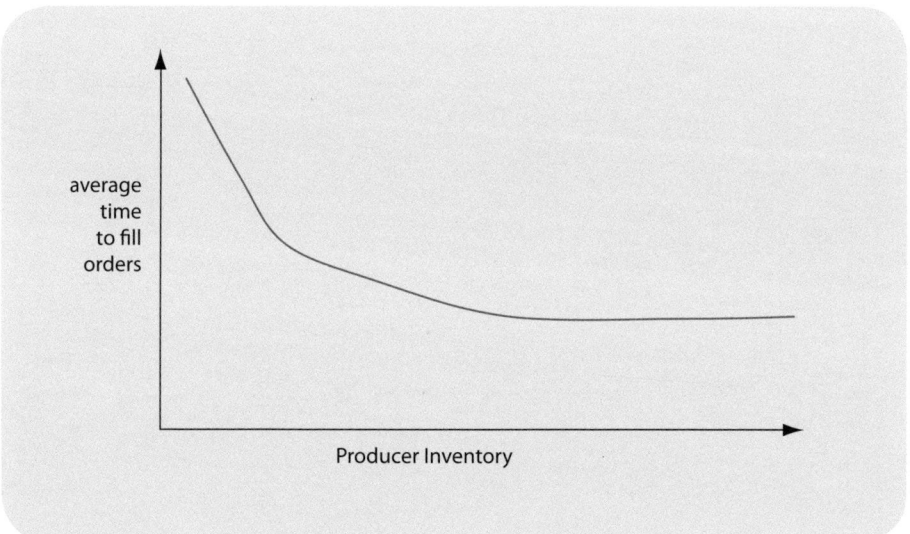

Figure 7-9. Average time to fill orders vs. Producer Inventory

resulted in positive changes in *Price*, whereas a high ratio caused *Price* to fall, as shown in Figure 7-10.

Again, Phil and I simply took the results of the data analysis, imported them directly into the variable called *fraction change in price*, and then simulated the results to ensure they still calibrated with a reasonable degree of accuracy to the historical data.

Closed-Loop Thinking

An interesting thing happened, however, when we tried to formulate the multivariate relationships for *consuming*. The team's hypothesis was that *consuming* would have a base seasonal component, but would also be influenced by *Price*. It seemed like simple Economics 101: high prices would tend to dampen *consuming* and low prices would encourage additional *consuming*. The data analysis did, in fact, show these relationships, but not to a significant degree. In other words, the simple relationship of *Price* either accelerating or diminishing *consuming* was not enough to explain the variability of that particular variable in the historical data. We reconvened the client team to show them the results; clearly we were missing some key relationship in the model. We poured over the data again to look for errors, but none were evident. Finally, one of the client team members related an anecdote from a market research study completed some years before

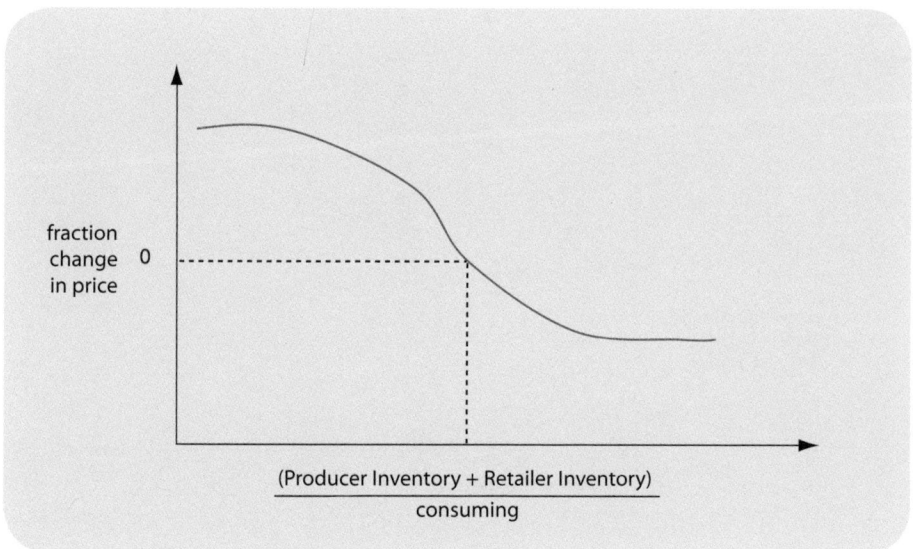

Figure 7-10. Fraction change in price vs. inventory to consuming ratio

in which a number of consumers had indicated they were more interested in how price was moving rather than where it actually was. A high *Price* would certainly have a tendency to dampen *consuming*, but this impact might be overridden if the expectation was that *Price* would be even higher a few months into the future. In other words, the market research study had indicated that at least some consumers have a decision rule in which speculative buying came into play. In times of rising prices, they would tend to purchase more in order to stockpile material at the current, lower *Price*, as shown in Figure 7-11.

In a truly "a ha" moment, the client team realized that this speculative dynamic might, in fact, be a key mechanism driving instability in the market. A simple mental simulation quickly confirmed this hypothesis, at least in theory. Low levels of inventory would cause the price to increase; consumers would see this signal of rising prices and increase their *consuming*, thus exacerbating the low inventory levels and pushing *Price* even higher. This type of feedback mechanism is called a positive (or reinforcing) feedback loop, and such relationships tend to exhibit out-of-control behavior and destabilize markets. Incorporating this dynamic into the decision rule for *consuming* was a true breakthrough, as subsequent simulated results once again tracked very nicely with historical data.

The effect of price speculation on behavior was seen in the decision rule involving orders as well. As hypothesized,

> This type of feedback mechanism is called a **positive** (or **reinforcing**) **feedback loop**, and such relationships tend to exhibit out-of-control behavior and destabilize previously well-controlled markets.

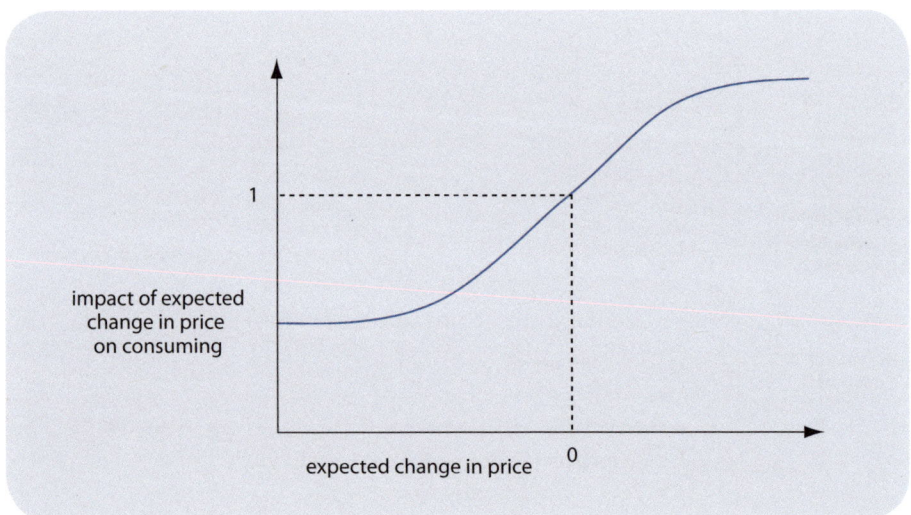

Figure 7-11. Impact of expected price on consuming vs. expected change in price

an analysis of the historical dataset showed that retailers set a value of *base orders* to replace *consuming*, which was then modified up or down based on the amount of *Retailer Inventory* and existing *Order Book*. The team's original assumption was that *Price* was another driving factor in this decision, but some extensive data analysis found that not to be the case. Instead, similar to the decision to consume, retailers appeared to be factoring in the *changing price* rather than the absolute value of *Price* (*expected change in price*) in their *ordering* decisions. In fact, retailers were forming an expectation of short-term forecast of *Price* and then adjusting their orders accordingly. Including this dynamic in the model introduced yet another reinforcing and de-stabilizing mechanism into an already unsteady market.

The exact same speculative dynamic turned out to be present for producers of wood pulp. High prices would indeed trigger increases in *producing* (via an increased *operating rate*), but the stronger relationship (as determined by in-depth data analysis of the historical data) proved to be the expectation of higher prices in the future. On the flip side, producers would tend to ratchet down their *operating rate* in a period of falling *Price*, all the while considering the relative magnitudes of *Producer Inventory* and *Order Book*. This dynamic on the part of producers, while speculative, is another example of a balancing loop. As producers see the *Price* for wood pulp increasing, they bump up their *operating rate*, leading to higher levels of *Inventory*, which tends to feed back and dampen the *Price* in the marketplace. The modified model, including all of the identified interrelationships, is shown in Figure 7-12.

When the strengths of the various influencers were incorporated and all parts of the model were calibrated to their historical data, this integrated simulation produced results that were amazingly similar to the observed behavior of inventories and price over time. Phil and I were pleased, not only that we had a model with both structural and numerical validity, but also that the process had produced a change of mindset on the part of the client. Identifying these feedback mechanisms allowed the client team to see and analyze the system from an aggregate perspective and to understand that much of the volatility of the market was produced by the collective decisions of the players in it, rather than the result of wild swings in demand from consumers or other various events within the system. In this way, closed-loop thinking provided a valuable shift in focus for the client team; the whole system now seemed both understandable and manageable, and it afforded the client the perspective of asking how they themselves may have been contributing to the problems (in this case, price fluctuations and lack of market stability) they were trying to solve.

> Identifying these feedback mechanisms allowed the client team to see and analyze the system from an aggregate perspective and understand that much of the volatility of the market was produced by the collective decisions of the players in it, rather than the result of wild swings in demand from consumers or other various events within the system. In this way, **closed-loop thinking** provided a valuable shift in focus for the client team.

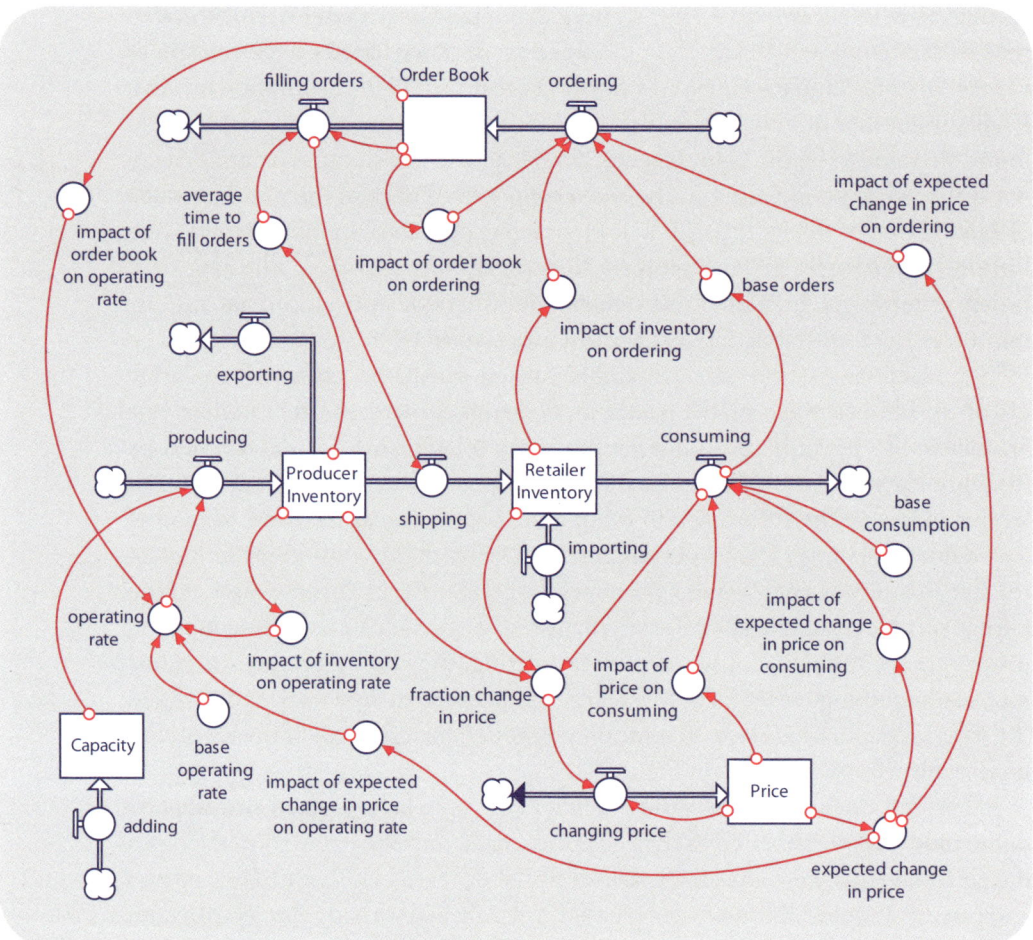

Figure 7-12. Adding the dynamics of expected price

10,000-Meter Thinking

With the insight from closed-loop thinking in mind, the client team next turned to analyze the collective decision-making processes of industry producers. Originally, the team had hypothesized that individual producers would have a very simple set of rules dictating their production decisions. If conditions were favorable (as determined by the influence factors identified previously), producers would utilize their entire *Capacity* (*operating rate* would equal 100%). If conditions were unfavorable, they would cut production significantly, but never below a certain "floor" *operating rate* of 90%. Directors of plant operations at various facilities confirmed this assumption, and this "on/off" dynamic was originally included in the model. This type of close-up, "gnat's eyebrow" focus on individual, discrete decisions can sometimes be useful, yet the process of pulling back and looking at the problem from an elevated, more aggregate view is often more illuminating. It was challenging to persuade the client team to take a 10,000-meter view of the system and examine the *operating rate* decision on the part of the industry as a whole. But when the data was examined from this aggregate perspective, changes in industry-wide operating rate never exhibited the sort of "spikiness" that a discrete decision rule implied. Instead, while the actual values for aggregate *operating rate* did exhibit significant variability, the functions that described the impact of various influencers on *operating rate* were themselves smooth, continuous curves as depicted in Figure 7-13.

> The process of pulling back and looking at the problem from an elevated, more aggregate view is often more illuminating. It was challenging to persuade the client team to take a **10,000-meter view** of the system and examine the operating rate decision on the part of the industry as a whole.

Because the inputs to the *operating rate* decision were continuous functions, the variable itself (while showing fluctuations over time due to varying market

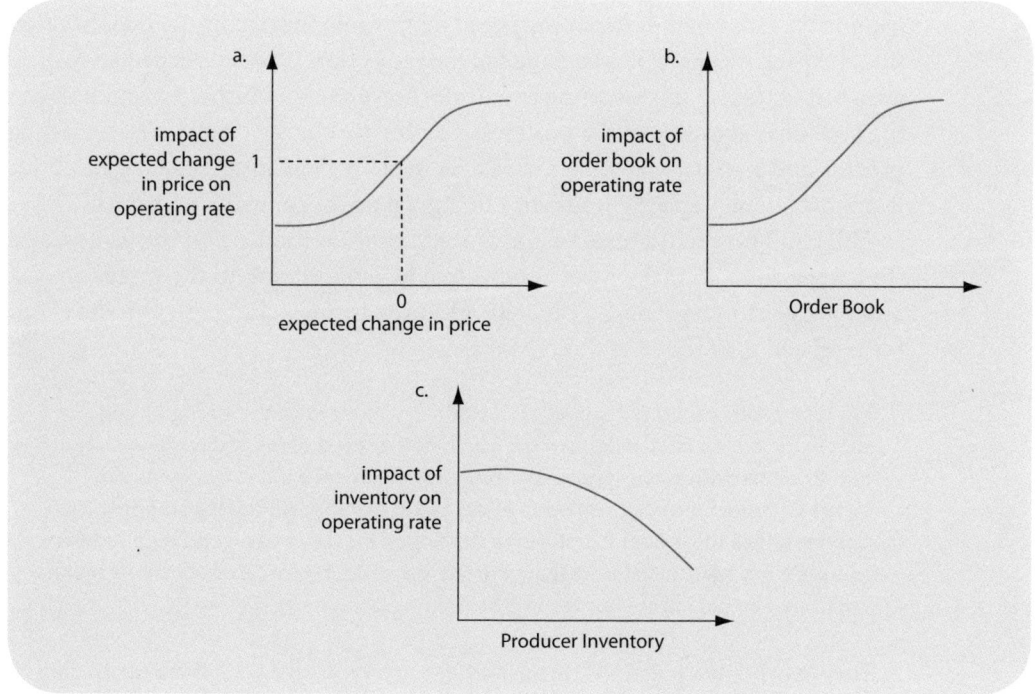

Figure 7-13. Continuous curves describe impact of influencers on operating rate

conditions) was continuous as well. In fact, the shape/slope of those influencing functions could be estimated by a thorough data examination of the input factors and resulting operating rates. So, instead of thinking about producing in a very discrete or discontinuous manner ("production facilities either run full out or at some lower set operating point"), the client team was now using continuum thinking to understand the broad, aggregate relationships driving marketplace decisions.

With the model structure fully populated and simulated results calibrated to historical data, the team was able to shed some light on the likely evolution of inventory and the corresponding market price for wood pulp over the next few years. Specifically, the simulation was able to project, to a fair degree of certainty (given the model's historical validity), what prevailing market conditions would be 18 months in the future. With this information in hand, the executive team was finally able to assess the financial viability of the proposed capacity addition. Although the industry-wide price was currently high enough to support such an investment, it turned out that the dynamics of the system (driven by the identified structure and inter-connected feedback relationships) would soon push price back down to just below the "break even" point regarding the financial viability of the capacity addition. Of particular interest was the fact that this result did not include the effect of the client's proposed new production facility. When that additional capacity scenario was included in the projection, price was expected to drop even further (since, all else being equal, more inventory would be accumulating in the system as a result of extra producing on the part of the client). The modeling process and associated simulation results made it clear to the client's executive team that adding capacity would not be a good use of company resources.

Phil and I now had a team of enthusiastic systems thinkers on our hands, and they were quick to make a key intellectual leap pertaining to the price forecast and the decision regarding a capacity addition. In an exciting session, the client team related the following thoughts:

> We have a fully calibrated model of the industry, along with the strengths and shapes of various inter-relationships which determine a series of decisions on the part of actors within the system. We also have historical data on our own company's decisions regarding operating rate, average time to fill orders, shipping, etc. Can we utilize the model structure we developed for the entire wood pulp industry and see if our own decision-making criteria are any different? And if so, how much might we (by ourselves) be able to "shape" the market?

The answers to questions such as these are typically very difficult to derive in a static, isolated context. But because we had developed a model structure which was in part generic, it could be disaggregated or broken up by individual producer. So instead of having an aggregate role for producers of wood pulp, our team amended the model structure to account for both the client and the rest of the industry individually. The relationships that formed the basis for decisions on the part of the client were separated from those dictating the behavior of the other producers in the market. Although at times these were remarkably similar, in some cases the data analysis showed marked differences. For example, the data analysis showed that the client much more aggressively changed its *operating rate* in response to price expectations, as shown in Figure 7-14.

Scientific Thinking

Lastly, the client was interested in using the finalized industry model and associated knowledge of how the market worked to see how much they could change the market by altering their decision-making criteria. Assuming no collusion, how much could an individual producer "change the future" by refusing to follow the herd and by making better long-term decisions? Could the client alter its own decision rules and reap the benefits of making better, more informed choices? For example, understanding the ordering rules of retailers might allow the client to separate speculative orders from actual end-user demand. The effect of expectations regarding price could suggest a pricing signal strategy or longer-

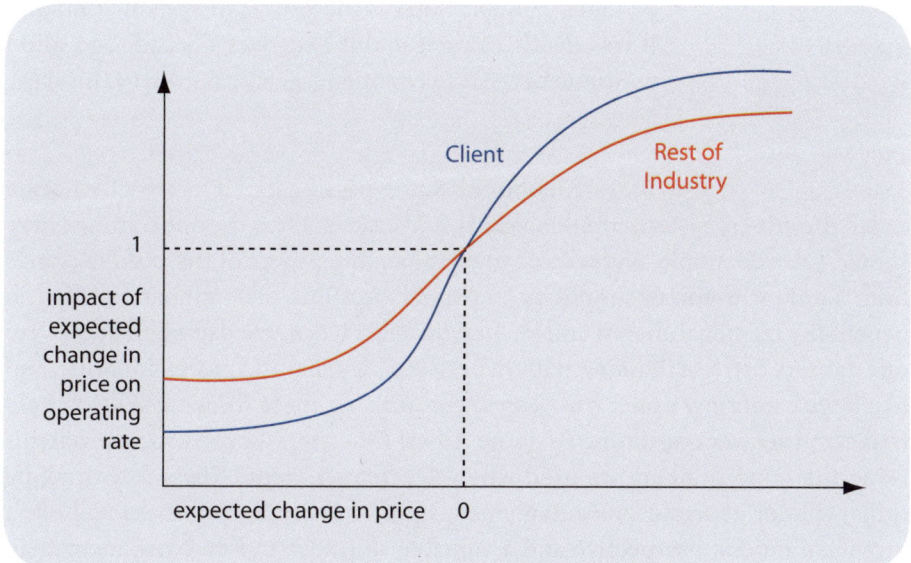

Figure 7-14. Impact of expected change in price on operating rate

term, fixed-price contracts with retailers. In some cases, industry producers might be able to better understand the market-wide dynamics and refrain from adding capacity indiscriminately. The modeling tool allowed the client to set up, simulate, and analyze these types of "what if" scenarios. By systematically testing these various options using the model, the client was able to arrive at a set of effective operational strategies. Doing so proved to be a great example of scientific thinking in which the simulation model provided a "virtual testing ground" for evaluating various components of company strategy.

> By systematically testing these various options using the model, the client was able to arrive at a set of effective operational strategies. Doing so proved to be a great example of **scientific thinking**.

From start to finish, Phil and I were involved in this modeling engagement for over a year, but its impact extended far beyond that window of time. At last report, the client was still using an expanded version of this model for decision-making purposes and as a training tool throughout the company. Although (as is often the case) the complexity of the model had increased in the intervening years, the basic operational physical backbone of the stock-flow structure remained intact. Perhaps more importantly, the client had made a concerted effort to communicate the insights from the model and also disseminate the key systems thinking skills upon which it was based. In the end, this engagement didn't just produce an "answer"—it also resulted in a client team now capable of seeing and thinking about their industry in new and more productive ways. Such is the power of systems thinking. It was clearly evident in this case over a decade ago, and I continue to see it in client engagements even to this day.

> This engagement didn't just produce an "answer"—it also resulted in a client team now capable of seeing and thinking about their industry in new and more productive ways.

Barry Richmond was a passionate advocate of what he called the critical systems thinking skills, and cases such as the one outlined here should provide ample evidence of their value. The power of these skills comes from a unique union of simplicity and sophistication—a combination that can benefit the technical analyst and lay-person alike. It is a rare day when I don't use one or more of these thinking skills in both my personal and professional life, and to a large extent my career has been spent utilizing these thinking skills to help frame and answer questions. To quote Albert Einstein, "we can't solve problems using the same thinking we used when we created them." These key thinking skills will not generate "instantaneous insight," but employing them will often provide a unique perspective and a valuable shift in mindset. Now, more than ever and in a wide variety of contexts, such results are incredibly important.

Notes

1. The client team ultimately was able to optain a more complete industry-wide estimate for historical data regarding exports through another source, and including this data fixed the simulation result error for *Producer Inventory*. The issue of imports was a more difficult challenge, and ultimately we used the simulation to "back solve" for what imports must have been to explain the historical changes in *Retailer Inventory* given the other operational dynamics within the system. This estimate turned out to be remarkably consistent with a later government report which identified overall imports of wood pulp and other paper-related materials.
2. See Forrester, J., *Industrial Dynamics* (Pegasus Communications, 1961), and Sterman, J., *Business Dynamics: Systems Thinking and Modeling for a Complex World* (McGraw-Hill/Irwin, 2000).

8

Finding System Dynamics: An Exploration in International Development

John L. Newman

> John L. Newman describes the effectiveness of systems thinking modeling to inform international development work, dealing with such problems as malaria control, malnutrition, and production of exports.

Over the years, I have come to firmly believe that systems thinking should help guide the way international development economists and practitioners approach a problem and that the toolkit of system dynamics should be included in their bag of tools. I didn't always feel this way. During my professional training in economics at Johns Hopkins and Yale, and in my first 10 years of work as a professional economist, I was not even aware of the existence of system dynamics; however, during my work in different countries trying to instill the greater use of evidence in public policy decisions and in taking a more systematic approach to improving performance, I have learned to appreciate the potential of the system dynamics approach.

Many people within the system dynamics community have also seen the potential in this approach for addressing problems in developing countries; however, many development economists, including my colleagues within the World Bank, and some within the large regional development banks, do not view the tools of system dynamics as useful complements to their other tools.

Does this imply that the idea of systems thinking and the use of system dynamics tools have failed a market test among an important group of potential users? Are the benefits from system dynamics outweighed by the costs of time, effort, and money to acquire the tools? I would argue that the verdict is still out. For the market test to be valid, however, the participants need to have adequate information. Most development economists and practitioners are probably as unaware of

> **John L. Newman** is currently lead economist in the Poverty and Gender Group of the Latin America Department of the World Bank. Previously, he was the World Bank representative in Peru and Bolivia and has held several positions in both research and operations departments at the World Bank. Prior to his World Bank experience, he was Assistant Professor in Economics and Latin American Studies at Tulane University.
>
> He holds a Ph.D. in economics from Yale University and B.A. and M.A. degrees from Johns Hopkins University. He has published in the areas of impact evaluation, labor economics, macroeconomics, and poverty analysis.

the potential benefits as I was when I found this field. To help fill the informational gap and to encourage others who focus on pressing problems in undeveloped countries, this paper tells the story of how I came to hold my particular views about the potential usefulness of system dynamics. In telling my story, I will weave in illustrations of the critical thinking skills related to systems thinking that Barry Richmond so usefully identified in the introductory chapter of this book and in other publications.

First Encounter: Social Investment Fund in Guatemala

In the early 1990s, I was in charge of a World Bank project that supported the creation and implementation of a Social Investment Fund in Guatemala. Social Investment Funds (SIFs) started in Bolivia in the mid 1980s as a tool to mitigate the effects of structural adjustment programs. At that time, the Bolivian government realized that it did not have the ability to move quickly enough to respond to the unemployment resulting from the closing of state-owned mines and the recession associated with the end of a period of hyperinflation. As a result, the government created a fund to finance thousands of small, employment-generating projects proposed by local and community groups and non-governmental organizations (NGOs). A small, responsive team was created to oversee the fund, operating outside the normal government bureaucracy. The team developed a menu of prototypical sub-projects, generated a database of unit costs, and received, reviewed, and approved thousands of small proposals.

After several years of operation, it was recognized that this approach provided a means of getting government programs to people in areas that had never before been reached. Other countries (especially in Latin America) began to adopt the SIF approach to tap into the installed capacity of NGOs to help deliver services. By the time the Guatemala SIF began in 1992, five similar funds were already working in other countries. As SIFs were replicated, some patterns of dynamic behavior, typical of start-up operations, became apparent. During the initial years of operation, an SIF often took a long time to come up to speed and involved many bottlenecks and delays. It seemed like every country had to learn

tracing connections

In the early 1990s, I was in charge of a World Bank project supporting creation and implementation of a Social Investment Fund in Guatemala. The bottlenecks in this process led to a search for management tools and, during this search, I stumbled across system dynamics. *iThink* proved to be ideal. Later we worked on a demonstration case—malaria control in Bolivia—to determine whether system dynamics tools would be useful in analyzing tasks with a specific goal. Encouraged by this work, we went to a modeling and *iThink* training session outside Washington, D.C., in 2001, where I met Barry for the first time. I discussed with him what we were trying to do to help developing countries achieve their social goals. Barry gave us several important pieces of advice and told us how committed he was to development and how pleased he was that his daughter, Joy, was in Paraguay as a Peace Corps volunteer working with early elementary education, health education, and youth groups. His support meant a lot to us, and his very generous offer of making 100 copies of *iThink* available to us at minimal price allowed us to explore the potential of system dynamics to address additional issues in Bolivia. It also allowed us to collaborate with many more people in Bolivia than previously possible. As I heard more about Barry from people who knew him, it was apparent that his combination of enthusiasm, insight, and generosity was something that he brought to his relations with many, many people.

all over again how to ensure that a large number of sub-project proposals could be submitted for funding and be evaluated quickly.

The management challenge boiled down to making a production line work effectively. Each sub-project proposal could be thought of as a product entering the production line, being reviewed, and exiting the production line as a fully financed and implementable sub-project. The bottlenecks in this process led to a search to find management tools, used by businesses, to avoid similar bottlenecks in production. The tools had to be simple enough to use for people who did not have strong management backgrounds. I stumbled across system dynamics, and *iThink*, with its graphical interface, proved ideal. Without realizing it, I was making use of one of the critical thinking skills of Barry Richmond's 1993 article on systems thinking: generic thinking: "apprehending the similarities in the underlying feedback-loop relations."

Together with the staff of the SIF management team, we generated a simulation model of stocks and flows for all the

As Social Investment Funds were replicated, some patterns of dynamic behavior, typical of start-up operations, became apparent. Without realizing it, I was making use of one of the critical thinking skills of Barry Richmond's 1993 article on systems thinking: **generic thinking**, "apprehending the similarities in the underlying feedback-loop relations."

steps of the sub-project review process. We showed that very early on in the process, the managers would have to shift resources from the promotion area (trying to convince groups to submit proposals) to the review process (dealing with the deluge of applications). Initially, it took some time for community groups and NGOs to learn about the existence of the fund and then to prepare proposals. Managers of the SIFs devoted considerable staff time to try to drum up proposals. But once a number of sub-projects were financed, more communities became aware of the program and more community groups and NGOs submitted proposals. Indeed, the large numbers of proposals soon swamped the SIF's ability to process them. The model showed very clearly that the very success of the operation created problems down the line. In practice, the management of the SIFs had been slow to recognize and act upon the time delay inherent in the launching of the programs.

This experience illustrated another aspect of the critical thinking skills of Barry Richmond: closed-loop thinking. "When exercising closed-loop thinking, people will look to the loops themselves (i.e., the circular cause-effect relations) as being responsible for generating the behavior patterns exhibited by a system." The use of the system dynamics model of the production line helped SIF program managers see the relations more clearly and, as a result, act to resolve the problems more quickly.

Proof of Concept: Linking Policy Actions to Results Using System Dynamics

An interest in the analytical challenge of linking policy actions to results led me to consider the use of system dynamics again several years later. In the early 2000s, the international development community began a movement to focus more on results: the impact of the investments rather than the inputs to the investments. The UN summit in 2000 created the Millennium Development Goals, an ambitious set of goals set in such areas as poverty reduction, education, and health that was subscribed to by most nations.

Setting goals brings a subtle but important shift in framing the analytical question of interest. If there is an interest in results, but no goals are set, the analytical question typically posed is, "What is the impact of the investment made by the government?" When goals are set, the analytical question typically posed is, "What has to be done to achieve the goal?" Answering this type of question implicitly assumes that one should work backwards from the goal to figure out what would be the best investments to achieve that goal. Then, with an explicit plan to achieve that goal, one would monitor what is done, what the impact is, and what should be modified during the time needed to achieve that goal.

In contrast to an impact evaluation, which had a ready-made set of tools and methodology, no established methodology existed to allow one to work backwards from a goal to determine what must be done to achieve that goal. At one extreme was the increasing demand coming from governments and aid agencies to be specific about the goals, the final outcome of the system. At the other extreme was the tradition among governments, development agencies, and NGOs to develop projects with extensive effort on specifying what was to be done. But there seemed to be a gaping hole in the middle: there did not seem to be a generally accepted approach to link policy actions to results.

Linking policy actions to results seemed to be an ideal application for system dynamics. It offered a structure to organize different elements that could contribute to achieving a result and the language of stocks and flows that allowed one to describe specific policy actions that might be undertaken. Once parameter values were provided, the system dynamics model could be simulated to gain greater understanding of the likely outcomes of different actions. In the ideal case, the parameter values would be based on hard evidence; however, even without hard evidence, informed opinions from subject matter specialists who had some understanding of how the system operated could be sought. Additional resources could be invested in data collection or in research to obtain more precise measures of the key parameters if insufficient information or a high level of uncertainty remained. The priorities for new data collection and research could be guided by simulations indicating where the highest payoffs to new and better information might be found. Over time, one would expect that working systematically to link policy actions to results would allow one to achieve the results faster than would be the case if policy choice is driven only by the mental models that are held tightly by the policy makers in charge.

> Linking policy actions to results seemed to be an ideal application for system dynamics. It offered a structure to organize different elements that could contribute to achieving a result.

Based on that logic and on the positive experience with system dynamics, we formed a team in the Bolivia Country Office to explore whether system dynamics might be a potentially useful tool to link policy actions to results. This effort was warranted because demand for this task was only expected to grow over time. John Sterman, at MIT, was instrumental in identifying a system dynamics specialist with an interest in international development, good interpersonal skills to interact at many different levels of government, the ability to work in Spanish, and a willingness to relocate temporarily to La Paz, Bolivia. Incredibly, he found someone who fit the bill—Leslie Martin. She came to play a crucial role in all the work that followed, providing additional training to me, to two key, young, talented staff members in the Bolivia World Bank Country Office, Maria Alejandra Velasco and Alavaro Mario Fantini, and to several counterparts in the government.

Malaria control in Bolivia

With a small team in place, we chose to work on a demonstration case to test the hypothesis that the tools of system dynamics would be useful in analyzing the tasks required to achieve a specific goal. Several practical reasons led us to malaria. First, there was a consensus on what indicator public policy should try to affect: decreasing the Annual Parasitic Index (API), which is widely considered a reliable measure of the severity of malaria in a country. Having a consensus view on the goal ensured that the team could concentrate efforts on helping determine what was needed to achieve that goal, not on the distinct (but often very important) task of deciding what goal to try to achieve. Second, the government had already set a clear goal to reduce the value of API to below 2, the threshold value used to define whether malaria is considered endemic in a country or not. Third, over the three years prior to embarking on the system dynamics modeling exercise, a strong decline in the API coincided with the government's launching of a malaria control initiative. This resulted in evidence that the technology to bring about a change in the indicator was known and, therefore, could be captured as data; however, at the same time, the country had not yet achieved an API below 2.

The task was to find out what had to be done, how much it would cost, and how long it would take for the country to reach its goal. In addition, it was important to find out how much it would cost to keep the API under 2 once the goal had been reached, since API fluctuations were very common. When the incidence of malaria was high, the malaria control programs would receive adequate funding and, because the technology for controlling malaria was known, the problem would be brought under control. With success, malaria control would be put on the back burner. The problem would grow, first slowly and then, following the typical pattern of an epidemic, more rapidly, until the cycle would begin all over again. Communication problems seemed to exist between officials from the Ministries of Health and Finance, allowing this pattern to continue. If the budgetary discussions could be based on a shared understanding of what drives the malaria problem, perhaps it would be possible to avoid this type of costly pattern.

Working with experts in the malaria control division in the Ministry of Health and in PROCOSI (a network of NGOs), a useful model was developed that was able to replicate past dynamic behavior and provide answers to all of the key questions posed above. The components of the system dynamics model are presented in Figure 8-1 and more details can be found in Newman et al. (2003).

Focusing on the "Mosquito Nets" sub-component of the model, one can observe the use of Barry Richmond's critical thinking skill: operational thinking. "Thinking operationally means thinking in terms of how things really work, not how they theoretically work or how one might fashion a bit of algebra capable of generating realistic-looking output" (Richmond 1993). Two very different units must be combined—numbers of mosquito nets and liters of insecticide—to ensure that *impregnated* mosquito nets are produced. Moreover, mosquito nets do not just appear. They must be physically acquired, requiring real resources. There is a distinction between the "stock" of mosquito nets that exists at any one time and the "flow" of services that a family receives from using the *Mosquito Nets*. The stock (*Mosquito Nets*) can physically wear out over time. Factors such as these must be taken into account when addressing the operational questions of what it would take and how much it would cost to control malaria in Bolivia. The stock and flow diagram for vector control is shown in Figure 8-2.

> **Thinking operationally** means thinking in terms of how things really work, not how they theoretically work or how one might fashion a bit of algebra capable of generating realistic-looking output.

Simulations were constructed to look at past, present, and future outcomes. By using actual information on the implementation of the different components

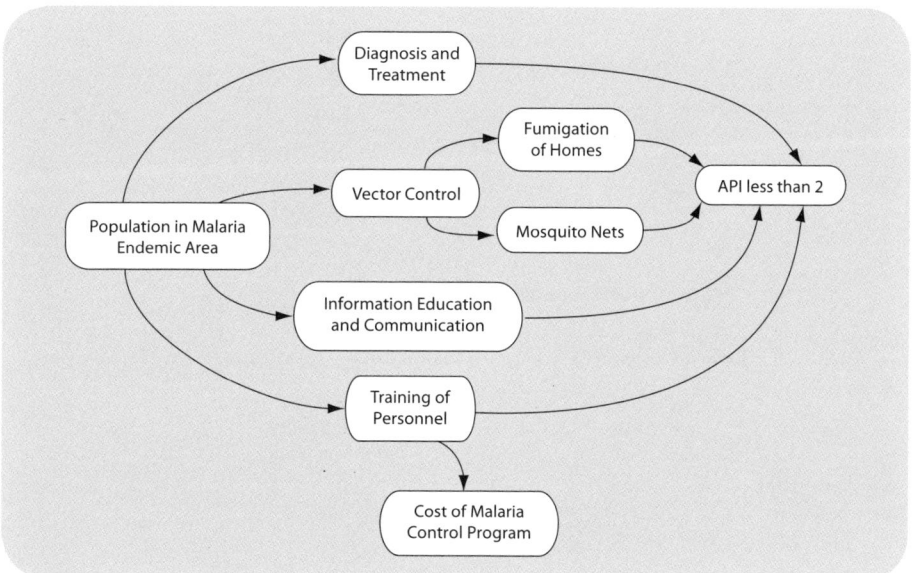

Figure 8-1. Components of the Malaria Control in Bolivia Model

of the malaria control program, the model reproduced the dynamic path of the API from around 25 in 1998 to around 5.5 in 2001. The simulations also allowed one to calculate how long it would take (around two-and-a-half years), how much it would cost over that period to reach the target of an API of 2 (around $8 million U.S.), and how much it would cost to maintain an API of 2 (around $0.5 million U.S.). In addition, the simulation allowed the user to consider any changes in policies that would allow the goals to be reached faster and cheaper. For example, one possibility was whether, for the same total expenditure, one could improve performance by shifting resources away from treatment of the sick and towards greater vector control; however, in Bolivia, such a reallocation would have actually increased the time and cost of achieving the goal. As the team explored the model, it was clear that, because vector control is imperfect, if the number of sick people is not reduced, more mosquitoes would be infected and the disease would spread more rapidly.

The model was extended and used by the Unit of Analysis of Economic Policy of the Ministry of Finance to consider alternative policy actions and financing alternatives in conjunction with Bolivia's proposal to the Global Fund for Malaria (see Narvaez et al. 2005). The Health Reform Unit of Bolivia's Ministry

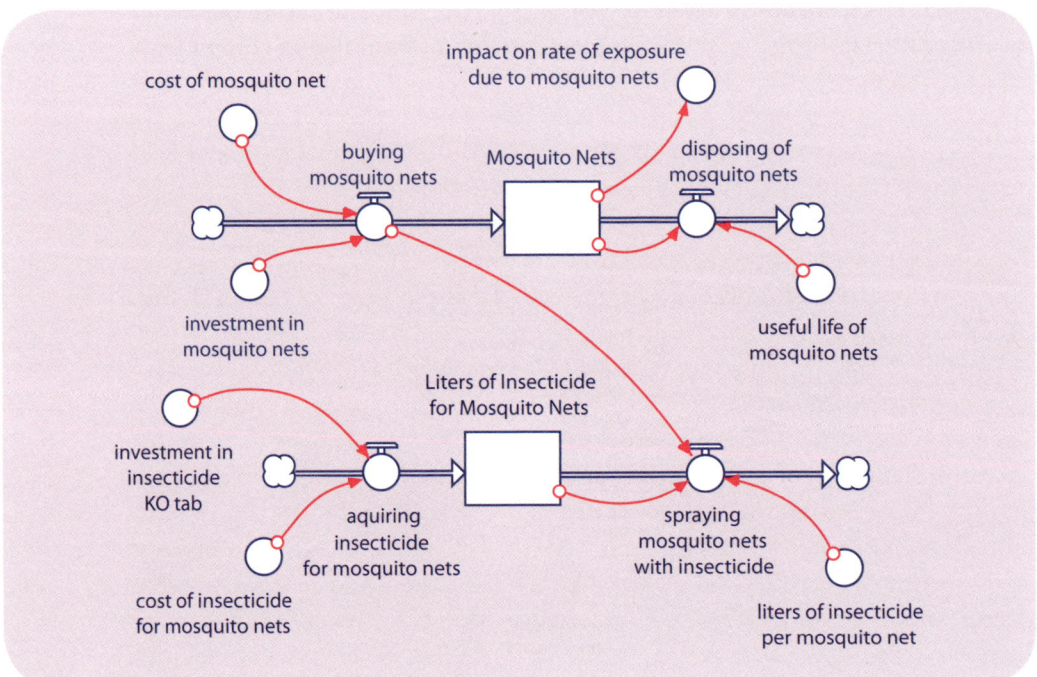

Figure 8-2. Vector control: Use of mosquito nets

of Health then commissioned some further work using system dynamics models to analyze the potential effectiveness of their programs to extend basic coverage on infant mortality.[1]

Education for All Fast Track Initiative

The team's second project with the Bolivian government was the "Education for All Fast Track Initiative," one of the first tangible programs coming out of the 2000 UN Monterrey Conference. Under this initiative, an offer was extended by international donors to a select group of low income countries. If the countries could come up with what was termed a "credible plan" to ensure that all children could receive a basic education of adequate quality, grant money would be made available to cover whatever financing gap existed; however, it quickly proved impossible to extend this offer to all low-income countries. But the first group of countries did have an opportunity to receive a significant increase in aid to education—provided they could come up with "a credible plan."

A Knowledge and Innovation Grant from the World Bank enabled us to conduct a week-long workshop in Bolivia for representatives from eligible Latin American countries to explore how system dynamics might help them construct their credible models. The participating countries were Nicaragua, Honduras, Guyana (the only English-speaking country), and Bolivia. We benefited from the presence of Chris Soderquist of Pontifex Consulting, who provided excellent training and guidance to the teams.

Although Bolivia never finalized their credible plan and never submitted a financing request, ironically, an educational system dynamics model was used to help estimate future costs of teacher salaries under different policy scenarios. Nicaragua did submit a credible plan. The Nicaraguan team at the workshop, led by Emilio Portas, quickly recognized the potential of system dynamics and based the preparation of the financing needs for the planned activities in their credible plan on a system dynamics model.

The Nicaraguan model was based on the flow of students through the educational system. To meet the goal of increasing the percentage of children who successfully completed basic education at an appropriate age, Nicaragua had to increase the intake of 6-7 year olds and reduce repetition and drop-out rates. The government proposed a broad set of actions ranging from improvements in infrastructure and increases in teacher salaries to changes in school autonomy and systems of incentives to school administration officials. Every action had a cost, which was tracked in the model. Even the change in school autonomy required some costs of re-training. The model consisted of some twenty-four sub-components, some of which were linked, but all of which contributed to the total cost of the initiative.

The system dynamics modeling exercise enabled the government to come up with a reasonable estimate of the financing costs over time, even as the nature of the educational system evolved over time. The student cohort component captured the flow and allowed for an adequate estimate of the scale of needed inputs, but did not provide much detail about improvement in quality because of limited knowledge about this function. The Nicaraguan model was then extended beyond basic education to include secondary education. In this extension, the model was used to identify financing needs that would be covered by a group of multilateral and bilateral aid agencies working in education in Nicaragua under what is known as a Sector Wide Approach Project, or SWAP. The ability to easily change assumptions of the model allowed the government to get some sense of how rapidly they could undertake the improvements and how much incremental financing would be required to do so.

Pension reform

Pension reform was a third area where the team applied tools of system dynamics to help Bolivia estimate how best to limit the costs of its transition from a pay-as-you-go pension system to an individual account system for public employees. The expectation in carrying out the reform was that, after a period of high transitional costs, the new system would become self-sustaining. The reform was undertaken because the pay-as-you-go system was essentially bankrupt. By 2002 (five years after the reform began) the transition costs were running at around 4.4% of GDP, almost twice the original estimates and equivalent to close to 75% of the entire national budget. In an effort to improve the situation, a consultant was hired to prepare a simulation model written in Visual Basic; however, the government users were not able to make modifications easily and so could not adjust to reflect the ever-changing circumstances.

As part of a Poverty and Social Impact analysis supported by the UK Department for International Development (DFID), Leslie Martin worked with the Ministry of Finance and the Superintendency of Pensions on a system dynamics model of the pension system (Martin 2002). The central part of the model was a population component that captured how different groups in the population aged over time. With the stock-flow orientation of system dynamics models, it is much easier to construct demographic models than, for example, with spreadsheets. Again, the graphical nature of the software was of tremendous help, allowing the users to understand what was going on in the models and allowing them to make modifications in the model to reflect changed circumstances. A sign of the interest in this approach was provided by the willingness of government staff to attend a five-week course held early in the morning before the normal work day to learn more about the tool. While the model does not fully exploit the power of system dynamics models because it was only a cohort simulation and did not have a behavioral component, it allowed the users to create their own projection model that was sufficiently flexible and powerful to capture how a fairly complex pension system worked.

Production chains related to income generation of the poor

"Production chains related to income generation of the poor" was the last area that the team worked on in Bolivia. The focus came from an effort by the World Bank and other development agencies to support the Poverty Reduction Strategy prepared by the Government of Bolivia. The Government argued that it was necessary to improve certain key production chains as a means of improving the livelihoods of the poor. Many mainstream development economists are leery about work related to production chains as they feel there are risks in "picking winners." This concern is well-founded; however, several arguments argue for working on this topic.

First, if 75% of the income of the poor comes from a few products (as it does in the Bolivian altiplano geographic region) and if it is unlikely that there will be a shift to producing other products or migration of the population out of the area, then the only way for incomes of these poor to increase in the near term would be for productivity to rise or for the production chain to work more efficiently. Of course, whatever gains from greater productivity or a more effective production chain must not be captured by the wealthy or lost in price declines.

Second, the possibility of market failure exists in the production chains related to what the poor produce. Market failures may not be detected and addressed if they are not identified. With large producers, considerable resources are devoted to resolving market failures related to informational problems and under investment in resolving technological bottlenecks. When producers are atomistic and poor, no one may actively be working on resolving their problems. The poor lack resources to devote to collective action and often have difficulty generating sufficient voice to lobby for government actions to resolve their problems.

System dynamics models are well-suited to analysis of the effectiveness of production chains. The problems are closely related to the problems of supply chain management, which have been analyzed extensively with system dynamics models. The team worked with the Productivity and Competitiveness Unit of Bolivia's Ministry of Development. While some analysis was done in all fourteen

System dynamics models are well-suited to analysis of the effectiveness of production chains. The problems are closely related to the problems of supply chain management, which have been analyzed extensively with system dynamics models.

identified production chains, the effort to develop system dynamics models was concentrated in the quinoa production chain. Quinoa is a highly nutritious Andean grain that is grown following both organic and non-organic practices. The organic quinoa has a market in the United States and Europe, while the non-organic quinoa is consumed mainly in South America. The strategy was to test out the usefulness of developing system dynamics models in one production chain and then extend to other chains if it looked promising. The high-level map for quinoa is reproduced in Figure 8-3.

Within each component, one could analyze the factors that influenced the production and profitability of the producers and refiners of the grain. The model was developed by talking to key actors involved in all parts of production—from the campesino farmers to the refiners and packagers of the final product.

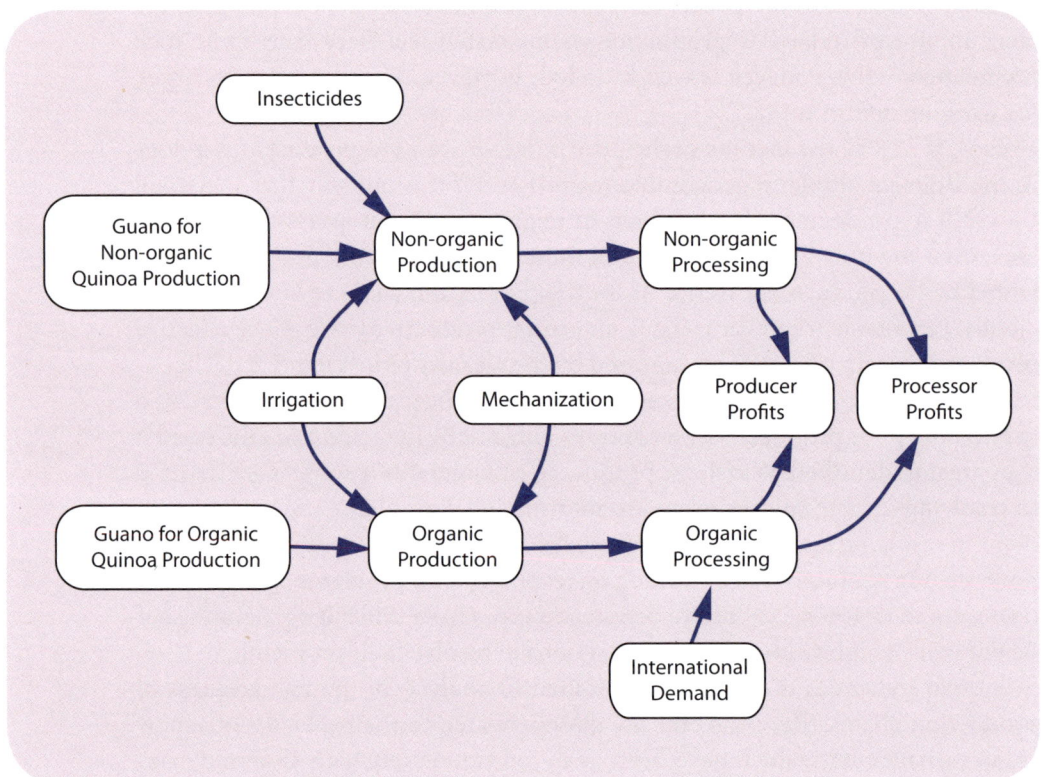

Figure 8-3. High-level map for quinoa

The system dynamics exercise showed benefits to both the World Bank and government team. As in other experiences using system dynamics models, one of the main benefits was simply the ease with which one could structure or organize the components that would have to be analyzed. A high-level map is a useful way of setting the boundaries of the problem and provides the opportunity to see the details, allowing one to keep track of both the "forest" and the "trees."

A second benefit was identifying possible reasons for low profitability. First, surprisingly, was the almost complete absence of a market for rental machinery. In the United States, before farmers were large enough to own their own machinery, mechanized equipment was rented. Some asymmetric information or potentially high legal costs may impede the development of a rental market. Second was the importance of guano (dung) from cameloids (as fertilizer) for production of quinoa and how much quinoa production depended on adequate supplies of dung at a low price.

A third reason for low profitability was how important misrepresenting non-organic quinoa as organic quinoa was on profitability for peasant producers. Producing organic quinoa is considerably more expensive than non-organic quinoa, but organic quinoa sells for a higher price. The Bolivian producers, used to producing for a non-demanding domestic market, were inclined to misrepresent the non-organic quinoa as organic. The system dynamics model showed how a nasty feedback loop, acting through decreased demand for Bolivian misrepresented quinoa, could dramatically lower profits from organic quinoa. Peasant farmers did not realize how easy it is to detect the presence of chemical fertilizers and how damaging misrepresentation could be to future demand. Especially in this latter example, a system dynamics model showed how it was possible to combine modeling of very different markets—the traditional production market in the Bolivian highlands with the globalized markets of the purchasers of quinoa—within a single analysis.

The experience using system dynamics in four quite distinct applications in Bolivia convinced me of its usefulness as a tool. Some of the people working in government and in NGOs who were exposed to system dynamics were also convinced of the potential usefulness; however, the work described above was done on a small scale and while working to a large extent under the radar, both within the country and within the World Bank. Convincing a wider audience is a pending future task and may or may not happen. The second option is one that presented itself in my next position.

John L. Newman

Uses of System Dynamics Models to Help Reduce Chronic Malnutrition in Peru

In 2004, I became the World Bank resident representative in Lima, Peru. In Peru, as in Bolivia, there was a growing interest in focusing on results and in linking policy actions to results, especially with the approaching five-year anniversary of the Millennium Development Goals (MDGs). The initial focus of our effort was achieving greater progress in reducing malnutrition, a serious problem in Peru, where one in four children still suffered from chronic malnutrition. In addition, there was hope that something could be done quickly. As with malaria, the technology to bring about reductions in chronic malnutrition is largely known. If the institutional complexities, which resulted in an inefficient dollar allocation and ineffective interventions, could be overcome, substantial progress was possible.

The work on nutrition is ongoing, with government and many other institutions engaged in a serious effort to bring about change. The President of Peru has announced explicit goals related to reducing chronic malnutrition. The government has made reducing chronic malnutrition one of the main objectives of a Conditional Cash Transfer program (JUNTOS) and attention to chronic malnutrition is receiving high priority within the Ministry of Finance. The Ministry of Health, Ministry of Social Development and Women, and the Interagency Committee on Social Affairs, supported strongly by the Nutrition Initiative, a consortium of NGOs, UN and bilateral aid agencies, and World Bank, are working extensively on interventions to lower chronic malnutrition.

System dynamics has been used in three of the problem areas to work on alleviation of chronic malnutrition and, at some point in the future could be used in two more areas. These uses are important as they point out how similar exercises could be used to bring about an improvement in a particular element of social welfare. It is important to note, however, that not just one system dynamics model of chronic malnutrition served all purposes. Rather, different models were constructed and different approaches were taken, depending on the problem at hand.

Development of a causal model of chronic malnutrition

A system dynamics model was created to capture the processes through which a child becomes chronically malnourished. The high-level stock-flow map is reproduced in Figure 8-4. One key process involves the ingestion of nutrients and then the ability of the child to make use of the nutrients, which depends on his or her nutritional status. Sickness affects both the rate of ingesting nutrients and the body's use of those nutrients. The vicious cycle between nutritional status and illness (particularly of diarrhea) must be broken if a child is to avoid becoming chronically malnourished. After five or six repeated spells of diarrhea, the risk of a child becoming chronically malnourished is very high. Evidence indicates that the critical time periods are the periods of pregnancy and the first two years of life. After two years of age, not much can be done.

The map depicted in Figure 8-4 attempts to capture the consensus view of the determinants of chronic malnutrition. Any public policy directed to improving chronic malnutrition must operate through one or another of the mechanisms identified in the causal model. This logic allows one to check all policies that are promoted as affecting chronic malnutrition. Several programs thought to be affecting chronic malnutrition are not, because they do not operate on the key transmission mechanism. School feeding programs are an example. They may

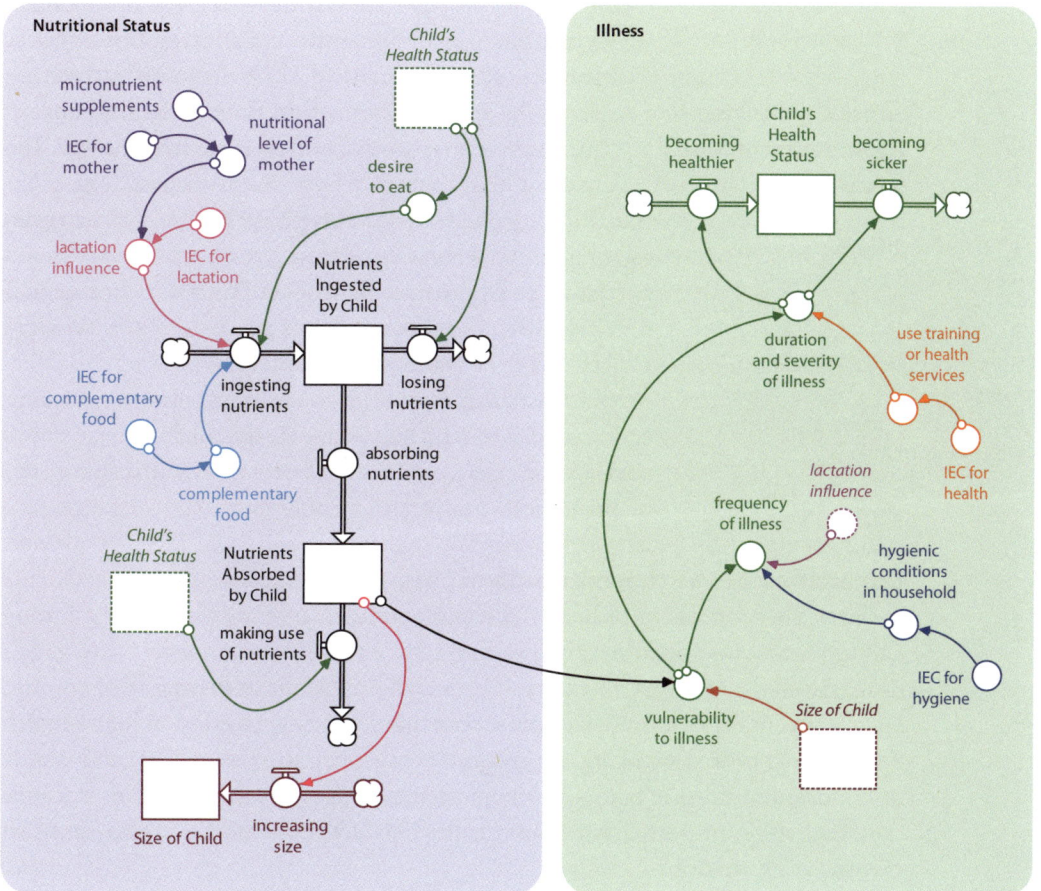

Figure 8-4. Stock-flow map of chronic malnutrition

affect the ability of children to concentrate during school or serve as an incentive to go to school, but they do not affect chronic malnutrition because they come into play well after the first two years of life, during which the window of opportunity to affect chronic malnutrition exists.

There are separate points of entry for public policy in the model, such as the IEC (Information, Education, and Communication) Program. A useful point about the model is that it clearly shows that tackling nutrition is not just about providing supplementary feeding. There are other possible interventions and the evidence shows that these other interventions are often more important than supplemental feeding.

The type of work related to developing a model from this type of map is an illustration of another one of Barry Richmond's critical thinking skills: scientific thinking. "Scientific thinking has more to do with quantification than measurement . . . Thinking scientifically also means being rigorous about testing hypotheses. The process begins by always ensuring that there is a hypothesis to test." The scientific thinking illustrated in this phase of the work involved forming a hypothesis concerning the way or ways that a particular policy would be expected to affect chronic malnutrition. By going through this process, it was possible to arrive at a set of policies that had the potential to affect chronic malnutrition and to dismiss others that logically could not. At a later stage in the analysis, one could address the relative mix and scale of programs that could be brought to bear on the problem.

Explanation of the dynamic path of chronic malnutrition

In Peru, the progress in reducing chronic malnutrition had come to a grinding halt ten years previously and had stabilized at a relatively high level. This stagnation existed despite vast amounts of money being spent in the name of combating chronic malnutrition. Peru was at that time entering a period of high growth, heading to a more promising future, and it was very worrisome that thousands of children could not take advantage of the improved opportunities because they had suffered permanent damage to their cognitive abilities as a result of chronic malnutrition.

The attempt to understand why progress had stopped, after it had appeared that Peru was on track to resolve its problems, gave rise to a second system dynamics modeling exercise. A multidisciplinary team consisting of representatives from government, NGOs, and bilateral agencies participated in a workshop focused on the stagnation problem. Discussion of the dynamic path of chronic malnutrition was very useful and elicited a lot of reflection. Has Peru always had this problem? What would likely happen if no changes in policy were made? Would the problem get worse or better? These types of questions were used to help the participants think in terms of the dynamics of the situation. The entire exercise was an illustration of another one of Barry Richmond's critical thinking skills: dynamic thinking. "Dynamic thinking is the ability to see and deduce behavior patterns rather than focusing on and seeking to predict events."

> **Dynamic thinking** is the ability to see and deduce behavior patterns rather than focusing on and seeking to predict events.

The facilitation at the workshop was done by Bob Wiebe and Dan Compton of The Boeing Company, who followed a very interesting process that they term "Focused Strategic Conversations" to try to get different groups with different perspectives to develop a shared understanding of the nature of the problem. This also illustrates a point made by many in the field that a consensus has emerged that modeling should be done not for managers, but *with* managers.

> This also illustrates a point made by many in the field that a consensus has emerged that modeling should be done not for managers, but **with** managers.

One of the interesting and unexpected insights coming out of this work was that part of the earlier success in reducing chronic malnutrition was a byproduct of the rapid migration to urban areas caused by people escaping the rural violence associated with the Sendero Luminoso (Shining Path) terrorists. In addition, following the terrorist period, the number of community activists operating in the rural areas declined. Fewer outreach activities were carried out by the Ministry of Health. Some of the effects of that dramatic period of violence in Peru were still being felt. The group felt that the new policy of using a conditional cash transfer program to increase the use of health services in the rural areas would be able to reestablish the level of contact that campesinos would have with the health system and that this would be an important approach to regain some of the momentum that had been lost. Under this program, known as JUNTOS, families would receive cash payments in return for guaranteeing that their children received preventive care, undertook growth monitoring, and attended school. These conditional cash programs have been shown, through rigorous impact evaluations, to have positive effects on nutritional outcomes.

While the shared discovery process had considerable potential, keeping the group together long enough to follow through on discoveries and translate them into actions was difficult. This reflects the institutional complexities in dealing with nutrition where the important participants come from very different sectors and the coordination challenges are considerable. Rotation of personnel is also typically high, which makes follow-through hard. In a business setting, if there is a champion who can compel the participants to make a sustained effort, the teams from different departments are probably more likely to continue the work.

Identification of implementation problems

The third use of system dynamics models was to try to help resolve implementation problems related to the operation of JUNTOS. A conditional cash transfer program provides an incentive for families to use the health system and will increase demand; however, the desired impact on nutrition will not take place unless there is an adequate supply response on the part of the health system. This is not automatic and requires some coordination in the expansion of the conditional cash transfer program and the upgrading of the supply of health services.

A workshop was held with representatives of JUNTOS and the Ministry of Health to map out what potential bottlenecks needed to be addressed. Based on this discussion, Chris Soderquist of Pontifex Consulting developed a small system dynamics model that captured the nature of the problems. This is another illustration of the operational thinking element of system dynamics. The model is shown in Figure 8-5.

A total of six distinct problems were identified:

1. Families had to be officially enrolled in the program and, in order to receive money from the government, they needed to have an official identity number. Many did not, so that registering to get a national identity number was important.

2. Some health clinics did not have enough human resources to respond to the increased demand for services. Such clinics had to be identified and the policy makers needed to look at the hiring and training processes involved.

3. The treatment protocols had been started, but had not been completed. Time and effort needed to be assigned to make sure that happened, as an essential part of the quality control system.

4. There were conflicting messages about nutrition delivered by outreach workers from the Ministry of Health and from the Ministry of Social Development and Women.

5. It was deemed important to set up some type of complaint system. Creating some mechanism to block Ministry of Health

workers from selling their signature indicating the families had brought their children in to receive attention when, in fact, they had not, was necessary.

6. The Ministry of Health and JUNTOS staff recognized that it was necessary to explicitly consider how information about a situation of excess demand was going to flow back to administrators. The system could have imbalances, but if no authority knew about them, they would not be resolved.

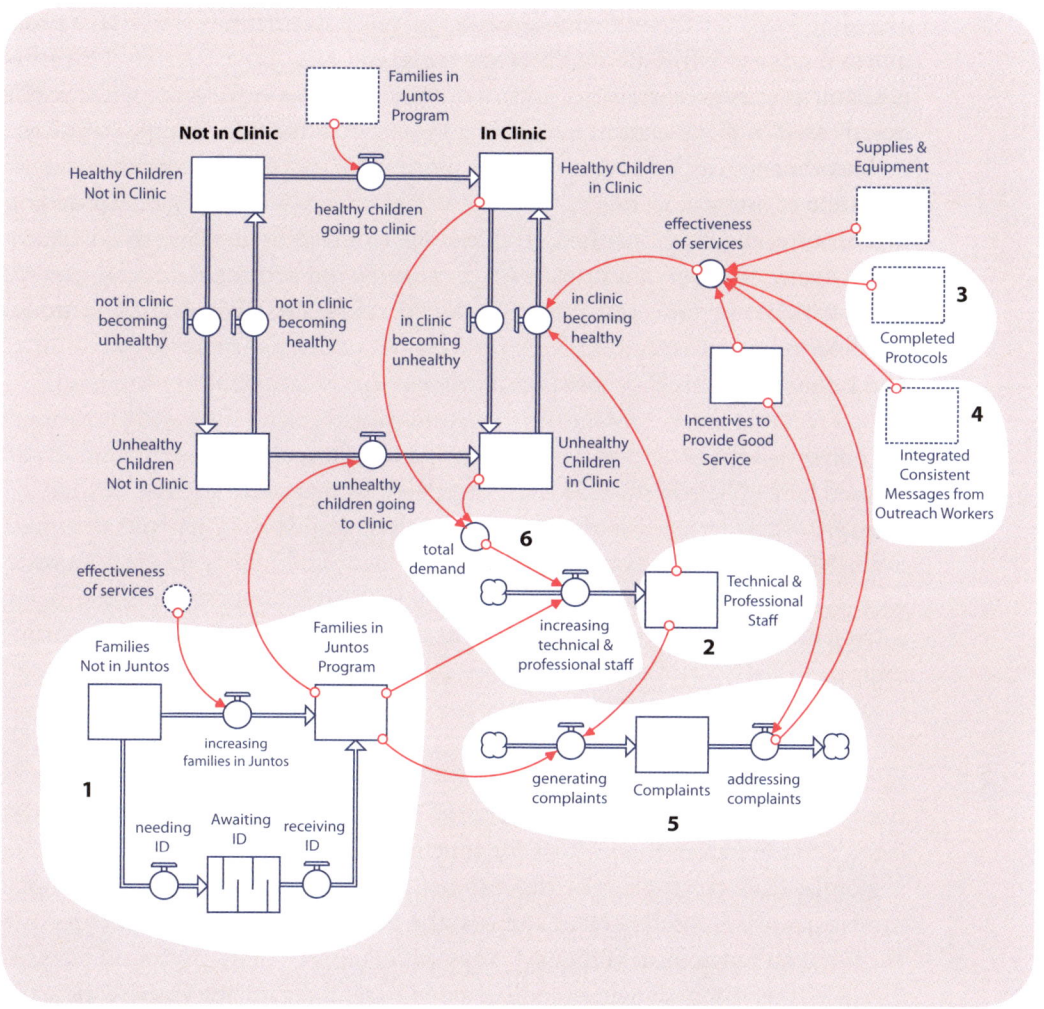

Figure 8-5. Implementation problems related to the operation of JUNTOS

Current Work and Next Steps

Currently, the Peruvian government is working specifically to resolve all the operational issues involved in making the activities of JUNTOS and the Ministry of Health fully effective. Once resolved, another possible use of system dynamics models would be to illustrate what would be required to take the intervention to scale as was done with the malaria model.

The use of system dynamics in nutrition as described above is closely related to the planning phase for the interventions; however, an important part of a results orientation is to think of a systematic process towards achieving results, not a one-shot focus on the planning process. In the implementation phase, system dynamics, when combined with other tools, can also prove helpful. Once the new nutrition interventions are up and running, monitoring district performance, as indicated by the change in the level of chronic malnutrition, is important. Data on performance can be documented by plotting the empirical distribution of the indicator of interest, in this case, the absolute change in the percentage of children chronically malnourished. This change can also be benchmarked against performance in other countries, with comparable international data on chronic malnutrition over time available from the World Health Organization. It is also possible to look at conditional distributions of performance, taking account of initial conditions or characteristics of districts that are thought to be relevant.

In a second follow-up stage, the questions involve what the good performers are doing that the poor performers are not and vice versa. System dynamics can be used here to help identify high leverage actions that could then be introduced to improve performance. A third stage of analysis could be to carry out an impact evaluation on the effects of introducing the identified high leverage actions to an entirely different population. To ensure that useful interventions are being carried out and to build political support for the interventions, such a rigorous impact evaluation could be conducted.

In closing, I would first like to say that it is an honor to be asked to contribute to this book in memory of Barry Richmond. He was a visionary, a great communicator, and a generous man whose life touched many people.

For the readers who may be development economists or practitioners, I hope these examples have illustrated some of the potential uses for system dynamics. The uses can range from fairly basic uses of the tools to more profound ones. At one level, the system dynamics tools provide a useful organizing framework to put different elements into buckets that can be analyzed in detail within the bucket, but then linked to elements in other buckets. Simply getting an organizational handle on complexity, though seeming mundane, is extremely useful. Many useful bits of empirical research provide only a nugget of information of limited usefulness by themselves but often become more valuable as part of a larger system.

Beyond helping to create a framework on which to hang other work, system dynamics tools can be also used to construct models that are used primarily for projections, as in the "Pension Reform" or "Education for All" examples. Because there is always an explicit dynamic orientation to system dynamics models, it can be easier to construct projection models using system dynamics models rather than Excel, for example. But, beyond the ease of use, the focus on closed-loop feedback makes it more likely that the person constructing the models may consider possibly important feedback effects that might otherwise be missed.

System dynamics can also be useful for more complex dynamic problems. Stephens et al. 2008 provides a good example of how dynamic processes describing biophysical relations and human decision making can be combined to increase understanding of real world experiences. The models developed by the Millennium Institute illustrate how system dynamics can be used for development planning.

Finally, system dynamics models have considerable potential for use in results-based management in development. System dynamics models have been developed to model the introduction and implementation of results-based management systems themselves (Grizzle and Pettijohn 2002). In addition, system dynamics models can be used to do some of the heavy lifting in implementing results-based management by making it easier to link policy actions to results and to allow for explicit characterizations of the production functions employed by good and poor performers. All of the examples discussed here have, in one way or another, been related to using system dynamics to improve the results orientation of work in development.

System Dynamics Outreach

For readers interested in seeing wider use of system dynamics, I have three suggestions that each involve collective action in the system dynamics community. First, concerted effort is needed to communicate better what system dynamics models can do. It is not easy to describe models nor can we automatically expect policy makers to make the investment to learn what system dynamics is and why it would be useful to them. Something like a professionally produced package illustrating ten system dynamics exercises (real-world cases) that could be handed out to people to convey what system dynamics is about and how it might be helpful to them is needed. A linked website would contain additional content and video content on the models.

Second, for system dynamics to be used more within agencies like the World Bank, the International Development Bank, and the UN Agencies, preparation of students who could work as interns would be valuable. Before system dynamics proves its usefulness, people will be unwilling to invest much money in pilot experiences; however, a few senior system dynamicists with a foot in the teaching community and directing pre-selected graduate student interns with a reasonable training in system dynamics and an interest in economics, international relations, or World Bank projects, could provide a good supply of people to carry out three-month projects.

Third, the potential advantages of the system dynamics approach could be elevated in the public's consciousness if there existed a real world "killer application" for system dynamics. The 2008 financial and economic crisis would be an obvious and almost unique opportunity to create this type of application. In congressional hearings, the financial crisis has been characterized as a system failure. Looking forward, there is universal recognition that the regulatory system must be fixed so that this problem does not happen again. What better opportunity to demonstrate how system dynamics can help increase understanding of the behavior of a system and be used to develop instruments (in this case, regulations) to help the system work better? With the understanding of what generated the problem gained from system dynamics modeling, the task would then turn to plugging the regulatory holes that allowed the system to fail.

For those interested in extending the use of system dynamics, the positive externalities generated for system dynamics for this type of work would be considerable and could justify some collective action. In order for the idea to gain any traction, it would have to be considered and proposed by the leading figures in the field.

Acknowledgements

I would like to thank Joao Pedro Azevedo, Leslie Martin, Paul Newton, and Chris Soderquist for helpful comments on earlier drafts of this paper.

The findings, interpretations, and conclusions expressed in this paper are entirely those of the author. They do not necessarily represent the views of the International Bank for Reconstruction and Development/World Bank and its affiliated organizations, or those of the Executive Directors of the World Bank or the governments they represent.

References

Flessa, S. 1999. "Decision support for malaria control programmes—a system dynamics model." *Health Care Management Science* 2(3):181–191.

Grizzle, G.A., and C.D. Pettijohn 2002. "Implementing Performance-Based Program Budgeting: A System-Dynamics Perspective." *Public Administration Review* 62(1):51–62.

Homer, J.B., and G.B. Hirsch 2006. "Systems Dynamics Modeling for Public Health: Background and Opportunities." *American Journal of Public Health* 96(3):452–458.

Martin, L. 2002. "The Cost of Pension Reform in Bolivia." World Bank, mimeo, October 2002.

McDonnell et al. 2004. G. McDonnell, M. Hefferman, and A. Faulkner. "Using System Dynamics to analyse Health System Performance within the WHO Framework." Oxford 22nd International System Dynamics Conference, July 2004. http://www.systemdynamics.org/conferences/2004/SDS_2004/PAPERS/337MCDON.pdf.

Narvaez et al. 2005. R. Narvaez, R. Bernal, and M. Vargas. "Escenarios de Proyeccion de Indicadores ODMs y Requerimientos Financieros." UDAPE Working Paper, Ministry of Finance Bolivia, April, 2005.

Newman et al. 2003. J. Newman, M.A. Velasco, L. Martin, and A.M. Fantini. "A Systems Dynamics Approach to Monitoring and Evaluation at the Country Level: An Application to the Evaluation of Malaria-Control Programs in Bolivia." In *Evaluating Development Effectiveness* by G. Pitman, O. Feinstein, and G. Ingram. World Bank Series on Evaluation and Development 7:249–262. http://ww.worldbank.org/oed/conference2003/papers/newman.doc.

Rwashana, A.S., and D.W. Williams 2008. "System Dynamics Modeling in Healthcare: The Ugandan Immunisation System." *International Journal of Computing and ICT Research* (Special Issue) 1(1):88–98. http://www.ijcir.org/specialissue2008/article9.pdf.

Richmond, B. 1993. "Systems Thinking: Critical Thinking Skills for the 1990s and Beyond." *System Dynamics Review* 9(2):113–133.

Stephens et al. 2008. E.C. Stephens, C.B. Barrett, D.R. Brown, J. Lehmann, D. Mbugua, S. Ngoze, C. F. Nicholson, D. Parsons, A.N. Pell and S. J. Riha. "Modeling Feedback between Economic and Biophysical Systems in Smallholder Agriculture in Kenya: The Crops, Livestock and Soils in Smallholder Economic Systems (CLASSES) Model." mimeo, October 2008. http://aem.cornell.edu/faculty_sites/cbb2/Papers/CJAE_Stephens_et_al_Oct2008_Full.pdf.

Note

1. In addition to this example, there are several interesting articles that look at health problems from a system dynamics perspective, including some that look at problems in developing countries, e.g., McDonnell et al. (2004), Homer and Hirsch (2006), and Rwashana and Williams (2008). Flessa (1999) developed an earlier model of malaria control using system dynamics.

9

The Power of the Situation: Modeling Classic Experiments in Social Psychology

James K. Doyle, Khalid Saeed, Jeanine Skorinko

This chapter honors Barry Richmond's remarkable contribution in crossing interdisciplinary boundaries by highlighting how system dynamics can realistically interact with social/psychological models for use in future research and psychological education.

The disciplines of system dynamics and social psychology would appear to have a natural affinity for each other. Despite their widely varying methodologies (computer simulation versus experimentation on human subjects), both disciplines offer similar explanations for human decision making and behavior. In system dynamics, modelers constantly make the claim that "structure drives behavior," meaning that the physical structure of the system—how the stocks and flows are interconnected—is often a stronger determinant of system behavior over time than the specific values of parameters. Similarly, social psychology experiments often reveal that the situation or role structure in which behavior occurs is a stronger predictor of cognition and behavior than the precise makeup of an individual's character, personality, or habits of thought. Thus, both fields see the individual decision maker as being embedded in an external system whose properties can have a strong influence over behavioral outcomes; however, despite the apparent similarity in theoretical approach, system dynamics and social psychology have rarely interacted. Few psychologists have made the effort to learn the system dynamics modeling approach and to apply it to the understanding of social behavior. In fact, social psychologists rarely use any form of computer simulation to develop and test their theories. At the same time, few system dynamicists have either attempted to apply the

> This chapter was written by three people with diverse backgrounds from the Department of Social Science and Policy Studies at Worcester Polytechnic Institute (WPI). Each was influenced by Barry in different ways.
>
> **James K. Doyle**, who grew up in California, is a social psychologist specializing in judgment and decision making. He received his B.A. from the University of California at Berkeley and his Ph.D. in social psychology at the University of Colorado at Boulder. In 1992, James joined the faculty of Worcester Polytechnic Institute, where he was first introduced to system dynamics by Professor Michael Radzicki, and got to know Barry who was Chair of WPI's System Dynamics Advisory Board. James is currently Associate Professor of Psychology and Head of the Department of Social Science and Policy Studies at WPI.
>
> **Khalid Saeed** grew up in Pakistan, and came to work on a Ph.D. in system dynamics at MIT in 1975 at the same time Barry joined the program. They developed a close friendship and kept in close communication thereafter. Khalid worked at the Asian Institute of Technology in Bangkok, Thailand, after he graduated from MIT. He spent a sabbatical year (1983–84) at Dartmouth College and moved to Worcester Polytechnic Institute in 1997. At WPI, Khalid oversaw the development of system dynamics undergraduate and graduate curricula and invited Barry to chair the advisory board of the System Dynamics Program.
>
> **Jeanine Skorinko** grew up in Allentown, Pennsylvania, and completed her Ph.D. in social psychology at the University of Virginia. She joined WPI in 2007, and she was introduced to system dynamics at that time. While Jeanine never met Barry, she is intrigued by the idea of applying system dynamics to classic and modern social psychology studies.

system dynamics method to socially relevant and standard social psychological topics (e.g., the nature of obedience, group dynamics, persuasion, aggression, or prejudice), or to reference the large experimental literature in social psychology.

Barry Richmond provided a particularly notable exception to this lack of synergy between the two fields by attempting to replicate two classic experiments in social psychology using system dynamics. Barry joined the system dynamics doctoral program at MIT in 1975 and, along with his fellow doctoral students in the Sloan School of Management (including one of the present authors), took a mandatory seminar in behavioral science. An intriguing part of this seminar was the presentation by Professor Edgar Schein of two classic social psychological studies: Stanley Milgram's obedience experiment[1] and Philip Zimbardo's prison simulation study, known as the Stanford Prison Experiment.[2] These two studies are often cited as the examples of a widespread phenomenon in social behavior referred to as "the power of the situation." This refers to the ability of external circumstantial or situational factors to overwhelm individual differences and personality factors, resulting in identical behavior from people with very different personalities and values.

Both experiments placed their human subjects in a difficult situation and set up a conflict between the values of the individual subjects and the demands of the situation. In the Milgram obedience studies, subjects were asked to deliver painful electric shocks to a fellow subject in obedience to the instructions of the experimenter. In the Zimbardo experiment, subjects were asked to play the role of prison guard in a simulated prison environment. In

tracing connections

Barry Richmond provided a particularly notable exception to the lack of synergy between two very different disciplines—social psychology and system dynamics—by attempting to replicate two classic social psychology experiments. Barry joined the system dynamics doctoral program at MIT in 1975 and, along with his fellow doctoral students (including one of the present authors), took a mandatory seminar in behavioral science. During the seminar, two classic social psychological studies were presented: Stanley Milgram's obedience experiment and Philip Zimbardo's prison simulation study, known as the Stanford Prison Experiment. These two studies are often cited as examples of a phenomenon in social behavior known as "the power of the situation." This refers to the ability of external circumstantial or situational factors to overwhelm individual differences and personality factors, resulting in identical behavior from people with very different personalities and values.

Barry, who held a master's degree in psychology, came away from these presentations with what, for the time, was a very radical idea: the experiments could conceivably be conducted on a computer using system dynamics modeling rather than employing real human subjects. He took on the challenge of building a system dynamics model of the Milgram experiment, producing a fascinating technical report describing the model and his experimentation with it. Later in his career, Barry also built a more elegant model of the Zimbardo experiment.

---

both, the question was similar: would the personal traits of the individuals matter more than the situational pressures created by the roles they were asked to assume? The surprising (and disturbing) result in both cases was that a majority of subjects took actions to harm or denigrate others—actions that, prior to the experiment, they would never have dreamed they were capable of doing.

Barry, who held a master's degree in psychology, came away from these presentations with what, for the time, was a very radical idea: the experiments could conceivably be conducted on a computer using system dynamics modeling rather than employing real human subjects. He took on the challenge of building a system dynamics model of the Milgram experiment, and produced a fascinating technical report describing the model and his experimentation with it.[3] Later in his career, with more experience under his belt, Barry also built a more elegant model of the Zimbardo experiment. Although this model was never fully written up, it is briefly described in a paper published by Barry in the *System Dynamics Review*[4] and the authors gained access to the original document through the assistance of isee systems.

The present chapter honors Barry's remarkable contribution by highlighting how system dynamics can realistically interact with social/psychological models for use in future research and psychological education. For both the Milgram

Experiment and the Stanford Prison (Zimbardo) Experiment, a synopsis of the experimental protocol and the overall results are provided.[5] Each synopsis is followed by a discussion of Barry Richmond's system dynamics model of the same experiment, along with sample computer simulation runs.[6] In the final summary, Barry's models are used as a springboard to address several important questions at the interface of system dynamics and social psychology, including lack of historical interaction, benefits of more future interactions, and the future potential of using system dynamic methodology for exploring social psychological topics.

The Milgram Experiment

After World War II, the world, shocked by the atrocities committed by Nazi soldiers onto the German Jews, wondered what could make the Nazis such an evil group of people. In the midst of this outrage against Nazi Germans, Stanley Milgram, who was interested in the influence of the situation on individuals, wondered if the Nazis were naturally evil people or whether anyone, given the right situation, might commit similar acts. It was from this question that he designed his now-famous obedience experiments.

The Milgram Experiment: Synopsis of the experimental design

Milgram set up his original experiment using individuals who were paid to participate in an experiment on learning and punishment. Besides the subject (also referred to as "teacher"), the other individuals involved included the experimenter (authority) dressed in a laboratory coat, and another person, Mr. Wallace, introduced as a participant (also referred to as "learner" or "victim"), but who in fact worked for the experiment.

Although apparently random, the experiment was set up such that the subject always ended up being the teacher and Mr. Wallace always ended up as the victim (learner). The experimenter explained that the subject would be teaching the victim word-pairs, and the victim would need to accurately recall the word-pairs. The subject was told that incorrect recall would result in punishment by electric shocks. With each incorrect response, the intensity of the shock increased by 15 volts. In addition, during the setup of the actual electrical shocking straps, the victim informed both the experimenter and the subject that he had a heart condition; however, the experimenter assured the victim he would feel pain, but that there would be no heart effects from the shock. (It is to be noted that no shock was actually ever given.) At first, the victim recalled the word-pairs correctly. But as time went on, the victim's performance declined; the shock intensity increased, and the subject's anxiety probably increased as well. Milgram hoped the experiment would indicate when the anxiety of doing something harmful to another person might override obedience to an authority figure.

To aid in the reality of the situation (and to make the harm on the other person more apparent), the subject began to hear (pre-planned) verbalizations from the victim based on the shock's intensity. As the voltage increased, the verbalizations changed from a mild "Ugh" to, eventually, "My heart's starting to bother me. I refuse to go on. Let me out," and then to "Let me out of here," repeatedly; finally, after 330 volts, the victim went silent. Thus, the subject likely began to feel two types of increasing anxiety: anxiety over the fact they had to administer increasingly powerful shocks to the victim, and anxiety over the reactions and screams of the victim to the increased intensity of the shocks.[7]

Often, after the first few reactions by the victim, the subject would look to the experimenter for guidance about what to do. The experimenter responded in one of four scripted responses, but did nothing else: *Please continue*; *The experiment requires you continue*; *It is absolutely essential that you continue*; or *You have no other choice, you must go on*. The experimenter's insistence that the experiment continue created additional anxiety in the subject. The subject needed to weigh four anxiety inputs: the anxiety felt for simply administering painful shocks; the anxiety felt for the pain being inflicted on the victim; the anxiety felt for obeying an authority figure (the experimenter) who stated that no real harm was being done; and the anxiety felt for not wanting to let the experimenter down so the experiment could be completed.

The Milgram Experiment: Results

What happened? Sixty-five percent (26 out of 40 men) of the subjects punished the victim to maximum voltage. Were there any limits to these findings? Milgram[8] ran several replications to this original study. One key finding was that gender of the participants did not affect the results; however, several factors did result in lowered obedience by subjects. First, the physical proximity to the victim slightly reduced compliance. Forty percent of the subjects gave the maximum shock when the victim was in the same room as the subject. If the subject had to also physically touch the victim (actor), and place the victim's hand on the shock plate, then less than 30% of the subjects continued the experiment to the maximum voltage. Anxiety may explain these results. The more the subject had to physically face the victim, the more anxiety the subject felt and the more likely they were to want to witness the effect of the shock, regardless of the presence of the experimenter. These results may be explained by the additional anxiety about the need for trusting and keeping the experimenter happy.

Second, factors relating to the authority figure also contributed to reductions in obedience. Just the presence of an authority figure played a key role. If the experimenter left the room, leaving only a staff member to run the experiment, then the subject only gave 20% of the maximum shock to the victim. The proximity of the experimenter also played a key role. If the experimenter administered the experiment from a different room, again only 20% of the subjects obeyed and used maximum shock. If the experimenter never gave any of the four commands described above, fewer than 5% of the subjects administered the maximum shock. In these cases, too, results may be explained by the decrease in anxiety felt by the subject if they did not have to face the disappointed experimenter.

The third factor was the presence of other dissenting/rebelling subjects, which led to increased rebellion on behalf of the subject. In the presence of other subjects who refused to continue shocking, less than 10% of the subjects would continue shocking to maximum voltage. In this case, the social influence of seeing someone else refuse to continue provided the subject with an excuse to stop. Initially, the subject may not have wanted to be the only one to stop the study, but then the subject may have believed that the other subjects had a reason to refuse to continue, or knew something else about the situation.

Milgram's obedience studies (and other studies replicating Milgram) have had important implications for a variety of social science disciplines. The findings raised awareness of the importance of the situation in possibly overriding personality traits. The studies also raised the issue of ethics in conducting research, and involved questions such as the delicate balance between the risks to participants (e.g., the emotional distress they felt at harming another individual) and the benefits gained from the empirical research. It is in this area that Barry's insight to use system dynamics modeling was particularly important.

> Barry originally formulated the dynamic hypothesis underlying the decision process in Milgram's experiment as shown in Figure 9-1. It consisted of two major negative feedback loops that described the behavior in the experiment, exhibiting **closed-loop thinking**.

The Milgram Experiment:
The system dynamics model

Barry originally formulated the dynamic hypothesis underlying the decision process in Milgram's experiment as shown in Figure 9-1. It consisted of two major negative feedback loops that described the behavior in the experiment, exhibiting closed-loop thinking.

We have reformulated the model in four sectors (using the *iThink* hierarchy): Punishment Delivered; Decision to Continue; Anxiety; and Termination (of the experiment). The structure and information relationships between Punishment Delivered and Decision to Continue are shown in Figure 9-2. The experiment is terminated when the *Total Punishment Delivered to the Victim* exceeds a value set by the experimenter. It can also be terminated due to the *Subject Anxiety Level* or his/

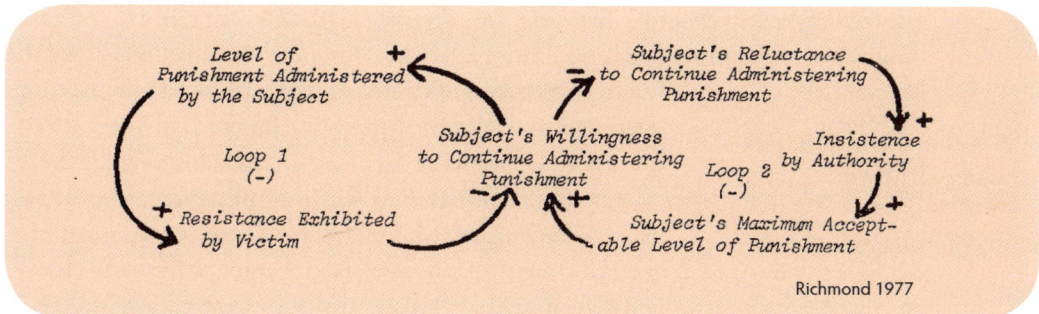

Figure 9-1. Barry Richmond's original causal loop diagram describing behavior in the Milgram Experiment

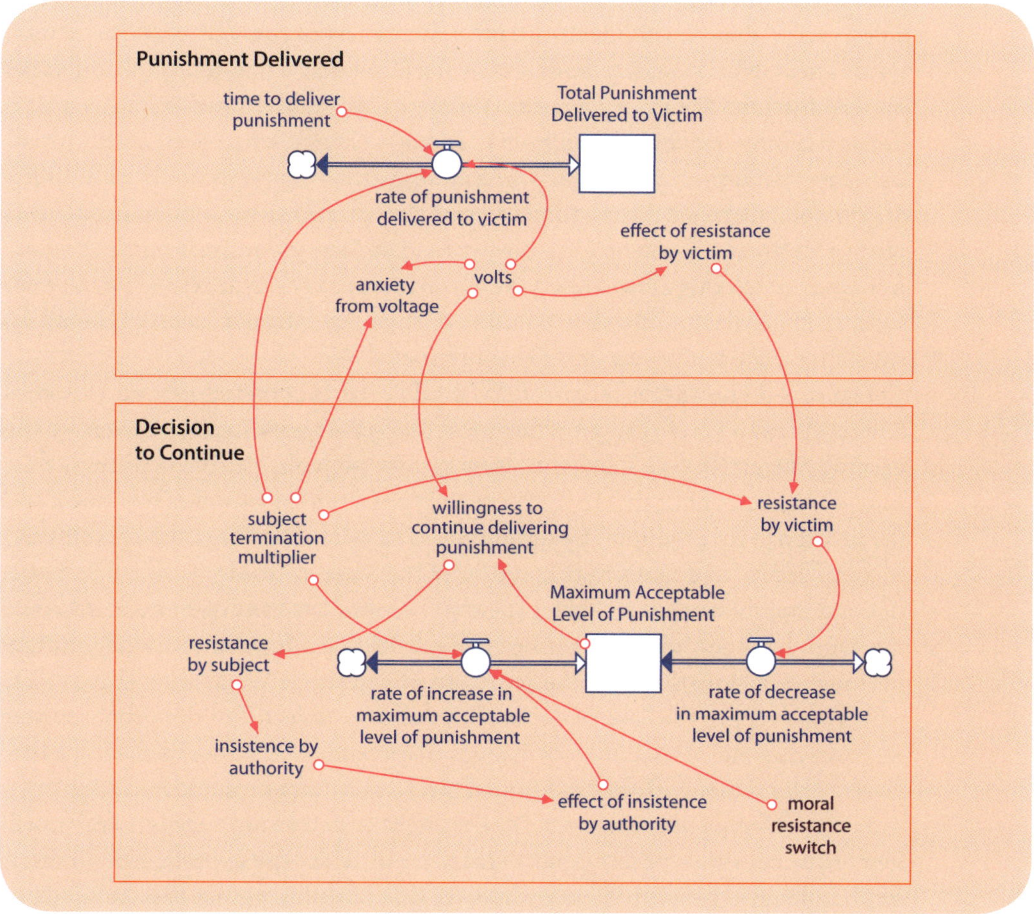

Figure 9-2. Punishment sector and Decision to Continue sector of the Milgram Model

her *willingness to continue delivering punishment* (Figures 9-3 and 9-4). The reformulation of the model uses operational thinking to make the structure clear.

> The reformulation of the model uses **operational thinking** to make the structure clear.

Termination ends Anxiety, Punishment Delivered, and Decision to Continue. Both Punishment Delivered and the Decision to Continue fuel Anxiety. The instantaneous *rate of punishment delivered to victim* is measured in volts/unit time. *Total Punishment Delivered to Victim* is accumulated in a stock (measured in volts) and that stock drives the *experimenter termination* process. The number of *volts* increases over time and is an exogenous input to the system as the experiment continues. The *anxiety from voltage* in turn creates *Subject Anxiety Level*, another stock, on the part of the subject (teacher), while also invoking *resistance by victim* (learner).

Volts and *Subject Anxiety Level*, together with a third stock, *Maximum Acceptable Level of Punishment*, determine the *willingness to continue delivering punishment*. The subject's *anxiety from voltage* is eliminated when the subject decides on termination. The increase in the *Maximum Acceptable Level of Punishment* is determined by *insistence by authority*, and can change when the subject resists or when the subject's *willingness to continue delivering punishment* wanes. The *Maximum Acceptable Level of Punishment* also drains as the victim shows resistance (*resistance by victim*). We have added to Barry's original model a *moral resistance switch* that slows down the *rate of increase of the Maximum Acceptable Level of Punishment*. This allowed us to change the intrinsic value of the moral resistance a subject brings into the experiment.

Figure 9-3 shows the sector of the model that is centered around the stock, *Subject Anxiety Level*. The growth in the *Subject Anxiety Level* is driven by the existing *Subject Anxiety Level*, the rising number of volts delivered (*anxiety from voltage*), the resistance shown by the victim (*anxiety from resistance by victim*), and the insistence (to continue) by the authority (*anxiety from insistence by authority*). Anxiety decays as a first-order function of the *Subject Anxiety Level* stock, but is drained rapidly when the subject (teacher) terminates the experiment. An *empathy switch* has been added to the original model that allows us to specify another personality factor: the empathetic nature of a subject. We assume that anxiety will grow faster in the case of a more empathetic subject. For the purposes here, we restricted our model only to changes in empathy and in the moral resistance levels of the subjects, though additional personality factors could be added.

Figure 9-4 shows how the experiment might end—through anxiety and unwillingness to continue by the subject (teacher) or when the experimenter (authority) has determined that the maximum level of punishment has been reached.

Figure 9-5 shows a computer simulation run of the experiment. An increase in *volts* delivered drives the system. The *Subject Anxiety Level*, *Total Punishment*

The Power of the Situation 175

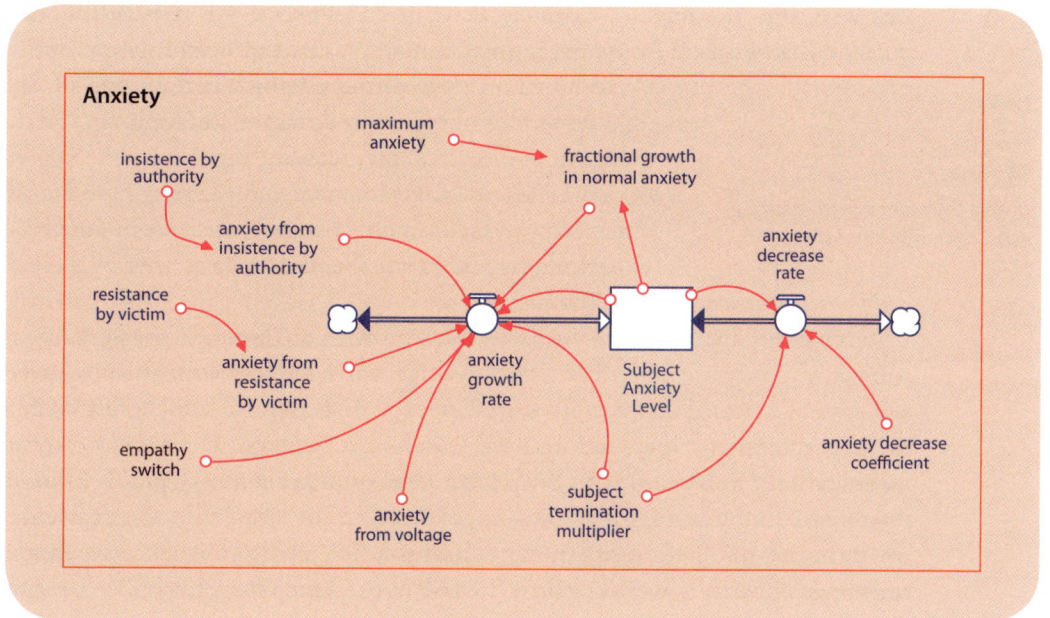

Figure 9-3. Anxiety sector of the Milgram Model

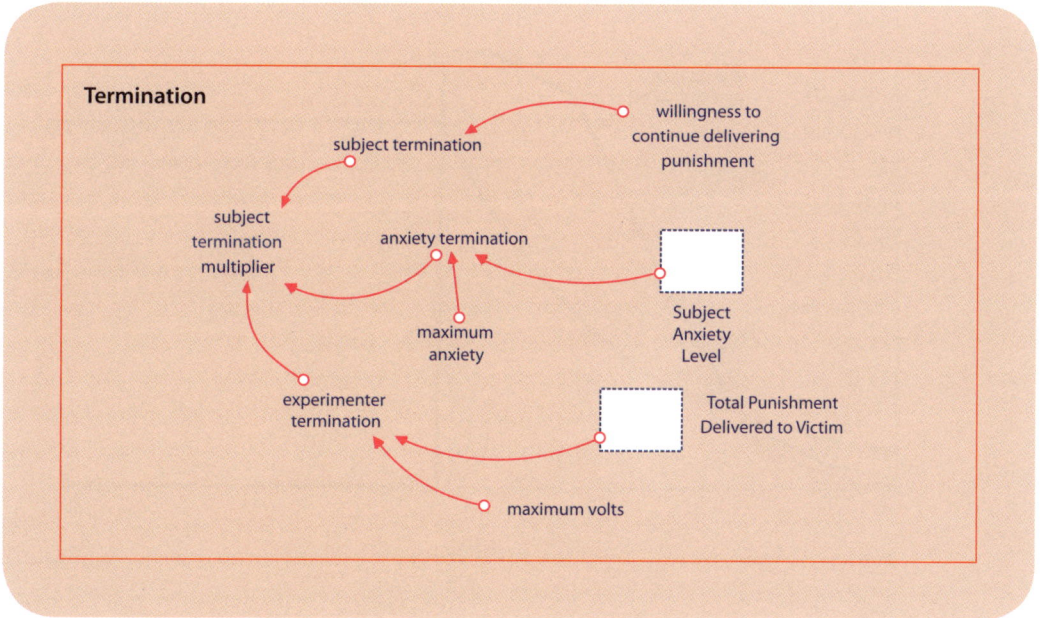

Figure 9-4. Termination (of the experiment) sector of the Milgram Model

Delivered, the *Maximum Acceptable Level of Punishment*, the *resistance by victim*, and the *insistence by authority* grow concomitantly until termination of the experiment. The use of these behavior-over-time graphs illustrate one of the eight system thinking skills: dynamic thinking.

> The use of these behavior-over-time graphs illustrate one of the eight system thinking skills: **dynamic thinking**.

Figure 9-6 shows the relationship between *Subject Anxiety Level* and *Maximum Acceptable Level of Punishment*, which grows concomitantly because *insistence by authority* (experimenter) mitigates the resistance created by *Subject Anxiety Level*.

Three cases are shown: a subject (teacher) with an "average" personality, a subject who is more empathetic than average, and a subject with an above average level of moral resistance. As would be expected, a moral subject terminates the experiment at a low level of *Total Punishment Delivered to Victim*; however, an empathetic subject gets to the design level of *Maximum Acceptable Level of Punishment*, but takes a longer time to get there. In the latter case, the insistence by authority mitigates empathetic behavior while in the former case, moral resistance effectively works against the rise in the *Maximum Acceptable Level of Punishment* delivered.

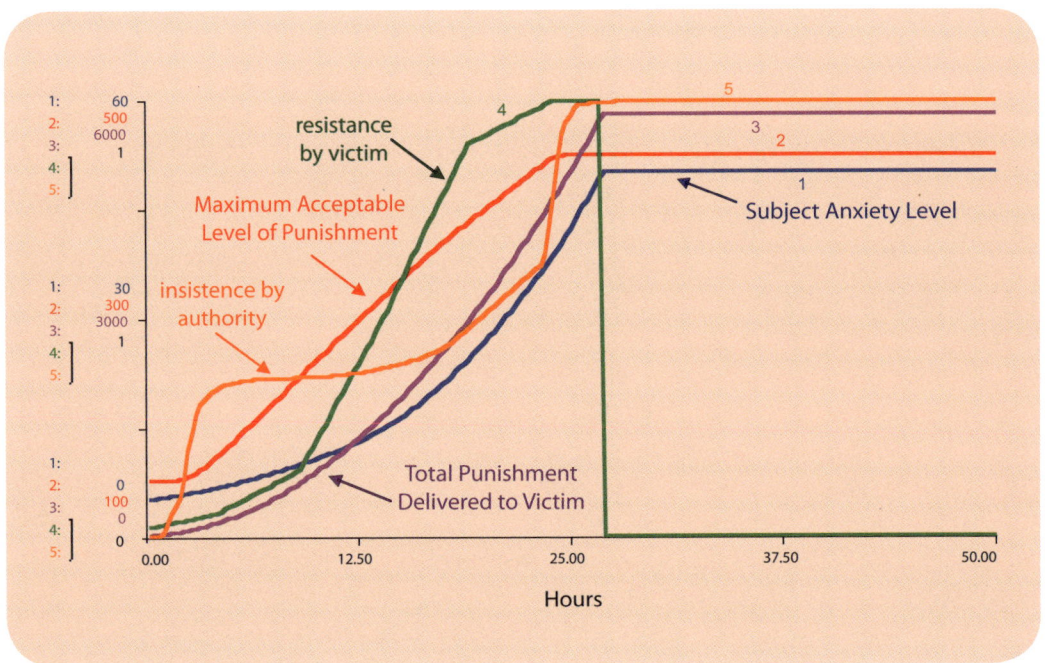

Figure 9-5. Simulation run of the Milgram Model

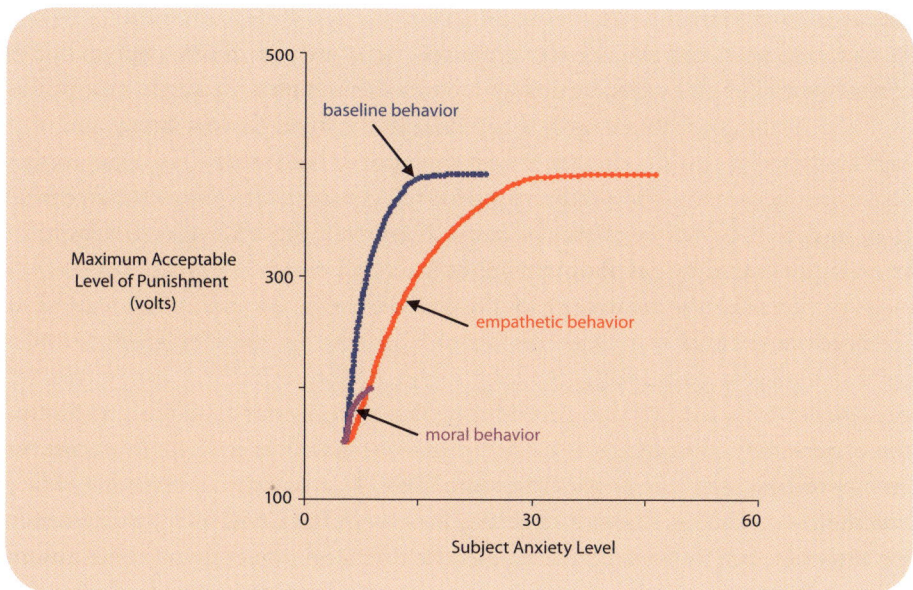

Figure 9-6. Relationship between Subject Anxiety Level and Maximum Acceptable Level of Punishment in the Milgram Model

The Stanford Prison Experiment

Because of interest in the effect the social situation has on individuals, Philip Zimbardo and colleagues decided to try to understand prison behavior.[9] Unable to put participants inside a real prison, Zimbardo created his own prison in the basement of Jordan Hall (the psychology building) at Stanford University. Interested participants were screened for mental illness and proclivity towards violence, to ensure neither of these variables would influence the results of the study. The participants who passed the screening tests were randomly assigned (by flipping a coin) to be either a prisoner or a guard.

The Stanford Prison Experiment: Synopsis of the experimental design

At the start of the study, the guards were given the following instructions: no violent acts towards the prisoners; prisoners must be called only by their ID number; lineups were conducted and prisoners were counted frequently; prisoners were to be allowed three bland meals and three toilet visits per day. Prisoners were unexpectedly arrested at their residences by the local police department. They were then officially booked into the prison, strip searched, given a prisoner ID number, given basic prisoner apparel, and chained around their ankle.

The Stanford Prison Experiment: Results

At first, the scene and the participant interactions were mundane, but gradually changes started to take place. Some guards started taking advantage of the power they had: waking prisoners up in the middle of the night to do a lineup and making the prisoners do manual labor (e.g., scrubbing the floors). As some guards took advantage of their power, more guards felt compelled to follow suit, whether to fit in with their fellow guards or because they felt that the other guards must know more than they did about how to act.

In response to the treatment by the guards, the prisoners at first started to rebel, refusing to do the ordered manual labor and ignoring requests to wake up in the middle of the night. As long as one prisoner rebelled, then the other prisoners felt as if they, too, could rebel; however, as the rebellions and number of prisoners involved increased, the guards started to retaliate by increased cruelty in language and prisoner treatment and by placing the rebels in solitary confinement. The rebellions and retaliations went back and forth, with increasing intensity. For example, the leader of the rebellion objected to the treatment by the guards; his complaints were received with even more abuse by the guards. The prisoner then started a hunger strike. In retaliation, the guards locked him in solitary confinement, announcing at the same time that all prisoners would have to surrender their blankets and sleep on a cold floor so the rebellious prisoner could be released from the solitary confinement.

With each failed rebellion, the prisoners started to feel an increased sense of learned helplessness that they could do nothing to remedy or escape the situation. Eventually, the prisoners stopped rebelling and started to become more reticent, more passive, and very unhappy. After six days, Zimbardo ended the study because several of the prisoners left the study as they started to exhibit signs of severe depression and anxiety. Ironically, the prisoners forgot, probably due to the situation and the effects of repeated failure of the rebellions, that they could have escaped the treatment merely by asking to leave the study.

The Zimbardo prison study along with the Milgram study were two of the first research studies to question the effect of the situation and demonstrate the power of the situation over personality traits. The results of both the Milgram and Zimbardo studies were pivotal in the history of social psychology and have stood the test of time and replication.

The Stanford Prison Experiment: The system dynamics model

Barry's original formulation of the Stanford Prison Experiment model has three main stocks representing *Prisoner Resistance*, *Prisoner Fear*, and *Repression by Guards*. A fourth stock, *Resistance Perceived by Guards*, is a complex exponential average of the *Prisoner Resistance*, with *perception time* also varying with the level of *Prisoner Resistance*. This basically means that low levels of resistance will go undetected by the guards, and high levels will be quickly detected.

Figure 9-7 shows *Resistance Perceived by Guards* leads to *Repression by Guards*, which invokes more resistance, creating an escalating process. At the same time, *Repression by Guards* also fuels *Prisoner Fear*. Both *Repression by Guards* and *Prisoner Fear* reduce *Prisoner Resistance*, thus creating major balancing feedback loops. While a major balancing feedback loop alone can create an overshoot and instability, a positive feedback loop coupled with this process will exacerbate such behavior; hence, the structure of this feedback system is bound to create escalation of hostilities between the prisoners and guards, regardless of the personalities of the two parties.

The model includes a switch, *remove John Wayne switch*,[10] which, when thrown, constrains the growth in *Repression by Guards*. With this switch, the model can be tested with different guard personalities.

Figure 9-8 compares changes in *Prisoner Resistance* with normal behavior and

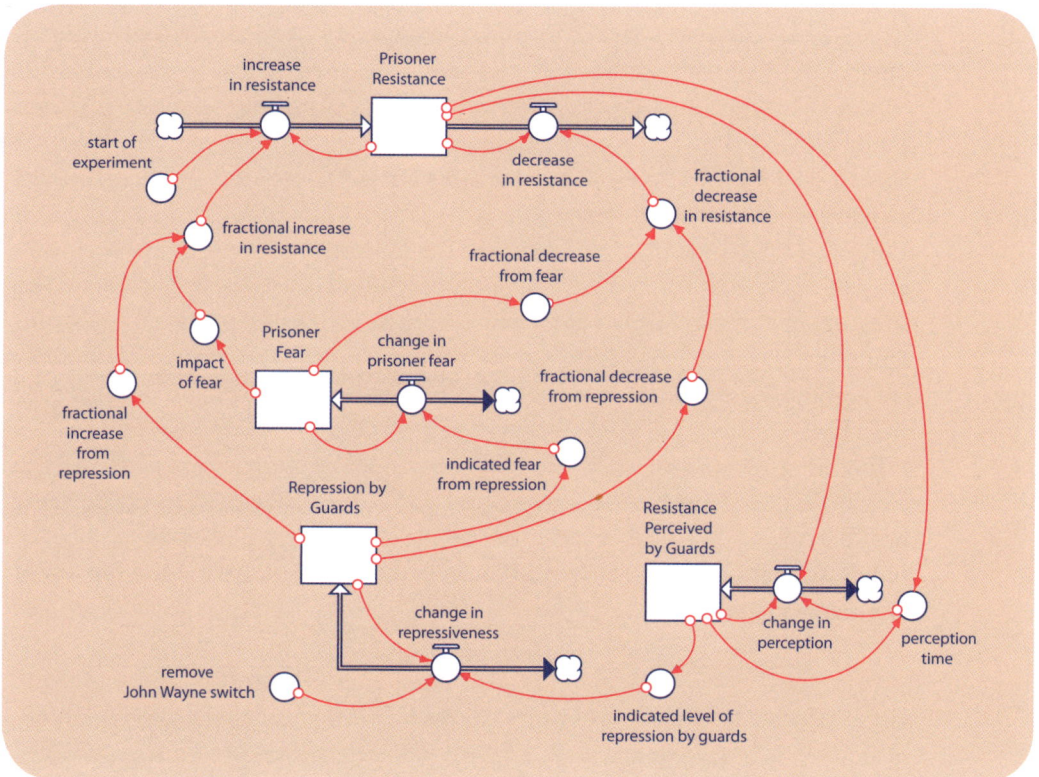

Figure 9-7. Structure of Barry Richmond's model of the Stanford Prison Experiment

"John Wayne" behavior. Figure 9-9 compares *Repression by Guards* with two different guard personality profiles. When *Repression by Guards* is 100%, then normal behavior is equivalent to "John Wayne" behavior (the "John Wayne" switch is turned on). Normal behavior for the guards without the switch turned on is considered to be 70% of the *Repression by Guards* that would be exhibited in "John

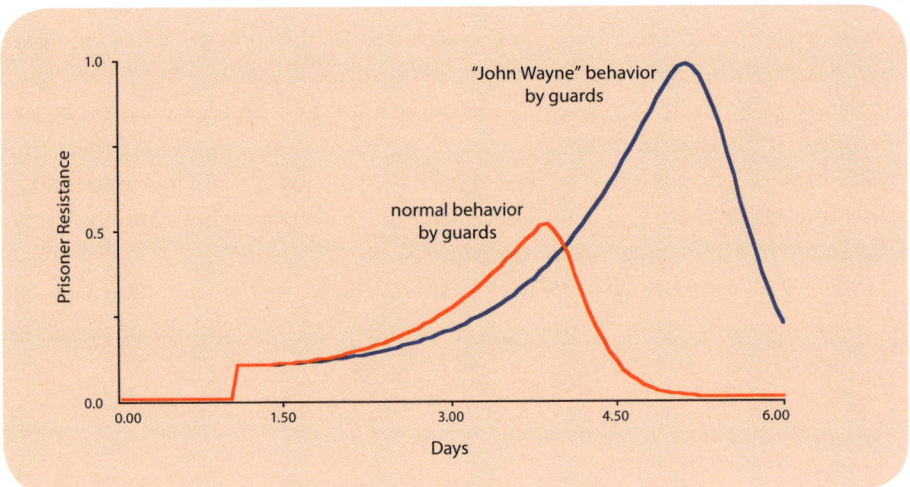

Figure 9-8. Changes in Prisoner Resistance with normal and "John Wayne" behavior by guards

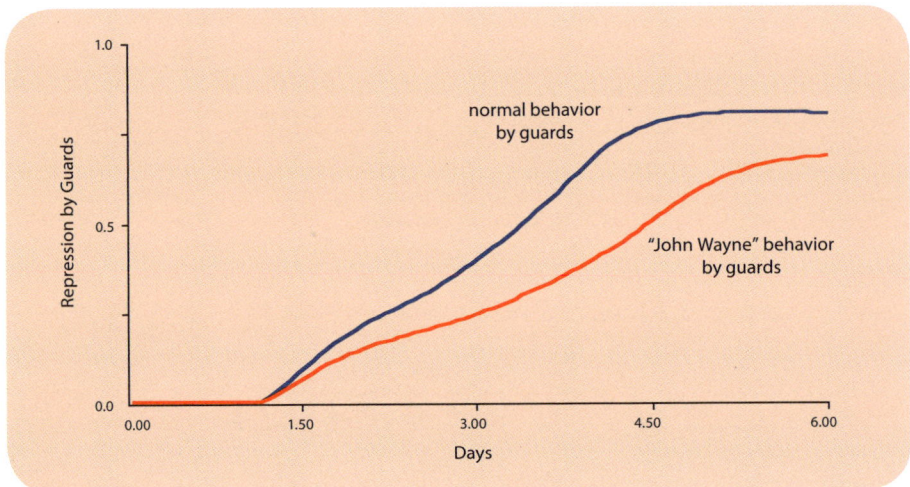

Figure 9-9. Changes in Repression by Guards with normal and "John Wayne" behavior

Wayne" behavior. When guards are more benign, *Prisoner Resistance* takes longer to break and rises to a higher peak, and as a result, *Repression by Guards* rises too.

System Dynamics and Social Psychology: Challenges for the Future

Barry Richmond's pioneering attempt to use system dynamics to model the underlying dynamics of subjects' behavior in social psychology experiments demonstrates both the feasibility of combining system dynamics and social psychology and the valuable insights such collaboration can produce; however, more than thirty years later, it remains a rare example of such interdisciplinary work. The lack of communication and interaction between social psychology and system dynamics is striking. On the one hand, for decades system dynamics has developed and improved techniques for modeling economic, policy, and business problems that are inherently social in nature without using the enormous empirical literature on human social behavior. On the other hand, social psychology has a long tradition of constructing inherently dynamic theories of human behavior, but generally resists using computer simulation as an aid to theory building and seems almost completely unaware of the system dynamics modeling tradition. The future challenge is to understand the differences and develop mutually beneficial interactions.

The answer to this dichotomy, we believe, lies mainly in the fact that researchers and practitioners in the two fields go about their business very differently. Social psychologists focus on conducting controlled experiments that change one variable at a time and employ random assignment of subjects in order to allow causality to be unambiguously determined. To a social psychologist, verifying the nature and magnitude of the relationships in a system dynamics model would represent a lifetime of work. Furthermore, the amount of time, effort, and expense involved in conducting experiments on human subjects means that the kind of time series data that lends itself to modeling is not often collected; most social psychology experiments are one-time snapshots of behavior or, at best, two snapshots (one before the experimental task, and one after).

By contrast, system dynamicists set aside the question of precise values for parameters and skip right to the big picture task of identifying the structure of the system in which behavior takes place. Since they theorize that it is primarily structure that drives system behavior, they believe it is unnecessary to identify the precise magnitude of relationships between variables up front; in fact, sensitivity analyses may ultimately show that system behavior is unchanged even with widely varying assumptions about parameter values.

Three important differences separate the two fields. The first involves the approach to data. System dynamicists would suggest that social psychologists are probably collecting a lot of unnecessary data. To which social psychologists would respond that system dynamics is "measurement without data." Social psychologists have a long history of combating "common sense" assumptions about human behavior that controlled experimentation has proved to be false. To such researchers, the system dynamics attitude of "model first, measure later" would be viewed as counterproductive and potentially harmful.

A second important difference is the relative importance assigned to different types of data for input to theories and/or models. Controlled experiments are held in high esteem by social psychologists for their ability to determine causality; however, external validity (whether results obtained in the lab also apply in real life) is an important concern as well. With this in mind, social psychologists employ a variety of additional data gathering techniques including survey research, naturalistic observation, field and case studies, and interviewing techniques. And with all techniques comes an overriding concern for systematicity in data collection and representativeness in the human subjects under study.

In contrast, system dynamicists often are not particularly interested in either formal methodologies or in the empirical psychological literature; instead, they simply go straight to the managers or decision makers who have the information they need and ask them for it. The modeling process determines the need for information, and the pressure to solve a practical policy problem often does not leave time to consult the empirical psychological literature. This approach suggests a high level of confidence in the ability of people to accurately remember and report on their own thinking and behavior; however, to a psychologist, the chance that information collected so informally will turn out to be inaccurate or misleading is simply too high.

A third difference between the two fields is the relative emphasis placed on theoretical versus applied work, resulting in the simple reality that their paths rarely cross. Social psychologists conduct applied research on a wide variety of socially important topics, but the emphasis is on developing and testing theories of human social behavior. In comparison, system dynamics modelers focus almost exclusively on social problem solving, as opposed to theory, and work primarily in collaboration with businesses and other large organizations. In addition to the above differences, since neither field is a typical (or even an atypical) component of academic training in the other, there is a profound, mutual lack of awareness between the two fields.

To fully realize the potential for productive interaction between system dynamics and social psychology, social psychologists will need to become more open to the advantages of the more holistic approach that system dynamicists can provide; to start applying the research they have already conducted and associated findings to many different models of human behavior; and to be more willing to leap into the modeling enterprise without waiting for data that may take years, if ever, to materialize.

System dynamicists, following Barry Richmond's example, will need to learn to find value in exploring and applying the empirical literature in social psychology and to discover the advantages of more systematic and representative data collection, and consequently more complex (and possibly more accurate) models. And, of course, researchers in both fields will need to find ways to educate themselves about the methods of the other domain.

The benefits of such interaction would be similar to the benefits offered by system dynamics modeling in any field. The discipline imposed by modeling would uncover errors, omissions, and inconsistencies in mental models of social psychological theories, as it has in many other fields. It could help strengthen the existing theories on human behavior by demonstrating their robustness (e.g., Barry's model on Milgram strengthened Milgram's claim that the situation played more of a role than personality). It would also help to make the theories less conceptual, more dynamic and complex, and more operational.

System dynamics modeling also has benefits unique to social psychology (and other experimental disciplines within psychology). Given the time-consuming, labor-intensive nature of each empirical test of a relationship in a psychology research program, use of simulation runs to test alternate hypotheses before using human subjects would allow directed use of limited resources for the most promising live experiments. The ability of dynamic modeling to combine many theories and variables at one time could also greatly enhance understanding of human behavior theories. Finally, as Barry Richmond suggested in his Milgram Model paper,[9] the simulation model could be used to test experimental conditions that would be difficult or impossible to reproduce in the laboratory or to put simulated subjects through procedures that would be unethical to duplicate in real life.

> Given the time-consuming, labor-intensive nature of each empirical test of a relationship in a psychology research program, use of simulation runs to test alternate hypotheses before using human subjects, would allow directed use of limited resources for the most promising live experiments.

Is there anything that makes system dynamics modeling particularly well-suited to the study of social psychology? Certainly the emphasis in the system dynamics paradigm on the inclusion of so-called "soft" variables, and the techniques that have been developed for incorporating them into models, is an advantage for studying social psychology, where concepts such as anxiety, obedience, prejudice, aggression, conformity, perception, and judgment may be the main topics of investigation. It would also allow the merging of the theories and concepts within many different domains with social psychology, psychology, and other disciplines (e.g., anthropology, economics, law, sociology). And other central aspects of the system dynamics tradition certainly offer an alternative to other modeling paradigms: the surfacing of underlying feedback relationships and the operational emphasis; the focus on learning rather than prediction; and the increased effectiveness of models when they are designed to help solve problems rather than exhaustively replicate systems.

However, the best reason to choose a system dynamics approach for the study of social psychology might be its suitability to study a long-standing problem at the heart of the field: the relative contribution of the person versus the situation in determining behavior. For any given topic of study or experimental situation, it is still not easy to predict or to tease apart the relative contributions of the person and the situation, how they may interact, and how that interaction may unfold over time. System dynamics modeling could be a very valuable tool, even ideally suited, to help simplify and systematize this effort. In system dynamics, situational factors can be incorporated into the model structure as causally related variables. Individual difference or personality factors can be represented as adjustable parameters. The test of the relative strength of situational versus personality factors thus reduces to the standard practice of parameter sensitivity analysis. Barry Richmond, in fact, took this approach in his models of the Milgram and Stanford Prison Experiments.

Conclusion

It has been inspiring for the present authors (one system dynamicist and two social psychologists) to have the opportunity to examine and reflect upon Barry Richmond's early effort to combine his knowledge and interest in social psychology and system dynamics. Our own thinking about the need for and benefits of productive collaboration between the two fields has been challenged, and our understanding of the obstacles that will need to be overcome to increase such collaboration in the future has been improved and focused. We are also pleased to play a role in bringing Barry's original models of the Milgram and Stanford Prison Experiments to a new audience, and hope others will be inspired to follow up or expand upon his work and, perhaps, explore other theories and applications of social psychology using the powerful tools of system dynamics. At the same time, we hope Barry's models will gain some use in psychological education. Students could be allowed to experiment with the Milgram simulation model themselves and see the effects of changing personality variables. This may be an effective way to drive home the point that in certain situations personality just does not matter that much.

We also believe there are larger lessons to be learned from Barry's work. Certainly, it paves the way for system dynamics modelers to make better use of an underutilized information source, namely, the results of controlled experiments on human subjects. In addition, as there are still those in the system dynamics community who are reluctant to model so-called "soft" or psychological variables, Barry's work serves as a reminder that such work, while challenging, can, and must, be done. And, finally, the topics of the Milgram and Stanford Prison Experiment models themselves serve as a useful reminder that the field of system dynamics began by addressing, and still can address, the great problems of society.

References

Haney et al. 1973. C. Haney, W.C. Banks, and P.G. Zimbardo. Interpersonal dynamics in a simulated prison. *International Journal of Criminology and Penology* 1:69–97.

Milgram, S. 1963. Behavioral study of obedience. *Journal of Abnormal and Social Psychology*, 67(4):371–378.

Milgram, S. 1974. *Obedience to Authority: An Experimental View*. New York: Harper & Row, 1974.

Richmond, B. 1977. Generalization with Individual Uniqueness: Modeling the Milgram Experiments." Technical Report D-2508-2. A DVD containing the complete D-memo series of the MIT System Dynamics Group is available from the System Dynamics Society (http://www.systemdynamics.org).

Notes

1. Milgram, 1963, 1974.
2. Haney et al., 1973; Haney and Zimbardo, 1976.
3. Richmond, 1977.
4. Richmond, 1993.
5. More extensive descriptions can be found at the websites: http://www.stanley milgram.com and http://www.prisonexp.org.
6. Note that, in the present paper, the models have been translated from the original *Dynamo* to *iThink*, updated according to current system dynamics practice, and modified to allow easier experimentation with parameters.
7. Milgram, 1974.
8. Milgram, 1963.
9. Haney et al., 1973.
10. Named after a particularly cruel guard nicknamed "John Wayne."
11. Richmond, 1977.

10

Education for an Interdependent World: Developing Systems Citizens

Peter M. Senge

> Peter M. Senge focuses on a new kind of thinking to educate youth that addresses the interconnected social, economic, cultural, ecological, and global challenges the world faces. In the process of recreating education, he advocates and cites examples of the use of systems thinking, authentic youth engagement, rethinking schools as learning communities, and engaging whole community action as the foundation for educating future systems citizens. Peter's chapter discusses our current education system and how it must change utilizing a systems perspective.

I believe that the industrial-age education system that has spread around the world in the past 150 years will change dramatically in the coming decades. This will not happen because such change is easy. Indeed, as most educators know only too well, few institutions are more resistant to innovation and change than is education in primary and secondary schools. It will happen because fundamental change is necessary if human society is to survive and thrive in the world in which we now live. The Industrial Age is ending, and the coming changes will not be possible without recreating the two central institutions—business and education—which have been the primary propagators of the industrial age world view and skill set.

Many have argued that the industrial age ended decades ago, as the world of smokestacks and mass production was replaced by that of bits and bytes. But this confuses shifts in dominant technologies with shifts in the underlying values and processes that defined the industrial age. More steel is produced in the world today than ever before. So, too, are more automobiles produced and more coal burned. Indeed, shifts in dominant technologies are a defining feature of the industrial age, what Lewis Mumford and others called the "age of the machine" (Mumford 1967).

> **Peter M. Senge** is a senior lecturer at MIT. He is also Founding Chair of the Society for Organizational Learning (SoL), a global community of corporations, researchers, and consultants committed "to increasing our capacity to collectively realize our highest aspirations and productively resolve our differences" through the mutual development of people and institutions.
>
> The *Journal of Business Strategy* named him a "Strategist of the Century," one of twenty-four men and women who have "had the greatest impact on the way we conduct business today." Senge is the author of several books, including the widely acclaimed *The Fifth Discipline: The Art and Practice of the Learning Organization* (1990). His most recent books are *Presence: Human Purpose and the Field of the Future,* co-authored with C. Otto Scharmer, Joseph Jaworski, and Betty Sue Flowers (SoL 2004), and *The Necessary Revolution: Working Together to Create a Sustainable World*, co-authored with Bryan Smith, Joe Laur, Sara Schley, and Nina Kruschwitz (Doubleday 2008).
>
> Senge has lectured throughout the world, translating the abstract ideas of systems theory into tools for economic and organizational change.

Educational Challenges for the World of Today and Tomorrow, not Yesterday

Economic globalization has brought extraordinary material benefits and unimaginable dangers. For the first time in human history, billions of people share a material standard of living previously unthinkable, just as so many more people share reasonable expectations of long life, democratic processes, and formal education than at any previous time. At the same time, human beings are destroying other species and ecosystems at unprecedented rates and altering their ecological environment locally and globally as never before.

According to Jason Clay of the World Wildlife Fund, it takes 1¼ earths to support today's global economy. Soon it will be more. But we have only one Earth, and the inevitable adjustment to living within the scope of her generosity grows more severe every year we continue down the "take-make-waste" industrial path. As one example, the average American causes a ton of material waste to be generated *per day*, including the gaseous waste by-products of industrial life like greenhouse gas emissions.

The challenges ahead will be social and cultural as well as economic and ecological—indeed they are inseparable. Globalization has caused a collision of cultures as well as economic systems, with many around the world fighting to preserve traditional cultural identity against the spread of western style consumerism, while massive joblessness spreads as rural economies decline and tens of millions are forced to migrate to cities. According to the World Bank, the poorest quartile of the world's people saw their share of global income fall from 2.5% to 1.4% from 1975 to 2000. Global terrorism, fueled by millions of disaffected youth with little hope for a positive future, is as inevitable a by-product of the spread of modern industrial development as is global climate change.

While most individuals and organizations are still largely in denial regarding the profound changes required to meet these challenges, more and more

tracing connections

Many years ago, Barry Richmond and I were doctoral students in the MIT System Dynamics Group that Jay Forrester had drawn together. Many eventual leaders of the field, including David Anderson, Ali Masheyekhi, Nat Mass, John Morecroft, George Richardson, Khalid Saeed, and John Sterman were also doctoral students in the group. We were all good friends and our families not only became close but remain so to this day. Our time together will always stand out as a model for me of what is possible in a truly collaborative, co-inspiring community within an academic context, something all too rare in universities.

Barry and I shared many wild ideas during those days, like the importance of systems thinking as a way of being and a broad set of skills, which system dynamics methods could help to develop in crucial ways. We talked about "systems thinking for the masses," feeling it was imperative to get the tools and principles of systems widely shared—in particular, embedding systems thinking in the key institutions that shape modern society, business, and K-12 education. In K-12, we believed this meant getting beyond the traditional teacher-centric schoolroom process, and enabling students to learn with and from one another. "There are so many more teachers that no one sees," Barry used to say, "if you can only let the kids learn from one another."

It seemed apparent to us both that seeing and understanding systems needed to be linked to the innate passion of people to learn, and that learning was not just a matter of the head, but of the whole person. Our friendship based on these common passions lasted a lifetime. This article is one small way for me to acknowledge that friendship.

---

business, civil-society, and governmental leaders (mostly in local government in the United States) not only see the changes needed but are busy bringing them into reality (Senge et al. 2008). Fortunately, this revolution also includes a growing number of educators and communities, examples of whom are given below.

These innovators are guided by imagining a different path into the future, one that leads toward a *regenerative* economic system in place of the *extractive* system that has dominated the industrial age. They are guided by simple but profound questions: Why could we not emulate nature in creating "circular economies" with little or no waste? Why could we not interact across cultural differences with the aim of learning rather than dominating, fostering a new renaissance as has happened before when established cultures were forced to face radical new ideas? Why could not globalization represent mindful stewardship of the Earth's treasures rather than mindless consumerism, awakening us to our sacred identity as *Homo sapiens*, the "wise species"?

The key, to paraphrase Shakespeare, lies not in our stars but in ourselves. Below the multiple symptoms of social and ecological imbalances sits a growing gap in awareness between the nature of our reality and the nature of our thinking, symbolized in Figure 10-1.

Global industrial expansion has woven a web of interdependence the likes of which has never before existed. For example, the average pound of food travels two thousand miles before it is purchased by an American consumer. Many of our every day nonperishable goods travel much further. Conversely, the by-products of our ways of living travel around the world. For example, the greenhouse gases emitted by American cars and SUVs, along with our video games, flat panel TVs, and web surfing, powered in large part by burning coal, constitute 20% of worldwide emissions, contributing to shrinking glaciers, reduced spring runoffs, and hundreds of millions of chronically dehydrated people in northern India. Weather instability, flooding, and rising sea levels affect a great many more.[1] In the immediate future, the same statement will be valid in reverse as the surging economies of China and India eclipse the U.S. economy in greenhouse emissions. Never before in human history have people's daily choices on opposite sides of the globe been so entangled.

But, as this web of interdependence grows, our capacity to understand interdependence has not; in fact, you could argue that it has steadily deteriorated over centuries. As humans have moved from tribal to agrarian societies and, more recently, to the modern industrial society, our sense of connection to the larger living world has progressively become more and more tenuous. For example, recent studies have shown that many American children believe that their food *comes* from the grocery store, and most have no concept of seasonality in food, since all foods are available at all times.

Because the decline in capacity to understand interdependence has happened gradually over many generations, it has largely gone unnoticed. Native peoples

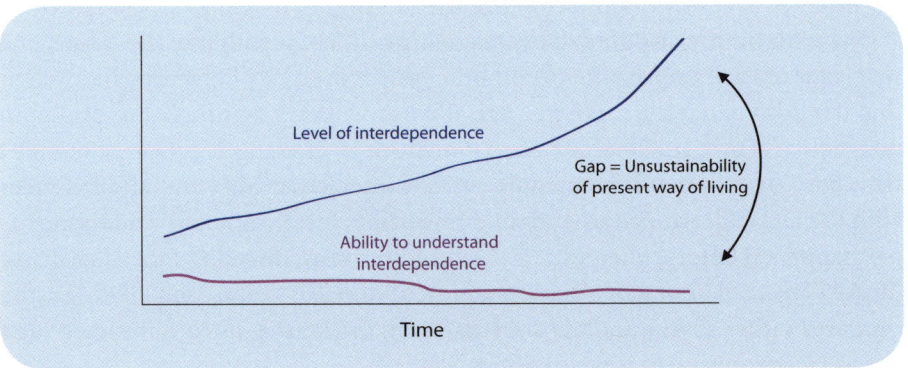

Figure 10-1. Growing gap between Level of interdependence and Ability to understand

do not need to read books to understand their dependence on and responsibilities to "Mother Earth"; it constitutes the very roots of their culture. Farmers likewise must understand the dance of sun, wind, rain, soil nutrients, and water flows or they cannot survive as farmers. The rest of us have no need to understand such natural rhythms, and consequently do not.

As the understanding of interdependence decreases, our way of living becomes increasingly unsustainable. Very few adults today understand the global economy, let alone where the goods they buy come from, or the social and environmental by-products of the global supply chains through which they move. Few know the effects of the worldwide expansion of industrial agriculture, mostly to serve middle class consumers in the north: displacement of tens of millions of rural residents per year due to falling farmer incomes; major source of greenhouse gases (not only CO_2 from shipping food around the world but methane from the expansion of livestock to meet growing demands for meat); and the loss of more topsoil in the past fifty years than the size of India and China combined.

> As the understanding of interdependence decreases, our way of living becomes increasingly unsustainable.

While there are many facets of the malaise of global industrial society, it is hard to imagine much real change without beginning to address this gap between our growing interdependence and our ability to understand that interdependence. No technological fixes are likely to solve climate change alone. No global government is likely to suddenly appear to deal with the growing stresses of food and water. No enlightened corporate responsibility movement will miraculously change the DNA of global business so that short-term profit comes into balance with long-term contribution to people and planet.

All of these changes, and more, *will only happen as our thinking changes.* The institutions of the modern world work as they do because of how we work. How we think and interact shapes their policies and practices, neither of which is likely to change on their own.

Thinking Newly: Educating for New Thinking

Time does not go backward. Our task is not to re-create yesterday's cultures of inter-relatedness but to anticipate tomorrow's. This will require deep change in all the primary institutions that shape modern society, none of which is more important than education because none has a larger long-term impact than education. This is why Barry Richmond believed that developing systems citizens must become the core purpose of education today—nurturing the next generation of young people whose capacity to understand interdependence is commensurate with the interdependence that shapes our lives.

"To be a teacher is to be a prophet," said Gordon Brown, former Dean of the MIT School of Engineering and a founding inspiration to systems thinking in the education movement. "We are not preparing students for the world of today, or the world that teachers have grown up in; we are preparing students for a world that we can barely imagine." Education is the one social institution with a 50-year plus time horizon. Business does not have this. Government does not have this. The media does not have this. But education, by its very nature, does. That is why education is always a key to the future direction of a society.

> Developing systems citizens must become the core purpose of education today—nurturing the next generation of young people whose capacity to understand interdependence is commensurate with the interdependence that shapes our lives.

When education is driven by incessant pressures to perform on standardized tests, get good grades, get into the right college, with the goal of a good job and lots of money, then education reinforces the consumerism and economic orthodoxy that drive the present global business system. When education is oriented around deeper questions of human and social development, it can contribute substantially to the larger needs of a society needing desperately to reorient its priorities for a different future. In this sense, education is a natural leader in this time of "great turning," when the industrial age is dying and, as Vaclav Havel put it, "something new, still indistinct, is struggling to be born."

While this might sound grandiose, I believe the kids in school sense the significance of the moment. More than ever before in history, today's young people grow up with an awareness of the world. They know about climate change. They know about our addiction to fossil fuels. They know about the persisting gap between rich and poor. They are often in direct communication with friends in other countries, and they know about the struggles of the world's cultures to live respectfully with one another. This is why they are disengaged when education does not address the imbalances that will shape their future, and why they thrive when it does.

> Young people know that the only citizenship that matters today is global citizenship and how the people of the world work together to, in the words of Buckminster Fuller, "create a world that works for everyone."

Young people know that we are "living into" a new global society. What they don't know is whether their teachers know. What they don't know is whether adults care enough and have enough courage to re-create education to match their world. Regardless of how they express it, young people know that the only citizenship that matters today is global citizenship and how the people of the world work together to, in the words of Buckminster Fuller, "create a world that works for everyone."

An education capable of developing systems citizens takes us all into new territory. No one knows how to do it. There is no set curriculum, any more than there is agreement on the processes of learning that will be needed. Moreover, it is not a job for educators alone.

The modern school is an expression of public priorities and sits within a complex web of societal accountabilities. Not only will the fragmented subjects that define the industrial age curriculum have to change, but also the fragmentation that separates education from the lives of the learners and the larger community will have to change (Senge et al. 2000). Recreating education will be a job for communities committed to a future that has a future, not just for professional educators.

Our efforts in the SoL Education Partnership[2] to explore this new landscape have focused on the following four foundational changes:

- systems thinking
- authentic youth engagement[3]
- rethinking schools as learning communities
- education for sustainability

The overarching aim is not educational reform but re-contextualizing the whole process of education: starting with young children learning how to be more responsible for their own school environment and gradually moving to interconnecting diverse stakeholders as they tackle complex real life community issues. In this process, students stop being passive recipients of someone else's curriculum and become active agents in developing a sense of responsibility and efficacy for an interdependent world—a start on the road to systems citizens.

Students stop being passive recipients of someone else's curriculum and become active agents in developing a sense of responsibility and efficacy for an interdependent world—a start on the road to systems citizens.

Systems Thinking at Work in the Classroom

In 1988, the first systems thinking classes were started at Orange Grove Middle School in Tuscon, Arizona, instigated by Frank Draper, a science teacher, and encouraged by Mary Scheetz, then Orange Grove's principal. When my wife, Diane, and I first visited Frank's 8th grade science class in 1991, it was hard not to notice that something was different. First, Frank was nowhere to be seen. In fact there was no teacher in the room. A couple of students had some questions about their library research, and Frank had gone to the library with them (remember, this was back before the Internet). But, to our amazement, the classroom had not descended into chaos. Instead, the thirty or so students were glued to their new Macintosh computers, two to a machine, deeply engrossed in their conversations with one another.

We learned that Frank and his colleague Mark Swanson had designed their semester science curriculum around a real project: the design of a new state park to be developed north of Tucson. After studying the sorts of conflicts that inevitably arise in park and wilderness area management, they were working with a STELLA-based simulation model that showed the impacts of different decisions. They had an overall budget and a prescribed mission based on environmental quality, economics, and recreation and education targets they had set out for the park. At the time, they were working on designing the park's trail system. Once they laid out a proposed trail, the simulation model calculated the environmental and economic consequences, prompting energetic debates over tradeoffs among different options.

We had only been standing in the back of the room for a few minutes when a couple of young boys came over and grabbed us. "We need your opinion," Joe said. "Billy and I have different trails. He thinks his is great because it makes a lot of money (routing hikers past the best views), but it also does a lot of environmental damage. Mine does less environmental damage, but he thinks it is too close to the Indian Burial Grounds and will stir up protests."

We listened for a while as the two boys explained their different trails and showed us some of the simulated consequences. There were no black and white answers, and it was clear that they understood this. This was about design and making choices. The bell rang, signaling the end of the period, and they said goodbye, agreeing as they left to come back after school to see if they could agree on a proposal to share with the rest of the class at the end of the week. (Eventually, the students' proposals and analyses were presented to the actual park planning commission at the end of the term.)

> The students were learning to see change—the consequences of how the park's trail system was laid out—as differing patterns of behavior over time, exhibiting **dynamic thinking**.

Barry Richmond has identified eight component thinking skills that comprise a broad definition of systems thinking. (See the introductory chapter in this book on Barry's system thinking skills.) In this particular project at Orange Grove, several of Barry's thinking skills were apparent.

First, the students were learning to see change—the consequences of how the park's trail system was laid out—as differing patterns of behavior over time, exhibiting dynamic thinking. Second, the students were practicing stepping back to see how one change can have many different effects as the change plays out in a larger system, exhibiting

10,000-meter thinking, and how that system has its own distinctive characteristics and generates particular forces exhibiting system as cause thinking.

Third, the students were practicing stepping back to see how that system has its own distinctive characteristics and generates particular forces, exhibiting system-as-cause thinking. Fourth, they were learning how to formulate a hypothesis—what consequences they expected from different changes—and then testing their expectations against a formal model of the system, exhibiting scientific thinking. The students were learning how to formulate a hypothesis, and then were testing their expectations against a formal model of the system, exhibiting scientific thinking.

> The students were practicing stepping back to see how one change can have many different effects as the change plays out in a larger system, exhibiting **10,000-meter thinking**.

The students also learned a variety of conceptual tools for mapping systems and for expressing and communicating with others about their understanding of the interdependence in developing a park plan. Today, tools like behavior-over-time graphs, connection circles, causal loop diagrams, stock-flow mapping, and system archetypes are introduced as early as kindergarten. These young children are invited to look at daily experiences like how the intrinsic value of trust builds or deteriorates in a friendship, or what happens during the process of breaking a bad habit (Quaden et al. 2008). As students get older, they can naturally extend these tools to more complex subjects, and start to write their own simulation models. This process develops not only deep content knowledge but thinking skills to see how common system dynamics can underlay very different situations.[4]

> The students were practicing stepping back to see... how that system has its own distinctive characteristics and generates particular forces, exhibiting **system-as-cause thinking**.

> The students were learning how to formulate a hypothesis... and then were testing their expectations against a formal model of the system, exhibiting **scientific thinking**.

"Our approach was to invite kids to consider a worldview of complex interdependent systems. Instead of abstract learning, we use simulations to begin to confront and to penetrate this world of interdependence as it is embodied in particular real-life situations, and how these systems relate to other systems," says Frank Draper.

This work is challenging and requires dedicated teachers like Draper and Swanson willing to wrestle with some timeless questions, as well as newer ones such as the following brought to light by the systems worldview. What if the education process throughout primary and secondary school continually built on children's innate curiosity and capacity to construct their own understanding rather than digesting and parroting back a teacher's understanding? Learning through doing is ultimately essential for retention and meaningfulness, but how can this learning be extended to more complex subjects where the consequences of our actions are no longer immediate? What really are our innate capacities to understand complexity and how far could this intelligence develop if it were really nurtured?

Authentic Youth Engagement

What was evident from the outset in the state park exercise at Orange Grove was the engagement of the students. What made them so involved?

First, the students were wrestling with real-world problems rather than artificial schoolroom exercises. They could identify not only with the challenges of developing a new state park but also with the benefits of designing the park well.

Second, the students were thinking for themselves. They knew there was no single right answer to the challenges they were facing. Ultimately, they had to understand more clearly what would happen if different decisions were made, and they had to frame the resulting trade-offs appropriately. No single formula was presented by the instructor to point to the right answer. Rather, the students had to sort out their own thinking about a real issue and explore different proposals, ultimately coming to their own conclusions.

Third, the teachers operated as mentors, not instructors. The teachers' role was not to give a prescribed method or guide the students to a pre-determined right answer. Indeed, the teachers did not know the best outcome and were co-learners with the students. But the teachers' roles were no less crucial: they had to help the students make sense of the outcomes of different scenarios. Having been involved in building the computer simulation gave the teachers important knowledge for this task, but no simple answers. A complex dynamic simulation model will often respond to changes in ways that its developers do not anticipate, as different feedback interactions play out over time.

As a result, both teachers and students became mutual learners. They had to recognize that it was *a model* and thus, by definition, incomplete. One of the teachers' roles was to help the students describe the assumptions upon which the model was based and to invite the students to critique those assumptions and consider the implications of alternative assumptions, a critical aspect of scientific thinking (for examples, see Fisher 2007).

Fourth, working with partners drew the students into a joint inquiry. This not only enabled them to get to know one another, but forced them to continually confront alternative views and assumptions. This drew students into a natural process of seeing how each individual reasons, based on past experiences and assumptions to draw conclusions that guide our actions, and as a result, to become more open to testing their reasoning.

Of course, human beings follow such processes of inferential reasoning all the time, but it is often easier to see how this works in another person, since our own reasoning is often "transparent" or invisible to us. Educators understand the importance of reflection (i.e., learning how to examine our own assumptions and reasoning), but it remains an elusive educational goal, all but completely ignored by traditional schooling. Didactic instruction by-passes it entirely. Teachers' efforts to try to get students to reflect is easily undermined by teachers' authority and formal power, which intimidates students programmed to seek correct answers. As Scheetz said, reflection requires safety, which benefits from an environment of mutual inquiry. In this sense, students helping one another reflect is a powerful approach that goes well beyond teacher-centered strategies.

For example, consider the following (slightly stylized) interaction between Joe and Billy working on their park trail system.

> *Billy:* Your trails are a bad idea because they are too close to the Indian burial grounds. You shouldn't do that.
> *Joe:* Who says? There are no rules that say we can't do that. They do a lot less environmental damage than yours.
> *Billy:* Yeah, mine *are* a problem. But what is worse?
> *Joe:* I didn't really think about the burial grounds. Maybe there is a way to avoid the burial grounds and also do less environmental damage?
> *Billy:* Yeah. Maybe, but I wonder how much less money we'll make; the park has to generate enough money to stay open. Let's try some other routes.

In this simple interaction, the two boys are practicing another of Richmond's thinking skills, operational thinking, understanding how specific features of the structure of a system cause its behavior (such as how trail location affects the hiking patterns of visitors, the environmental effects, and park revenues) and how changes in that structure can change system behavior.

> The two boys are practicing another of Richmond's thinking skills, **operational thinking**, understanding how specific features of the structure of a system cause its behavior.

Equally as important, these two students are engaging in a critical collaborative learning process—probing each others' ways of thinking through the design problem they face and, in the process, making their own thinking more explicit. They are helping one another; neither is right or wrong; both are learning. Joe hadn't really thought about the Indian burial grounds as a constraint; this was outside the assumptions upon which he was operating. Likewise, Billy had not paid a lot of attention to the environmental damage of his trails because he was focused on maximizing hiker traffic and park revenues. Both conclude that there may be still better overall designs if they expand their assumption sets. In short, the boys are mastering the basics of reflective learning, becoming more aware of their own taken-for-granted assumptions as they think through ideas together.

Of course, such interactions only work if there is mutual respect. It is easy to imagine two young boys simply arguing about who is right, and never challenging their own reasoning. This is why educators like Scheetz understand that realizing the benefit of systems thinking tools is inseparable from deep and broad engagement of students, and that how, in turn, this depends on the overall school environment. "An environment where learning is likely to occur is one that is safe and secure, and where taking risks is OK."

What if we saw *learning how to see systems* as inseparable from *learning how to see one another*? What if we saw the foundation for systems citizenship as a seamless blend of cognitive and inter-personal skills in learning about complexity, anchored in learners' ongoing discovery about what it means to grow as a human being in relationship with one another? What if teachers, as well as other adults working with kids, saw themselves as mutual learners along with the students?

> What if teachers, as well as other adults working with kids, saw themselves as mutual learners along with the students?

Rethinking Schools as Learning Communities

Early on in Orange Grove's movement toward adopting systems thinking and "learner-centered learning," the staff realized that their success depended on the overall learning culture at the school, starting with how they, the teachers, interacted with one another.

Of all professions, teaching is among the most individualistic. Teachers often espouse an ideal of collaboration, but lack practical experience at creating a true collaborative work environment. Whereas most people in business or architecture or law have an acute sense that their accomplishments are the result of a team effort (even though some individuals may have more visibility to a customer or a client), teachers typically operate in a highly fragmented world of their courses and their students. Working cooperatively as teams does not come easily to teachers who have spent most of their lives in an educational system that emphasizes individual performance and competition, reinforced by a professional work environment that forces them to practice their craft alone much of the time.

It takes time and commitment to go beyond platitudes about collaboration. "Of all the changes I tried to lead as principal, helping teachers learn how to team was probably the most difficult," says Scheetz. She personally led several-day retreats where teachers began to reflect and

> Of all the changes I tried to lead as principal, helping teachers learn how to team was probably the most difficult.

listen to one another more deeply and to build different capacities for dealing with the inevitable conflicts that arise between different teachers' lesson plans or strategies with particular kids. "There is so much more potential for collaborative solutions than normally gets realized given the professional isolation common to most schools," says Scheetz.

Scheetz and assistant principal Tracy Benson (who later succeeded Scheetz) made sure collaboration became part of teachers' daily lives by redesigning the school schedule so that each day all teachers had 45-60 minutes free to "clinic" with one another. "Collaboration only starts to make a difference when teachers have time to practice coordinating in real time," says Benson. "They need to know what Billy's teacher found out in his first period class or how a new systems idea that is supposed to integrate across civics and science is actually playing out for the kids. This is what actually helps teachers feel like a team."

Gradually, Orange Grove's teachers began to build a larger vision of the type of school culture they wanted to create. "We have to lead by example," said math teacher Kelly O'Connor. "If we show respect to the kids and to one another, the kids see that." Over time, the Orange Grove teachers found that their hard work in developing themselves as a learning community started to reshape how they interacted. "Any topic we talk about is a process of building a community," said Jay Barwell, English teacher. "Dealing with all our differences is the key to building our shared vision."

As the teachers developed as a team, so did their understanding of how specifically to move toward the overall school environment they envisioned. In the end, this came down to one idea: respect. With this as their guiding rule, they were able to create trust amongst themselves as well as with the students.

Extension of Learning Communities from School to the Larger Community

Building learning communities does not stop at the four walls of the school. School cultures, based on genuine respect and student engagement, affect how people think and act and naturally start developing a bridge that can encompass the larger community. Ironically, building this larger community is often more common in poorer settings, where resources are scarce and people must work together.

The Murphy School District in Phoenix, one of the founders of the SoL Education Partnership, is one of the poorest in America. Yet, the members of the community have succeeded in creating networks of mutual support that have led to delivery of food and clothing to those in need, a decrease in youth violence, domestic abuse and substance abuse, and an increase in student achievement over the past three years. A recent study by SoL researcher Dennis Sandow found that the "Students and their families, as well as the neighborhoods within Murphy School District, all benefit from a large, collaborative social system whose members include, but are not limited to, not-for-profit, government, faith-based and business organizations, teachers, counselors, parents, and Murphy School District graduates. There is a single (although unstated) purpose to this social system: to generate health and well being for Murphy School District students, families and neighbors" (Sandow 2006).

Traditionally, the professional isolation of teachers is mirrored by the way schools see themselves as isolated institutional entities sitting apart from the larger communities in which they are embedded. Tragically, this often becomes a self-fulfilling prophesy: isolated schools contribute little to their communities and in turn fail to tap the potential engagement and support from those communities. As this happens, the reciprocal benefits from acknowledging and cultivating the interdependence between school and community are lost.

"Maybe it is the harsh circumstances of Murphy, but it has always been obvious that if school here is to succeed, it must become a hub for community building," says superintendent Paul Mohr, a founding member of the SoL Education Partnership. "When that happens, the benefits for students as well as adults can go well beyond what educators can do on their own." Over the past five years, student achievement at Murphy has increased significantly because, according to Sandow, the larger "social system (is) supporting the Murphy School District student's academic achievements."

What if "school" were defined not by institutional geography but by the geography of students' lives? What if the "teachers" were not just the professional educators but all the adults (and the older youths) with whom a student interacts? What if we assumed that sustaining innovation in education will only occur to the extent that we develop collaborative networks linking local business, local social services and government organizations, and families, all of whom share a common vision of supporting kids in their development? What if we realized that whatever shortage in teachers we perceive is only an artifact of the fragmentation of school from the larger community—that in fact there are a vast number of potential teachers waiting to be asked to help? What would this mean for how education works in general and for nurturing systems citizens in particular if, by re-connecting school and the larger communities, we created a rich laboratory for students learning how to build healthy interdependence here and now?

Education for Sustainability: Making Systems Citizenship Real

The Monte del Sol charter school in Santa Fe, New Mexico came up with a simple way to start to re-connect the school to the larger community: the school's innovative "community learning project" requirement. Here's how it works.

Every 10th grader at Monte del SoL can identify something she or he wants to learn that someone in the community can teach them. The resulting project then constitutes one of their five required courses for the year. I have met students at Monte del Sol who have learned carpentry, consulting, and community organizing. As important as what they learn is how they learn it. Freed from the classroom, they re-create the oldest form of education: apprenticeship. Not only does this lead toward learning that has real meaning to them, it connects many adults with students and gives them a sense of being meaningful contributors in the school, paving the way for both to work together for building healthier and more sustainable communities.

Jaimie Cloud of the Cloud Institute, a national leader in education for sustainability for over a decade, identifies several "habits of mind" to be cultivated in education for sustainability, including the following (see http://www.cloud institute.org; Cloud et al. 2003).

- Intergenerational Responsibility: The extent to which one takes responsibility for the effect(s) of her/his actions on future generations.
- Protecting and Enhancing the Commons: The extent to which one works to reconcile the conflicts between individual rights and the responsibilities of citizenship to tend to the commons.
- Assumption of Strategic Responsibility: The extent to which one assumes responsibility for one's self and others by designing, planning and acting with whole systems in mind.
- Paradigm Shifting: The extent to which one recognizes mental models and paradigms as guiding constructs that change over time with new knowledge and applied insight.

Cloud sees education for sustainability as the integration of ideas and approaches from many different content areas such as the following: "ecological literacy" (science principles and natural laws that help us to understand the interconnectedness of humans and all of the Earth's systems); system dynamics and systems thinking; "multiple perspectives" (truly valuing and learning from the life experiences and cultures of others); "sense of place" (connecting to and valuing the places in which we live); "sustainable economics" (study of the connections between economic, social and natural systems); citizenship, participation and leadership (the rights, responsibilities, and actions associated with participatory democracy toward sustainable communities); and creativity and visioning (the ability to envision and invent a rich, hopeful future).

> Education for sustainability is more than just a new curriculum. It is about how the content and process of education can be interwoven with real-life contexts to create opportunities for young people to lead in building sustainable communities and societies.

Obviously, education for sustainability is more than just a new curriculum. It is about how the content and process of education can be interwoven with real-life contexts to create opportunities for young people to lead in building sustainable communities and societies. In short, real education for sustainability is only possible in concert with systems thinking, authentic youth engagement, and rethinking schools as learning communities to catalyze a radical shift. No longer is education something that adults do to kids. Education becomes a joint learning process for communities learning to become more sustainable.

As one example of this process, before I knew of the Monte del Sol charter school in Santa Fe, local businesspeople had given me an impressive local magazine, *Sustainable Santa Fe*. In addition to high quality articles focused on community sustainability challenges and innovative responses by local organizations, I noticed the editorial by-line: in order to advertise in the magazine, companies had to first meet certain criteria of waste management and energy efficiency. So, not only did the magazine feature sustainability-oriented stories, it fostered healthy competition among local businesses for positive brand image. It was only later that I discovered that the magazine was in fact a product of a group of Monte del SoL students teaming up with local community mentors in desktop publishing. Indeed, it was the students who had the idea of the advertising criteria!

> No longer is education something that adults do to kids. Education becomes a joint learning process for communities learning to become more sustainable.

In such projects, students become catalysts for engaging their communities—as they have at Brewster High School in New York. Brewster science teacher Scott Beall created a novel way to teach 10th and 11th grade science: Do Right Enterprises. Beall told his largely conservative school board that he was connecting meaningful science education with developing entrepreneurial skills. In fact, he had a bigger aim. In this program, for example, Beall teaches students how to conduct energy audits and then engages local businesspeople as clients. Not only do the students learn how to apply science to practical analysis, local businesses start to reduce their energy (and carbon) footprint. Along the way, the students discover the difference they can make to their community.

"We thought we were doing the students a favor by letting them come in and gather some data from our restaurant," said one local businessperson. "We had no idea how much waste they would find, and how much money we could save."

The difference for student learning, even as defined more traditionally, is dramatic. "There is no doubt that the kids in the Do Right course learn as much science content as counterparts in more traditional science classes," says Beall. In fact, their New York Regents' science exam results tend to be as high or higher than counterparts in more traditional classrooms. "There are many ways you can design meaningful service learning sustainability projects with particular curricular content in mind," says Beall. "The big payoff is student motivation and a completely different understanding of what it means to *do science* rather than do schoolroom exercises."

When education for sustainability is connected to community engagement, learning becomes intertwined with youth leadership development. "I think we tend to greatly underestimate young people's capacities as leaders," says Les Omotani, superintendent of the Hewlett-Woodmere district and another SoL Education Partnership founder.

For the past several years, Omotani has invited high school students to serve as facilitators for the community dialogues hosted by the schools. "What the young people learn is that they can help adults have meaningful conversations about how to make the community, including the schools, more healthy," says Omotani. "What the adults learn is to accept the young people as thoughtful and committed community members—it is a huge win-win for everyone." For example, out of a recent dialogue, the students started a "bag it" project to introduce reusable shopping bags throughout the community with the goal of eliminating many of the plastic bags that inevitably end up in landfills. Stories like these raise very basic questions about education for sustainability and fundamental developmental needs.

> When education for sustainability is connected to community engagement, learning becomes intertwined with youth leadership development.

For most of human history, by the age of thirteen to fifteen, children have gone through some sort of rite of passage that signals that they have joined the adult community. In the past, such rites of passage emphasized the importance of how young adults could contribute to their larger community. Confining students in their mid-teens to classroom instruction and traditional academic exercises not only fails to tap their creativity, but it also ignores fundamental developmental needs that deepen their sense of personal purpose and allows them to learn how they can make a difference. It is impossible to know how much of the anomie and developmental anxiety young people encounter later in life, in their twenties and thirties, has its roots in neglecting these developmental requirements in their teens.

Noted anthropologist Edward Hall, who had spent his life studying child-rearing in diverse cultures, felt that confining young adults to schoolroom learning "(ignores) the primate base we are built upon. Until a generation ago, males were warriors at the age of 18 . . . with all that energy, those glands going like mad, they shouldn't be in school. They're tearing things apart! We should educate them before and after" (Hall 1988; 1976).

> Confining students in their mid-teens to classroom instruction and traditional academic exercises not only fails to tap their creativity, but it also ignores fundamental developmental needs that deepen their sense of personal purpose and allows them to learn how they can make a difference.

What if we learned once more how to create meaningful rites of passage for entering young adulthood, and this were integrated into the educational process? How much of the frustration for students and teachers alike would be alleviated if we stopped seeing traditional classroom education as the anchor in secondary education, and school became more a sort of base camp for young people. Our young people could explore how to deepen their own sense of responsibility and efficacy supported by the content of the curriculum organized around this core developmental need. What if we stop seeing them as school children and, as Omotani says, saw them as important leaders in building more sustainable communities? How much would this contribute to the shifts desperately needed in awareness, understanding, and values needed to build a more sustainable world?

Learning that Lasts

One of the reasons for using several examples from the Orange Grove Middle School was that it affords a rare opportunity to glimpse the longer-term consequences of education for systems citizenship. Orange Grove was one of the first public schools in the U.S. to adopt systems thinking, authentic youth engagement (what they called "learner-centered learning"), and building schools as learning communities, starting in the late 1980s. (Education for sustainability was not a term used explicitly then, but many of the school's projects focused on these priorities.) Now, thanks to a recently released video documentary (Morrison 2008), we can see some of the longer-term effects.

Filmmaker James Morrison and former Orange Grove teacher Joan Yates recently brought together seven former Orange Grove students, including several who had been part of an earlier PBS satellite video program when they were students, fourteen years earlier. The former students' reflections indicate powerful life lessons tracing to their experiences as middle schoolers.

"My overwhelming positive recollection was one of being involved in what I was doing; there not being a set outcome; of learning on the go; of presenting at the end of the day a result that was *totally mine*, that didn't conform to a typical school-sheet form," says James, now an attorney. "I remember that as a very powerful thing. I really felt like I was seeing real world results."

The systems perspective was very real for the kids when they were students, as evident in these quotes from the original video: "I like the flexibility." "You use it almost automatically: just like that, you analyze a problem as a system." "We are so much more motivated than kids in other schools." "You learn so much more than you would if it was just paperwork."

And, it clearly had stuck with them fourteen years later. Dave (a high school teacher today) talked of seeing a classroom as a system: "From the minute they walk in from home, managing thirty kids in a room five times a day is all about the systems."

Nat (now a medical resident) commented: "(I notice) how often people use the word 'system' and why the levers people try fail. In a recent documentary on New Orleans (after Hurricane Katrina), I was struck by how often people said that we need to use a systems approach so that this does not happen again: the failure in the levies happened because multiple parts of the system that should have been considered were not, whether it was wetlands or the height of the levies or whatever—people just didn't consider how all of this would interact."

"(Systems thinking) really made us think out of the box, rather than just follow the easiest answer or the first answer that comes to you," according to Athena, a dentist today.

Interestingly, one of the lasting effects of their systems thinking work as teenagers was a sense of humility that had carried into their careers as adults: "Systems thinking teaches you to not take the straight line path between point A and point B," said James. "That's such an important lesson, not just for children, but for everyone. The ultimate lesson of systems thinking is that it's always more complicated than you think. As a parent, I cannot think of anything more important I could teach my children, because it goes to addressing so much in our society—not just what we do as professionals, but for who we are as people and how we interact with our community and how we interact with the world at large. I think systems thinking is an imperative for how we educate our children, both now and in the future."

> Systems thinking teaches you to not take the straight line path between point A and point B . . . That's such an important lesson, not just for children, but for everyone.

In the original video, Scheetz talked about the importance of creating "simulations where students learn how to make decisions to improve a system." Interestingly, when the adult former students got together, several reflected on what they had learned from the systems simulations they had done years earlier.

"In an ideal world, patient care would work like a good simulation," said Nat. "You come with your set of knowledge, but you have access to people you consult with. A cohesive approach is especially important with complicated patient illnesses."

Others talked about a city planning simulation they had done as students and the lessons it had left, like understanding tradeoffs in making decisions. "I had located the school next to a shopping mall," said Kelly, now studying to go to medical school, "because I thought getting kids to shop would be good for the economy. But it also promoted truancy. I hadn't thought about that."

As adults, the former students also talked about the importance of collaboration and learning from one another as a defining feature of their Orange Grove experience. In the original video, many of the students' comments had focused on the importance of working together: "Working together we get to know one another. You learn more trust." Another commented, "You had a partner and you could converse a lot . . . there was so much freedom, but you also had a goal."

Fourteen years later, Andy (now a trade negotiator at the Department of Commerce) commented, "(In order to get things done) you are completely dependent on your ability to understand other people's thinking . . . (for example, in negotiations with the Chinese) to understand their positions, what sorts of pressures people feel domestically from their constituents. It's really hard to shift from a 'push' type of argument, trying to convince someone, to 'pulling' them towards you. Making that sort of mental transition was really beneficial in my work." Interestingly, in the original video, thirteen-year old Andy had commented, "You really have to start to learn to listen to other people . . . because you may actually be wrong." Seeing this, Andy commented, "I had not realized how much of this insight came from the 8th grade."

> Appreciating collaboration is rooted in understanding the limits of each person's mental models, starting with your own.

Appreciating collaboration is rooted in understanding the limits of each person's mental models, starting with your own. "You have your perspective and you have to seek others' views," said Nat. "You learn pretty quickly that the docs are pretty knowledgeable, but so too are the nurses and the support staff, and many have been in the trenches a lot longer than you have. You need to pay attention to one another and actively seek their advice."

Clearly, for these young adults, systems thinking and learning collaboratively had shaped their world views in profound ways. In Andy's words, "The real question is: Are you, when you are the person in a position of power, willing to let it go? Are you willing to ask, I don't know—what do you think?" For Athena: "Yes, we learned to look for more complexity, but also to look to our peers." For Nat: "I think we learned how to actively seek out knowledge together." For Dave: "When you look at other middle schools and you talk with other people, this really was a different place."

"Education is the most powerful weapon, which you can use to change the world," said Nelson Mandela. As concerns grow around the world around "sustainability" and the overall path of global industrial development, businesses, NGOs, and governments are stepping forward to confront increasingly critical issues around food, water, climate change, destruction of ecosystems, waste and toxicity, and growing gaps between rich and poor. But if you believe that the shifts ahead will be cultural, not just technical, the potential role of education looms large.

> If you believe that the shifts ahead will be cultural, not just technical, the potential role of education looms large.

Hoping to direct attention to this role, the United Nations declared 2006 the year of "Education for Sustainability." This is encouraging, but the response to date is tepid. Today, what passes for sustainability education is mostly reworked environmental science curricula. Few school systems have re-prioritized their goals. Most teachers remain focused on "teaching to the test," seeking to improve student achievement in traditional subjects. Few business and public-sector leaders have stepped forward to "connect the dots" between essential long-term societal changes and a fundamental rethinking of the aims of primary and secondary education. Lofty sentiments do not make a revolution, yet a revolution is exactly what we need.

In my view, two things are critical to the future. First, we must build a meaningful consensus about the scope and substance of education for the twenty-first century and how it differs from education in the past.

Perhaps the vision of systems citizenship can help focus this budding consensus. Whether we are ready or not, young people will inherit a world in which they are, first and foremost, global citizens, not national citizens. Unlike any time in human history, young people today grow up with an awareness of the world, and with increasing connections to other young people around the world. It is irresponsible that they should leave secondary school without understanding how the global economy works, or without an understanding of the basic interconnections between healthy economies, healthy societies, and healthy ecosystems. It is tragic that they should leave without genuine curiosity about, and engagement with, other cultures, for which, often, they just need to travel across their city.

I believe that *systems thinking provides the missing intellectual and cognitive underpinning for education for global citizenship.* This is starting to be understood among business and civil society leaders. "If I reflect on what many organizations have been going through, the whole awareness of sustainability has been growing because systems thinking, in different forms, is enabling us to see many more interdependencies than we have seen in the past," says Andre van Heemstra of the Unilever Management Board. He adds, "It is those interdependencies which make you conclude that it is more than stupid, it is reckless to think of commercial sustainability in isolation of either social or environmental sustainability." (Senge et al. 2008.)

Barry Richmond's systems thinking skills offer a starting point in translating the need for systems thinking into the curricula and pedagogy needed to achieve it. By building upon the foundations of critical thinking and scientific reasoning, Richmond offers a bridge to mainstream ideas that are widely accepted. He extends these to incorporate thinking and learning skills almost completely missing in education today: namely, "the endogenous viewpoint" and learning how to identify feedback dynamics and understand the non-linear ways complex systems can respond to simple changes. Long regarded as the stuff of graduate education, twenty years of evidence now exists to show that, done well, these skills can be nurtured in primary education and developed to remarkably advanced levels in secondary education. These skills are not just for elite students, but are powerful educational tools for the majority of students.

Today, many educators embrace general goals such as: students "should know how to think systemically." But little will change without rigorous programs of study, teacher training, and curriculum development. When combined with developments in education for sustainability and reflection and youth engagement, I believe there is much to build upon to create such programs.

Second, we must face the fact that it is unlikely that basic innovation in education will be accomplished by educators working alone.

The failures of endless "educational reform" movements to produce large-scale, lasting changes offer mute testimony to forces that work to conserve the status quo in public education. The problem is not that educators do not have new ideas. The problem is that we, as a society, demand that education continue to operate in the same way as it did when we were children. This immense cognitive anchor becomes the source of the political movements that inevitably rise up to squelch meaningful experimentation, the sine qua non of innovation. This inherent conservatism

> This inherent conservatism will continue to thwart innovation until communities of leaders from education, business, civil society, and local government start working together to support ongoing basic innovation, not status quo and remediation, in public education.

will continue to thwart innovation until communities of leaders from *education, business, civil society, and local government start working together* to support ongoing basic innovation, not status quo and remediation, in public education.

We do not need to have all the answers worked out in advance in order to build these coalitions. We do need to have the capacity, as communities, to prioritize and persist in supporting new thinking and new practice. We don't just need teachers who are "prophets," as Gordon Brown called for. We need diverse leaders from all sectors willing to travel together into a future we can only begin to imagine. Education for life after the industrial age requires realizing that humans will actually be living together differently in the coming decades or they will not be living much at all—and that young people often have deeper intuitions than do adults regarding the changes coming.

Through the SoL Education Partnership, we are working together to embody and explore, in several communities around the country, what these new partnerships can look like. In particular, we are working to connect innovators from business and civil society with their counterparts in education. Many businesspeople live in a world where either you innovate or die. They understand how to manage the risks that come with experimentation; how to focus on testing new ideas in local ways before they are extended prematurely to broad application; and how to finance and assess innovation. But to date, the businesspeople drawn into working on education have mostly been reacting to perceived shortcomings in schools, rather than focusing on the real needs of creating sustained innovation.

A natural alignment exists between innovators in the private sector and innovators in education, but this alignment has not yet developed sufficiently to have large-scale impact. Leaders in the private sector know that they need people who can think for themselves, solve complex problems in creative teams, work effectively with people from different cultures, and maintain a global, longer term perspective while dealing with immediate problems at hand. And yet, relatively few of our schools are focusing on these requirements in educating students, and most school systems and state departments of education are still sadly out of touch with these very real needs.

> In a world of growing interdependence, what is the purpose of education?

Pursuing both this new consensus and building these new cross-sector partnerships will, I believe, bring us as a society to confront a core unasked question: *in a world of growing interdependence, what is the purpose of education?*

There is a timeless aspect of the purpose of education, enabling young people to grow as healthy and contributing human beings. Most people drawn to teaching as a life work are drawn because of this calling, to be part of how children and young people grow and develop as human beings. This is the love of learning for its own sake.

But there is also a timely and contextual aspect of education, which starts with recognizing the specific challenges society faces and how education must be part of solving these problems. This is the aspect of education that Nelson Mandela reminds us of, and it is to this aspect that education for systems citizenship points.

No one works consciously to destroy ecosystems, or to worsen the gap between rich and poor, or to use water and topsoil more rapidly than they are replenished, or to increase concentrations of greenhouse gases to the point of destabilizing global climate. All these changes occur as unintended by-products of business-as-usual. The problem is that, whether as businesspeople, consumers, or voters, we tend to operate with blinders. Individuals make decisions, like the products we buy, with virtually no awareness of the consequences of their choices for others. Companies maximize profits with little attention to the larger social costs, like the costs of climate change. Governments pursue national interests with little regard to the fact that all nations' interests are now increasingly bound together.

We have the sustainability issues that we have because, as individuals, organizations, and societies, we are unable to see the larger systems we have created that shape modern society, and we are unable to work together across institutional and national boundaries to create alternative systems.

Our core task is simple—to create a truly regenerative economy and society, one that operates based on the defining principle of all interdependent living systems: life creates conditions for life. It is time to recognize that young people have the largest stake in the unsustainable future we are now shaping, and they are more than ready to share in creating an alternative. Are we?

Acknowledgements

My heartfelt gratitude to the many pioneers of the systems thinking movement in public education and the founders of the more recent SoL Education Partnership: Shelburne Farms and the Burlington Vermont School District; Murphy School District in Phoenix, Arizona; the Hewlett-Woodmere District in Long Island, New York; the E3 Initiative and the Washington Sustainability Education Association; Sustainable St. Louis; the New York City Empowerment Zone Initiative; Jaimie Cloud of the Cloud Institute for Sustainability Education; and Lees Stuntz of the Creative Learning Exchange, dedicated to fostering networks of collaboration among systems thinking educators. A special thanks also to Linda Booth Sweeney, who has served as coordinator of the Partnership in its formation and now supports capacity building and research in several of the sites. See: Creative Learning Exchange, http://www.clexchange.org; Cloud Institute for Sustainability Education, http://www.sustainabilityed.org; isee systems, inc., http://www.iseesystems.com; and Waters Foundation, http://www.watersfoundation.org.

References

Cloud et al. 2003. J.P. Cloud, C. Federico, J. Byrne, et al. Kindergarten through Twelfth Grade Education for Sustainability. *The Environmental Law Reporter News and Analysis* 33(2).

Fisher, D. 2007. *Modeling Dynamic Systems: Lessons for a First Course*, 2nd ed. http://www.iseesystems.com.

Hall, E. 1976. *Beyond Culture*. New York: Doubleday, 1976.

Hall, E. 1988. The Drive to Learn. *Santa Fe Lifestyle*, Spring 1988:12–14.

Morrison 2008. J. Morrison, and Creative Learning Exchange. "... that school in Tucson." Video DVD. Acton, MA: Creative Learning Exchange, 2008. http://www.clexchange.org.

Mumford, L. 1967. *The Myth of the Machine, Vol. 1: Technics and Human Development*. New York: Harcourt Brace, Jovanovich, 1967.

Quaden et al. 2008. R.A. Quaden, R., A. Ticotsky, and D. Lyneis. *The Shape of Change*. Acton, MA: Creative Learning Exchange, 2008. http://www.clexchange.org

Quaden et al. 2008. R.A. Quaden, R., A. Ticotsky, and D. Lyneis. *The Shape of Change: Stocks and Flows*. Acton, MA: Creative Learning Exchange, 2007. http://www.clexchange.org.

Sandow, D. 2006. "Murphy School District's Learning Communities," Piper Foundation Research Paper.

Senge, P. et al. 2000. P. Senge, N. Cambron-McCabe, A. Kleiner, T. Lucas, and B. Smith. *Schools That Learn*. London: Nicholas Brealey, 2000.

Senge, P. et al. 2008. P. Senge, B. Smith, N. Kruschwitz, J. Laur, and S. Schley. *The Necessary Revolution: How Individuals and Organizations are Working Together to Create a Sustainable World*. New York: Doubleday, 2008.

Notes

1. In 2007, Oxfam estimated that the costs to the world's poor of adapting to global climate change (including costs due to loss of crops, spread of tropical diseases, and migration) exceeded $50 billion. (See http://www.oxfam.org.) This figure is expected to rise sharply in the coming years.
2. The SoL Education Partnership is a coalition of the Society for Organizational Learning (SoL), the Cloud Institute, the Creative Learning Exchange, Peter Senge, and Linda Booth Sweeney which focuses on creating a National Learning community among schools and communities.
3. Authentic youth engagement is getting students involved in real-life problems and activities that have meaning and purpose.
4. The idea of "generic structures" is a cornerstone of systems education and ranges from simple dynamic structures like delays that arise in virtually all social systems (and confound decision makers expecting immediate results from their actions) to more involved structures like "aging chains," which arise in diverse settings from demographics to product life cycles.